THE
SOUTHERN
POETRY
ANTHOLOGY

VOLUME X

ALABAMA

THE SOUTHERN POETRY ANTHOLOGY

VOLUME X

ALABAMA

William Wright, *Series Editor*

Taylor Byas, J. Bruce Fuller, & Adam Vines, *Volume Editors*

PREVIOUS VOLUMES

William Wright, Series Editor

Volume I: South Carolina
Edited by Stephen Gardner and William Wright

Volume II: Mississippi
Edited by Stephen Gardner and William Wright

Volume III: Contemporary Appalachia
Edited by Jesse Graves, Paul Ruffin, and William Wright

Volume IV: Louisiana
Edited by Paul Ruffin and William Wright

Volume V: Georgia
Edited by Paul Ruffin and William Wright

Volume VI: Tennessee
Edited by Jesse Graves, Paul Ruffin, and William Wright

Volume VII: North Carolina
Edited by Jesse Graves, Paul Ruffin, and William Wright

Volume VIII: Texas
Edited by Paul Ruffin and William Wright

Volume IX: Virginia
Edited by J. Bruce Fuller, Jesse Graves, Amy Wright, and William Wright

CONTENTS

Series Editor's Preface

In the ever-evolving landscape of literature, this contemporary anthology of poetry from Alabama emerges as a crucial and timely endeavor. This tenth volume of The Southern Poetry Anthology features a wide, diverse compilation of verses, penned by the best of contemporary poets associated with the state and serves as a poignant reflection of the state's present moment, capturing the nuanced experiences, emotions, and narratives that shape the lives of Alabama's poetry, one often neglected in national literatures.

At its crux, this anthology is a testament to the power of diverse voices. Alabama, like any place, is a tapestry woven from various threads of culture, history, and identity. Through the pages of this collection, these threads come together to create a rich and vivid tableau, one that encapsulates the struggles, triumphs, and everyday moments that resonate with people throughout the state. In a world increasingly connected yet often divided, such an anthology reiterates the importance of empathy and understanding, fostering a bridge between readers and poets who have vastly different backgrounds and epistemologies.

Indeed, this anthology offers a valuable opportunity for reflection on the trajectory of Alabama's cultural and social evolution. The state has a complex history, marked by both progress and challenges, and this collection of contemporary poetry becomes a mirror to its current state of being. Themes of heritage, tradition, progress, and change intermingle within these verses, providing readers with a nuanced exploration of the state's identity.

Furthermore, the anthology extends its significance beyond regional boundaries. The voices captured within its pages transcend the physical borders of Alabama, delving into universally resonant topics such as love, loss, nature, and human connection. This intersection of the local and the global reaffirms the timeless nature of poetry as a vessel for shared human experiences, allowing readers from various backgrounds to find common ground.

As with the entire series that appears before this volume and the ones hereafter, I am indebted to the co-editors of this volume. Without J. Bruce Fuller, Taylor Byas, and Adam Vines, this anthology would simply not have become as well-wrought as it is. Their help has proved not only helpful, but necessary, and I cannot articulate adequately the vastness of my gratitude. Thank you to the co-editors, the readers, and the excellent poets herein.

William Wright
Dahlonega, GA

Introduction

Though I consider Chicago to be my hometown and the place that raised me, it was in Birmingham, Alabama that I was made again, recast in that sticky heat as a poet. I went to college at the University of Alabama at Birmingham, ten hours away from home, sure that I wanted to write but not yet sure how. I flitted through my undergraduate years as first a pre-med student, then as a fiction writer. Finally, an ekphrastic poetry workshop changed the entire trajectory of my life and writing career. But that is the simpler version of the story.

The fuller truth is that Birmingham was an active character in my life, working overtime in the background to change the way I saw the world. Away from the hustle and bustle of big city life, and even the busy south suburbs of Chicago, I felt Birmingham grasp me by the shoulders. Slow down, it whispered, look. In that ekphrastic poetry workshop, and in the first poetry project I'd ever put together, I studied the work of famous Alabama photographer William Christenberry. Most of his photographs feature abandoned and dilapidated buildings, nature tangled with man's interventions. I'd never been to any of these places, and yet I felt their nostalgia, felt like I knew their stories. Looking at them, I always held my breath, half-expecting someone I knew to come bustling into the frame. I recognized something in these photos, the shadows and ghosts of the long gone, their presence lingering in church pews and grassy fields. Another feeling ran like a river beneath this strange identification; I felt like I belonged. As a result of studying Christenberry's work, the page became a place where I wanted to recreate that same emotional recollection I experienced as a viewer—I was called again and again to write about how Alabama reached out to me through time.

In 2016, when Donald Trump was elected president, I was forced to grapple with my complex relationship with Alabama as a Black woman. During that tense period, I looked to Birmingham's rich history for comfort. I sought out books and art. I wandered the near-silent galleries in the Museum of Art. In the Birmingham Civil Rights Institute, I walked through the Procession Gallery filled with replica statues of people walking, and weaved my way through the stationary bodies. That, I realized, was what poetry was becoming for me—a careful tiptoeing through history into the present. Into an unnamed, hopeful future.

The poems in this anthology walk alongside one another in a procession, bump into one another, converse, join hands. These poems make you remember a place you've never been, draw you in so close that they sew you into their history. Putting these pages together was a welcome return to my poetic home, and this anthology is a necessary illustration of Alabama's polyvocality and its loud, beating heart.

—Taylor Byas, Volume Editor

Unlike Taylor, I have lived fifty-two of my fifty-four years in Alabama. Since I was a very young boy, I've waded and boated and fished its streams, rivers, lakes, quarries, swamps, bays, and sixty miles of coastline. I've camped and backpacked and trail-run and hiked throughout Alabama and where the foothills of the Appalachian Mountains begin. My family likes to joke that we Vineses crawled out of the Warrior River in Walker County, Alabama, where my family worked the coal mines and tipples three and four generations ago.

I grew up in Birmingham, a post-Civil War city named after Birmingham, England, because of its prodigious steel and iron production, which also led to its nickname, Pittsburgh of the South. Birmingham is infamous for its civil rights history, with Bull Connor and firehoses and Dynamite Hill and the tragic Sixteenth Street Baptist Church bombing, which took the lives of four little girls. Martin Luther King wrote his famous letter from the Birmingham Jail, and just sixty miles southeast, Governor Wallace stood in front of the door of Foster Auditorium at the University of Alabama, blocking the entrance of two black students as a physical manifestation of his nefarious speech at the Capitol in Montgomery where he said, "Segregation now, segregation tomorrow, segregation forever."

Today, Birmingham owns the sins of its past but has become more progressive and is lauded for its great food and cultural and artistic attractions. At its foundation is the University of Alabama at Birmingham, or UAB, which I heard a friend humorously claim is an acronym for the "University that Ate Birmingham." UAB is a world-renowned medical and research university that is the state's largest employer and the third most diverse university in the country. I am forever indebted to UAB for what it has provided for me. I hold bachelor's and a graduate degree from UAB that I acquired while working as a landscaper full-time and going to UAB part-time, and I am now, somehow, a professor at the university.

Editing this compilation of poets whose sensibilities have been influenced by this state I adore is especially meaningful to me. Four of the poets in this anthology were and are mentors to me and guided and encouraged me as I learned to write poetry. One of these mentors convinced me, at twenty-six years old, to stay in his poetry writing workshop when I was walking out after looking at the syllabus on the first day. I thought the class was a literature class. I had never written anything creatively in my life and didn't think I had any interest in writing, of all things, poetry. He changed the course of my life. Many of the poets in this anthology mentored me through their poems and essays on prosody and poetics. Some I have met. Some I only know through their extraordinary writings. Some of these poets grew up in Alabama then moved away, while others grew up in places and now live in Alabama. Some of these poets were students of mine who have gone on to become accomplished poets and teachers and are mentoring young poets. The cycle continues.

All of us in this anthology have a collective anxiety about and affection for Alabama, which has a horrific civil rights history and still disappoints us politically and socially many times but embraces us with its natural beauty and weathered resilience in the face of adversity. The two years I left this state was my most productive time of writing. I took for granted what enticed and bewildered and thrilled and terrified me about this state. Living away allowed me to miss my home and my fellow Alabamians, to see what I thought I knew so intimately from another perspective. Whether a surrogate or birth mother, Alabama helped raise me and these poets. Enjoy!

—Adam Vines, Volume Editor

Palavi Ahuja

Aping

Maa's nightgown snakes through
her legs when she walks,

folding only at the slits. And, I
rest, that sored tangerine

printed on the frill of the neck
while she kneads and stirs.

Maa massages, forging a
pulse from dough—

juicing a counterfeit chant I've
hummed before:

Om bhūr bhuvaḥ suvaḥ
tatsaviturvarenyaṃ bhargo
devasyadhīmahi dhiyo yo
naḥ prachodayāt *

I imitate Maa's tongue,
folding mine up like a
lawnchair when she stops,

crimping the edges at every pause,
unwrapping when she purrs.

Yet, when Maa blurs into leftovers, dusted
coriander and clove,

I am soring.
Massaging my own wrist,

tallying the hush between
each pulse.

*****Gayatri Mantra**: Mantra from the *Rigveda*; It is believed that by chanting Gayatri Mantra, you achieve
success and happiness in your life. Regularly chanting it ensures stability in your mind. It is a declaration
of appreciation to the sun and the Divine. (From *Times of India*.)

1

*Theremin**

Like an altar,
I am   played
without touch.
The antennae,
two   koi fish
meditating while
the performer,
thrumming air,
finds the thumb
too   broad
for   thin wind
and pulls out a
pair of forceps,
gives birth to
new sounds,
forgetting old
purrs.   Such is
my tongue, clutching gum,
lugged out of the
normal   classroom,
plucked and rewired,
scrubbed until white.
English as a second language,
they called it as if it were not
two divets   forged in the mud,
one without   touch and
the other echoing   the air that maimed it.

*an instrument controlled without physical contact

2

Gorging on Names

—For the boy who, when asked his name, could not come up with one.

shrapnel clanking down your throat /
instead of answering / *what are you?* /
you hiss / at this threat / in pronouncing /
a cut-glass paperweight name /
fingers / leashed away from you /
do you know your tongue is yours?

*

the heavy tread of your eyes / its sloshing apology /
outlines my breath / when you beg /
*do they pander your name /
just like mine?*

*

as an answer / some foggy syllables /
those / blood-rattled gums /
names / swathed / in the white of /
tongues / we cease / giving back to /
offer me your slaughter / i will offer you mine /
let us both walk away / guzzled / by mistranslation

Daniel Anderson

Friend of a Friend

Though he and I had never met,
he hugged me anyway.
We're all buds here, he said, and slapped my back.
His fashion-model girlfriend hugged me, too.
How did I ever wind up there,
that nineteenth-floor apartment with a view?
Manhattan. Was it thirty years ago?
He made us gin and tonics, which we sipped
before three tall, wide windows.
Then out of nowhere someone said,
cocking a thumb at me,
You know who he looks like?
Hell yes, he does! somebody whooped.
In the moment I was flattered,
more than a little pleased
that I reminded them of their old pal
who'd also gone to Yale.
We'll have you to the Vineyard in July.
You're single, right? We'll fix you up
with Katsy McIntosh, my cousin.
She's a teacher just like you,
only richer than God himself!

Weehawken winked and glittered underneath
the evening's sapphire, pink, and lemon sky.
I gazed out of those windows.
I let myself forget
they probably all banked more in a month
than I made in a year.
I let myself forget
about my crappy car and credit cards.
Instead, I fell head-over-heels
in love with Katsy McIntosh.
I saw a tennis-playing blonde
with sun-bronzed, squared, and shapely calves,
the green eyes of a cat,
and a kindly, wry forgiving smile.

OK, why not? I fantasized
about our wedding and our honeymoon,
the purebred puppy we would raise,
and our brand-new Mercedes Benz.
I met her perfect parents,
Robert and Anne Marie,
who'd love me like the son they never had.
I even saw the handsome, smart, polite,
athletic kids we one day would conceive.
Wouldn't that be the life? I thought.

What was it then? A shattered cocktail glass.
The sound of high heels clacking down a hall.
That fucking bitch breaks one of those a week!
It's OK, man, somebody said.
Yeah, take it easy. Take it easy, Ted.
Don't ruin everybody's night.
Then Ted looked up and growled at us
to get the fuck out of his home.

                    And so
we did, in awkward, quiet haste.
Down on the street below,
our stunned and drunken gaggle frayed.
Some shambled off to hit the bars.
A couple went for Chinese food.
I caught the last train back to Morristown.

I haven't thought about that night in years.
I couldn't tell you who the others were
but I remember Ted,
the upturned collar of his polo shirt
and the glossy, haystack yellow of his hair.
A poet, right? he asked.
Indeed. The self-effacing, dreamy sort.
Naïve enough to ache for something grand.
Sometimes, I wonder where he went,
that gently haunted soul I used to be.

Right now, it seems, he's sitting next to me
with something like the glint
of disappointment in his eyes
or maybe just benevolent surprise.
Where are the wife and kids?

He sizes up my paunch and my bald head,
the crummy posture and the scowl
as if he can't quite understand.
Where's all the glamor and the fame?
Late golden lanes of sunlight fan the room.
Our silence grows. He shrugs.
I mean, it looks like things are pretty swell,
just maybe not like we had planned.
He leans back in his chair,
his legs outstretched and crossed in front of him.
A gin and tonic sparkles in his hand.

One of Us Tells a Joke

It's bawdy. Some would even say
it's a crude, disgusting joke.
But never mind the joke.
It doesn't matter if the punch line was
I could have saved my mom! Or
I thought you said you were a leprechaun!
Or *All you have to do is fuck one goat?*
Forget the filthy joke.
Listen instead to how we laugh.
As children laugh. We're stricken with surprise
by just how raucously we laugh,
how we snort and cackle,
how tenderly we sigh, then laugh again
until we're lost in laughter
and only laughing now because we laugh,
crying because we laugh,
laughing because we can't not laugh.
We're absotively, posilutely gassed
with laughter, tickled pink.
None of us can recall
the last time we laughed so long,
so helplessly, so goddamned hard.

The fire-flame dies. It's getting late.
All evening we have watched
the world outside the window fill with snow.
Stacked lawn chairs on the patio,
a picnic table, and old charcoal grill
surrender underneath

a drifting, moth-like weight.
Everywhere this January night
exaggerates itself.
On car hoods and the toppling peaks of roofs,
high up in the shaggy cedar trees,
and there along the proper picket gate,
one sees immaculate hyperboles,
grand, powder-blown absurdities in white.
It's getting late
but no one wants to leave.
We could get lost in looking out
on all that star-flake and snow-drop have made,
lost in that perishable arcade
of combed and quiet shapes.
In different homes on nearby streets
this weather settles on more solemn lives.
The widow Alice Murdock takes a pill.
Katz tipples one more brandy in the glass.
Harold Crockett wipes his weeping eyes.
Another dreadful silence thrives
between the Baxters in their sexless bed.

We have our sorrows, too,
troubles that others surely half-surmise.
Something, we know, is always *there*.
The skeletal, the sad, the strange
are never far away. Although tonight,
if only for a little while,
as snowfall webs the dark and frosty air,
they seem just slightly further out of range.

Lana K. W. Austin

Blood Harmony

A single larynx halved,
        that's how I perceived it

when I sang with my half
        brother—same mother,

long gone. She is
        where it came from,

our ability to blend,
        unique notes in a chord,

but still one voice. His tenor
        a ginger effervescence,

and my aubergine alto
        painting what felt like

caverns-deep undertones.
        In heavier hues,

our voices fused. Even
        in measures when one grew

more dominant on lead
        and the other receded,

growing hybrid harmony,
        counterpoint shifting,

we were rivulets divined
        from a vast river.

Creek, brook or stream—
        water from the same source.

Walking the Manassas Battlefield, September 14th, 2001

We've walked late afternoon through
      early evening once a week for months.
            Three days ago my new husband didn't die
      like his friends at the Pentagon,
          so we've come to walk here
      like always,
          for the normalcy of it.
Each week the deer materialize at dusk—
      but this twilight teems
with more movement than before, not
      just in the corner of my sight
          where the animals normally flit
             along the forest's outskirts,
          sometimes butting up against
the walking trails, or sloping
          down, clustered in the middle
of a field far from peopled paths.
      They fill my vision
          when they walk right up,
      a hushed sentry. Nineteen deer, so far,
I could have
      touched if only they'd stepped or I'd reached
just a few feet more. We've finished
          hiking the yellow trail and turn
      back towards the cannons. Four more deer
approach. One, the twenty-third—
          a prime number and a psalm—
      moves next to me, not tentative, but with the smell
      of soil after hail.

Nick Barnette

That Much

The difference between *it doesn't matter*
and *it really doesn't matter that much*
is, really, that much

You, your presence, is not
the leaking washer or fritzed wifi

You, your presence, is the extra
zero in the launch code
that solsticizes nuclear winter
where we cabin cozy curl
abreast our chthonian
fireplace, recounting
every word we've said since *mom*.

Bachelorette Sonnette

I want a reality TV love,
producers always telling me what face
to make, when to smile, compulsory
STI screenings for all my lovers—
at least 4 lawyers and 2 cornerbacks.
Swab my asshole, sew me into a jewel
tone gown. Oh...no? It has to be a suit?
And there's another Nick? That's fine! Brand me
Nick B.! When you drop us out a biplane
we'll scream each other's names to earth, dummies
in love. I said it: love. That's what it takes
to get the sponsorships: *right reasons* love.

Can you steal me for a minute? Steal me
forever, or until the season wraps.

Caroline Parkman Barr

Our Communion

She tells me: if you open it, you finish it.

The first time wine touched my tongue
I was too young to know, in communion
you shouldn't smack your lips and say *ahhh*
when the priest tips the chalice back.

Then, 18, I felt the bitter warmth that tasted like
Sunday. So similar in memory, I wondered if St.
Thomas shopped at Kroger.

My friend put her finger to the bottom of
the glass, pushing it up to find home on
my mouth. Finish it.

This is what we have to do—open, swallow.

Two Episcopalians and their wine—I think
there's a joke in there somewhere—drinking not
the blood of Christ, but fermentation paired
well with fettuccini alfredo.

I felt like I should be kneeling, knees pressed into
a needle-point scene of the Nativity
or an ark. I took the last drop and she released
the glass—I wanted her to say: peace be with you.
And I would say: and also with you.

Moorland Hawker Dragonfly

When faced with unwanted male advances
the female moorland hawker dragonfly is known to
plummet to the ground, lying motionless

until the male flies away. *Sexual death feigning*
as way of choosing her mate, of laying her eggs
in peace. Avoiding yet another copulatory wheel–

biologically necessary 69 of the insect world–she
performs her own sequined death drop, heels
to the sky. If only we could all embrace such drama.

Women falling to the sidewalk, dance-floor-slick, kitchen
tile. Landing without grace or injury, eyes closed and hair
splayed. As if this stillness would be enough.

A man touches the small of my back
and I wonder if I, too, could end its trajectory.

Gabrielle Bates

Dear Birmingham

I've been visiting again
the cemetery
with a sunken southern corner.

Fish smaller than first teeth, birthed from the soil,
maneuver in the glaze
where rain pools, covering the lowest stones.

      Behind him, in a cracked white tub,
my knees to his sides,
left ear pressed to
the stack of bones in his neck,

I was once so terrified of my own contentment
I bit my shoulder
and drew blood there

         to the surface—past it—

What I have wanted most
is many lives. One for each longing,
round and separate.

Sometimes I bring figs here, asphyxiating
in plastic, for their distant echo
of your humid, ghost-flesh air—
that almost-a-human
air—

      I was born in autumn
as it fled underground
to be fed to a body
of water that only swallows.

Strawberries

A car's tires thu-thunk
over the rubbery black tripwire at the oil change,
triggering a fat bell,
and a group of girls in silver leotards are reflected
like spatters of sap in its windows—
liquidine, firm, gleaming.
It's a game day; they are the girls
chosen to split in tempo to the brass band,
heel of a front foot sliding over Astro-Turf,
top of a back foot grinding over lit green,
cervix slapping the fifty-yard line
like a fried egg flipped down on a griddle to burn.
Behind the bleachers, a boy takes off the shirt of another boy,
paints a letter there in red paint
(*R*, and then another boy, *I-O-T* . . .).
When the sun goes down over the ridge
all the painted boys will make *PATRIOTS*.
For now the sun rises, sanctioning the street:
Jiffy Lube, pet store, the Sam's Super Samwiches
teens file into, practicing the joke of language.
The morning is cool on the outside
and hot in the restaurant, the war in the words
playful as a war can be, meaning
each gut bleeds out like a slit pig's,
filling the cracks in linoleum, spilling over, becoming smooth.
The layers of red dry and build on one another,
and for years the gap between ceiling and floor lessens;
backs hunch as the mind saws downward, revealing rings.
In the parking lot, *Are you asleep?*
says the boy who is not my boyfriend,
running his fingers along the band of my underwear.
Across the street from this, for years,
an ancient tortoise roams the floor
of the pet store, closing his army-green beak
around the red toenails of sandaled women,
thinking them strawberries.
I feel ashamed
for all the moments
I've been kind
knowing kindness is all it would take.

In the Dream in Which I am a Widow

I have carried a portion of your ashes overseas
to the Spanish statue of the falling angel,
its snake of stone wrapped twice around one leg's ankle
and coiled around the thigh of the other, stone jaw
unhinged and reaching for the humanesque hand.
We lived, remember? Briefly, near it. One wing arcs up in the sky
erecting an honest steeple, one that points not straight,
but upward and curving. As faith goes.
Back to earth. I've scattered part of what you were
from the mouth of my black jacket sleeve onto the field across,
watched over by tall and leaning trees, the field
from which you returned to me so many nights
cold as ice and glowing, your socks full of grass.
I heard the door open, blessed the opening,
blessed the stench you brought inside our home,
blood tangled in the hair on your shin,
bits of another man's flesh in your cleats.
I was curious about this forbidden felt language.
I rubbed my thumbs into your muscles,
the salt of you softening as it entered me. You were a wonder
with your bones and skin on. You focused your violence
with a pipette's precision, and it never spilled
in my direction, never though I lapped at its opening
determined to get a taste from the source.
Years before we went north, before your bed was my bed,
there was a garden in the south we snuck to
where spring made us a headboard out of heady jessamine,
the poisonous vine's scent sweet, aneurysmal sweet,
swelling our brains against our skulls.
I remember, even in that giddy upward state,
I always knew truth was somewhere not in that sweetness.
Now I've made of you a figure
always falling. What sort of monster
does this make me?

Anniversary

A little boy's starched white collar.
An insect traversing the curve.

Dusky pearls strung on a wire in my hair
wound low in a bow at the cerebellum,

the brain's wing-shaped center for balance.
It's April. There's no balance here.

Not in the arch twisted from an ice storm-
struck tree, the bluegrass grabbing my lace.

Scent of smoked meats mingling with the sugar-sweet
confections just burst on the apples' limbs.

Hands. Fingers. Ring of rough steel he bought
for $35, whose ends don't fuse but overlap

like an overbite—the symbolism isn't
lost on a woman like me:

There is a beginning and an end, April,
and one of us will go before the other.

Bees as a species are already dying
but we have tons. There, today,

we have a live bee for every lapel.
A bride should have a veil, they said

and so I bought one. Paid and left it;
like the skin of a fetal lamb

piled on the counter, it was
too finely made and traditional to be mine.

The sun dims and it's April again.
I can see a fire station now from our bed.

Sirens come and go all night.
On his left hand, the steel is gentle

as the shadows of emergencies cast on our wall
a procession of soft, bright bursts.

As we pulled away in the long black car,
our friend who would die the next year

tried to hand us a lit sparkler through the window.
What happens to our questions when we die?

I wondered aloud on our wedding night
about the origin of Daylight Saving Time,

and he told me. It's dawn, dark, April.
He blinks and apple blossoms fall all over my face.

What's the name for the way we wake
to sirens and each roll inward on the frame?

It wasn't us this time, I mean.
We're still alive, sleeping in our bed,

candles cool and unlit.
Small menace makes sweet the body

of April and that's the meaning of bees.
But the mind's shape is simpler.

When I say he hammered the ring to make it fit,
I mean the ring fits.

Sabbath

Round white mushrooms emerge in clusters overnight,
soil scattered across their brows
like Catholics bearing ash. It's taken me

almost a decade to admit it: I miss. I've missed
feeding all my thoughts through that revolving blade
so thin it could only be felt.

I've missed that arrowing of the—I
almost said *soul*—But it was the mind,
mostly, wasn't it, that winnowed?

I knew God listened. And I knew where to aim.
All the time, every second. I lacked
but with aim.

John Bensko

Independent Miner

Dead now, gone back into the hill
where you dug for coal far deeper
than where you lie, you've left behind
the same sloping hillside of yellow crumbly shale,
and above, the pines whose green comes clear in winter
from brush and scrub oak, and the dog's sharp bark
which echoes from the shacks
lining the creek. We stand beside your grave
as mourners. It's hard to think of ourselves
being up here, where the light goes on.

Then, the light came with you
in the brass carbide lamp, its pop of flame
as your thumb rolled steel over flint.
You clipped it to your helmet
and walked into the shaft, pushing
before you the cart, emptied of its coal
the evening before, and now filled with timbers
for shoring, down the seam's drift
of played out coal through the layers
of cap rock to the deeper veins, the new work.

There at the end, you told me once,
and I didn't know whether to believe,
where the night before
you'd shot the charge to loosen the next day's
haul, you found the opening
to the older shaft from another mine
and there the picks and timbers and lamps,
the iron rails of the cart track,
and the two dead men trapped,
preserved in the sealed air
from a rock fall. No one knew
who they were or when they'd disappeared.
Their clothes were from years
before the turn of the century.

I try to imagine you with them now,
preserved, still alive. But then
where would you be? Trapped,
digging the endless tunnels,
every day more of you, more of us
coming to join you?

It was then your story turned
from belief to disbelief. How the next day
you returned to the opened chamber
to retrieve the old tools and timbers.
They'd crumbled to dust. Not only the wood
but the metal, the steel and iron
lying in ghostly shapes of rust.

Maybe it was true, some alchemy
of carbon and pyrite, of air
breathed down by dying lungs
and held for years, until suddenly
the mouth is opened. The fresh life
breathes the held death to dust.
Or maybe it was just an old miner's tale,
meant to tell a grandson
that in a world of rock hard work
where the water drips the time
through a day you never see,
the imagination finds its way.

Brookside, Alabama

Long after most films went to color
they were still without sound
in the Brookside theater.
The grainy black and whites were matched
by the owner's daughter at the piano
pounding out the chase, or lilting through
gentle cascades of love.

Even the people had voices far
from the drawls of downtown
Birmingham, only twenty miles away.
Weekends, I'd ride with my parents

to my father's family
down the deadman curves
of Cat Mountain and along Five Mile Creek
which, as far as I could tell,
ran forever. Past the barren shale
of strip mines, and the clear
acid water pits, we'd come to a valley
where the sulfurous water of the treatment plant
announced slag covered streets
of unpainted high porches, where
the eyes of men and women
stared deeper than the mines.
They still kept to dark clothes from the old country
as proudly as their language I didn't know.

Once, with my grandfather in the silence
of the Russian church, I gazed at smoke
glazed icons of the grim, yet passive saints
and whispered: What is heaven?
Nothing we know, he said.
It's where the dead live.

In Brookside, they walked the streets,
or so my father swore,
having seen himself the woman
nine feet tall who guarded the footbridge,
and the man whose coffin would not allow itself
to be carried into church.
Like the coal mines, they're
played out now, all they
whose language was wrong, who stalked
street and porch in black and white
past their time and place.
They're silent stars, piano gone,
claimed by color and sound.

Snow Day

A winter day cannot avoid its snow.
Can I accept that I do not belong to myself?

On the street at night a flurry of shadows falls
across the light. Can I think that I will not be?

My feet leave impressions
that the snow itself cannot remove.

Things melt. Hair grows gray, then white.
Disappearing, can I think those I love will be gone too?

I love the snow, when it falls fast and thick,
when the wind takes it and throws it up against itself.

To explain me to me. To know
exactly what I am, and am not.

Snow does not worry.
Its only order is to fall and deepen.

When we unbecome ourselves, when we melt
in moments we cannot bear, who do we become?

I like to watch the snow melting leave the footprints. The icy
remainders where I've gone down the walk are the last to go.

People like to speak of the soul, and the soul's awakening.
It drifts, it rises and falls, it deepens.

Watching it at night, I wonder how thick it will be by morning.
In the day, I hope it will not stop before night.

Randy Blythe

For Aunt Louise, Who Never Liked Me

Some days when she was working in the garden,
    she liked everything. July afternoons,
with the tomatoes weeded and the light just right,
    she could convince herself she *loved* everything
and that maybe things were the way they were supposed to be,
    especially when she squinted through the apple orchard
for red and yellow shapes soon in the leaves, round and glossy
    with the sun behind them. For a second, even
the sweaty little nieces and nephews
    napping on the screened-in porch were dear,
the box fan humming next to them
    making what little breeze there was on Sand Mountain
some afternoons with the tent revival
    two lots over and one back and the traveling preacher
hollering in the faint hazy distance over the PA
    like he wanted the apples to grow
and Aunt Louise to stay the way she was,
    schoolmarm-hard, brusque and gray in the eyes
because part of her didn't care
    there was so much beauty in the world
and God had made her with a cold disposition
    like she had a rock in her flats,
while zinnias spread out from the center
    and the hosta flayed and sprung up
in the sandy ground by the swing
    that Uncle Wayne whitewashed before he died.
So she'd had to get old alone
    and indifferent about sister's grandkids staying with her
for a day or two in the summer
    when she'd never been able to have any of her own
except for the ones she'd taught history forty years
    at the high school. Asleep on the porch,
I was staying with my aunt, dreaming about an ocean
    that didn't have waves, that just roared
like a box fan on HI, then dreaming so what
    if my cousin Jimmy's chest was broader than mine,

which Aunt Louise had pointed out in front of everybody
　　when what was bothering her was probably Wayne
not worth flip, drinking behind the store
　　so he could work up the patience to wait on those
mouthy town kids from Section on credit and be nice to them
　　so their parents would trade with him
and then having the gall to die.

Fluke

Maybe God was inspired but impulsive,
　　not knowing how good creation would be.
Maybe his luck held out.
　　　　　One *Zap*
(celestial finger-point—one second, millenia;
　　deus ex, circumstance; reality, metaphor—
　　　　split gray hairs any old way)
and there were whales singing through the water—
　　deacons up continental aisles,
　　　　cetology's etymology—
at home in one pole's ocean or another.
God looked at them singly and in pods
　　(together rhyming with God's)
and thought (thinking in trumpet sounds),
　　　　"That's what I want: good, slow, gray: ·
　　　　　　loll and hum in the sea
　　　　　　where there was nothing so big before."
One dam surfaced and rolled
　　on a whim like the one that made her.
Her casual fin broke the water,
　　and her eye that had not seen
　　　　that way gazed at the blue.
She upended, tail signaling a sounding,
　　to leave the air world kindly
　　　　to those who would later ponder the pattern:
one motivated spore in a zillion: a fungus underfoot;
　　one spinoff ember-cloud in a zillion: a planet;
　　　　that planet one in a zillion distances from a star:
　　　　　　oceans full of ambitious microbes.
Now you: forget yourself and time: rise into the air.

Instinct

If you behave like a wasp,
God will broom you down
since, if you were a wasp,
you'd only know
how to behave like a wasp
and not like a human behaving
like one, so you wouldn't know
that to build a spit-paper nest
on God's back porch
is a bad move. Every ounce
of wherewithal you have
told you to build there,
and it was the very
wherewithal God installed.

So you already know
the situation is strange,
you're already pretending
the sky is a mirror,
and you can't not stare up.
There's no fun in realizing
you can only be here.
Next thing you're moving 10 ton
blue stone or porphyry 150 miles upriver.
You're carving
giant poses into a mountain.
You don't know
foolishness from ambition.
You're brewing twisted tales
in exasperation tea
because you're sure
there are mysteries in your cup.
Then the blind man
comes to your back door
selling brooms.

Those Many Years

The tremor in his voice,
his eyes, his playing,
the actor playing Sam singing

"just a sigh" softly enough
to bring Ilsa to the point of tears,

the scene about more, you'd think,
than old Dooley Wilson
playing upright and sympathetic

and again on command
because he'd been given little choice as an actor,

the pay was good enough,
and nobody else could downplay grief
like the dark-skinned friend

who understood self-torture
in ways Rick wouldn't know himself,

acting a comfort to our comfortless
and courageous hero who would
put her and her kisses

and the matter-of-factness of sacrifice
on a plane and watch it fly away.

Sami Painting

Moose upside-down wants
snow to touch him and make the sky
as wide as sunlight.

For this desire, it's said
there are nine names,
for snow twenty-three, for sunlight one,

for Moose a season of flakes.
Houses and people are still
houses and people. A man

with a hemlock twig claims horizon.
Everything but meaning returns.
Meaning cannot be eaten,

not even gnawed, says Beaver.
Beaver is Moose small with big teeth
but no antlers.

Night's houses have teeth,
but in the day their mouths are closed.
You cannot fold up sunlight

because it's not paper.
The sun is happy this is so
so is all day.

Emma Bolden

Shower Season

I sickened with sugar. I needed to clear the sky, stop sinking
my teeth into the corners of the ocean, into the blue

that curdles the peel of a clementine, sweet as the smile
on a news anchor's face after the cut back from a televised

disaster. Perhaps it's natural, my need to take home a meaning
not a moment, smooth & buttered, napkined over, a prison

of mints set out to celebrate two people promising to be
the same, or one person stringing together a new tune inside

the swollen cello of her body. Under the false-hooded winter
of every store's air I was conditioned to look through the pinks,

the peonied cards standing in toothed rows that grinned
greetings, belled lilies stretched over the valley of sympathy, so

I began to believe in believing, the way they told me to live. Silked
& unsuffered. I necked the tender loop of a narrative's noose.

Hum City

> "... several residents of Hueytown, AL, began hearing what they referred to as a mysterious sound. This
> sound, which became known as the Hueytown Hum, was alleged to be so disruptive that one resident
> claimed it made it impossible to hold a prayer meeting in his house."
> —T. Novak and S. J. Vitton, "A Case Study of Acoustics and Vibration of Mine Fans"

When the god of whatever finished his map
of Alabama, he blew pollen that settled it,
sent yellow dogs to paw at the doors of mines

that locked black lungs into Baptists. Bosses
hushed canaries then hustled hard to the bank
where coal, when planted, grew green as a dollar

leaves the hand of a worker, cold as coin. There,
Hueytown cited itself. There, men coughed,
hate-hangered. Lard-liquored, they swore

their lives on moonshine by and by
Lord as their wives swore the city's stills away
and with them dancing, bade that song stay holy,

safe as a Sunday serviced by the good preacher's gaze.
In church parking lots, the women gathered
calico, flowered through the gathers of their skirts.

By nails bared, they slicked matches against their heels
then gave fire to photos of the four mop-topped apostles
their daughters followed, throat-hollering, losing all

their lovelies to march by blasphemy's beat. At last
every exiled radio took its rocking, rolling away.
Silence stayed, blooming in victory like a garden

armed with okra and ugly tomatoes. Then they began
to listen: there, with their own breath, their own lungs
winged raven. The children hushed and their hush turned

into the direction each road rumored with its arrows—
it sounded like *away*—and because the law can't reach
through the throat to the heart, to the center that stayed

steady, souled, in its new stillness the whole city
heard it. A hum. Steady, unhurried, lush and long
like a lingering touch behind the barrier of a church

pew, loud as the silence that lit the night and stayed
stuck even in the shaft of the holiest throat.

Beatitudes

Blesséd be the first loves over ochre crayons, the girl who tried
to hide the fact she'd placed forest green in her mouth and chewed,

    the first time light took her greened tongue and gave it beauty
    in my memory, the first time weed felt like an early tree greening and

my mouth and I wanted to fell every self I had been
before I understood the primary language is silence. Blesséd

    be the silence. Blesséd be the quiet nightmares, like the dream when I woke
    up in the passenger seat to see my mother wasn't driving the car, no

one was, and my feet couldn't even reach the pedals. And blesséd
be my mother, loosing my childhood hair from the bristles' grip

    before leaving the brush to soak clean in sinkwater
    foamed with shampoo, and blesséd be my father, blesséd too

the pacemaker pumping my father's heart. Blesséd be
the heart itself, the symbol of the heart, the red construction paper

    suffering the touch of a child's safety scissors
    on its way to becoming a myth, which is a word

we made for the words we use to make ourselves believe
the world is a thing we can sentence into our own understanding.

    And blesséd be the thousand understandings passed
    by glance between girl and girl in a bar: *you are not safe*

with any him, never unwatch your drink, walk with your key
between your fingers, I do not know you but in the bathroom

    I will hold back your hair if need be. Blesséd be the girls
    the girls the girls singing oldies at the stoplight, braiding

their voices into the ribbon that reaches out
their cracked windows, a standard, a bright flag

    to say in this moment I am still
    singing, in this moment I am still afraid.

Finishing School

Couldn't sugar. Couldn't sweet right. Couldn't rat-
comb, couldn't tease the boys with a belt and a bra, Madonna

coned. Couldn't talk lady. Couldn't coo. Couldn't bless

the heart of Jesus till he bleached down to Southern, blonde.
That season slick and sudden, every man was gold and greened

unringed women into rot. I watched fat diamonds dew

the girls' fingers. Then they floated. Chiffoned, sherbet.
Loving like their mamas, like a good pack of bones.

Dogged Virginia slim in the bottom of my pocketbook.

Couldn't magnolia, moon. Couldn't sheath dress. A'blossomed
beneath the sick of shower and sweet each m'am said

would woman us. Couldn't honey the tongue. Couldn't sponge

with syrup the acid of a sentence held up for the savior'd
to sip on. Crossed them traintrackers. Sweat in the skirts.

I hung around till babies borrowed their bodies. Blued,

they hung by their tulles, a ring of bad roses throwing
flat notes into a dumpster. Sixteen satin'd. Twenty-one

a glove. No matter the norths or souths I prayed no

fine boy picked my back for his bullet, but I wasn't a lady
in waiting. For what? Beer breath. Buckshot. Pissed

vinegar, chained the table on which I offered my wants

to the chair. Cornmealed. I toughed grits. Growled
moonshine. Catalogued the ladies like a Sears. Bought

myself a little square of green and squatted, toothed

and rifled. Rocked the porch till every nail
shook loose. I never walked their plank.

Tabitha Carlson Bozeman

Sanatoria

I.

The locker door slammed
closed as my nervous fists,

      and I,

patted down and de-parceled,
walk into the green walled
quiet of your new reality,

          the one you conjured
      one
        foiled
          wisp
at a time,
up a pocket-knifed Bic pen,
into your lungs.

Your busy hands
tap the table,
eyes darting past mine,
    not
       quite
         connecting
as you explain
how your mind is too busy
to readorthinkortalkorsit

still—

I listen.
And watch.
And wonder what to tell your son.

II.

Patina-green copper
coils
    wait,
water wrapped,

while kettled cornmeal
steeps its sugared
soak, seeps up
one round,
drips down another—

drops of mountain moonshine
made for madness.

Meth Adaptation

Aluminum
foil,
soda can,
    metal
        rings
           of a stove eye:
marbled glass
broken coffee cup
shards of terra cotta—

All hot enough
to melt
and
burn—
a crystal incantation.

Shannon Bradt

Guilt

After an abstinent age
I smoke a Marlboro Gold
and my dad looks at me like

I torched the Amazon myself,
face daubed by charred
sterile soil as I count

rancher's profits—limp
bills spritzed with human
blood. There's nothing

to say, and if there were
I'd mute myself anyway:
it's humid enough without

me panting into this hothouse.
Charged with feeding
my neighbor's dog, I

cross the rift between suburban
edifices. The gray old girl
pants frantically, delirious

with my appearance. Dogs
don't sweat, they pant—
so don't blame us. We're

just two bitches without
a uterus between us trying
to stay cool during the hottest

summer on record. Maybe
it's for the best I won't
bear any grandchildren.

Tweaker's Aubade

"A poem should always have birds in it."–Mary Oliver

She leaves you for dead
in badlands etched

with fishbone-fossils,
her parting words

replaying as though
from nicked vinyl:

the birds in this poem
will be vultures.

A puzzler at the time,
but by the sixth

couplet they appear—
black ideograms reeling

overhead, needing no
transliteration.

Who can blame them
for fulfilling a criterion

or marking a corpse
that'll make a good meal?

No answers, just
Star Peyote cackling.

You want answers?
Cross-examine a Boy Scout.

The Devil's no
metaphysician, just

a guy with a ledger, and
even those buzzards

know you gambled
wrong this time.

Relapse

I'm running my fingernail over
the notches that score a Coors
bottle's base, which clinks
as it kisses the wrought iron

mesh of the only table outside
the Burly Earl. From within,
the muffled chorus of *Home
Sweet Home* chides the lost

and I imagine Nikki Sixx sober,
slamming back a cup of chamomile
and massaging the Maltese unmooring
in his lap on a quiet night in.

Here, beyond the black molars of
office buildings crenellating the
horizon, another sunset unknots.
I-65's rush hour exhaust is

the frosted lens of a kaleidoscope,
dicing Sol's deathbed into
blood-orange diamonds and
bruised-lavender trapezoids.

After a few rotations, the backlit
geometry becomes a muted
starscape. *Everyone needs a little
oblivion now and again,* my sponsor

tells me later, waist-deep in
cheese-dip at Los Amigos. I
never could "share" like others
did in meetings—which seemed to

them as easy as unstopping the
spigot of a cask. Suddenly
principled, I wouldn't lie and claim
some newfound joy, not even as an

iterative prayer. Between
confession and absolution winds
the copper coil of a Lee County
whiskey still. We are the

fermenting mash. *Confess*
your faults, one to another—
"give up what's volatile in you
to me," says Saint James

the alchemist, capping a jug.
Having boiled on barstools and in
Spartan folding chairs, I cool
on the psychiatrist's couch,

where threadbare buttons
punctuate the garden
of a fading floral pattern.
Wandering in, I pluck and

taste its lily petals, whose musty
cream recalls hazelnut liqueur.
Orange anthers emerge from
the foliage in glowworm-constellations.

"Do you look forward to anything?"
asks the doctor, disembodied,
but I've come too far. He's mantled
in static and the garden is only

drawing me deeper—down
its pea gravel path, which yields
to yellowing gingko fans
and a colonnade of soft-spoken ferns.

Tina Mozelle Braziel

Dandelion

My first trip, I scoured every floor
of the MoMA, winding around other patrons
before they could read "Alabama" on my tee.
I lingered over *Birthday's* lovers
levitating into kiss, then moved as if driven
until I found, unreal and gleaming,
an Airstream. I made myself at home.
I took a seat. I cranked the slatted glass
open and peered out at the nearby Eames
and Starck. You'd think I had never seen
metal rivets before. I had never seen anything
from where I come from hailed as art. I want that
trailer-inside-the-MoMA feeling again now, I want
dandelion seed valued as much as tulip bulbs.
So I'm buying this packet of what most want
to poison. And the dream of putting down
roots. It has nothing to do with dandelions
that sprout and blossom into suns and moons
as bright and mythic as any Chagall.
Or how their greens fill bowl and belly.
Or how my bees will ferment their nectar
into honey. That's all free and easy.
Those seeds I could harvest from any lawn.

    It's worth I'm after.
    And always paying for.

To the Coosa River at Clear Springs Marina and Trailer Court

Come evening, all tilts towards you,
light sifts down until your waters hold
more sheen than the sky.

Herons lift their backward knees
along your banks as egrets flock
to festoon the pines.

Like an outboard whining its way
across your slough, then settling
into an idle hum beside its pier, I linger,

wanting to hear your whisper hushing
the trailers and me. I long to stay
and feel the boat's wake kiss the fall-away shore.

Today I swam to the island, scratched
between the horns of the goat who baas
his lonesomeness and again

I was young and at home. I walked
beneath pines once whitened
by so many birds, their weight bent

the boughs beyond buoyancy.
Tomorrow I drive cross county,
making my way to settle beside another river.

I hear its waters run north and cold, too cold
for swimming. Don't hold on to me
like a mother, don't lay out this silken shine.

Let me go, but come with me,
set my body atilt with your sway
each night. Can't you shift like the egrets

who rearrange themselves from one branch
to another, each nearness shining
as perfect as the last and the next?

Joel Brouwer

Lines Written in Memphis, Tennessee

Defying the prominent signage, I took
a picture of the flophouse from the balcony
and a picture of the balcony from
the flophouse. School group kids with juice boxes.
Disgusted because I couldn't make it
poignant. A fucking dandelion growing from
a cracked brick wall. A thousand clouds.
The waiter urged me to select my choices
of mini pastries, juices, and hard fruit
from the breakfast bar. A man in the paper
dreamed of building a new house to replace
his old house. He wouldn't tear the old house
down, he'd build the new house up inside
the old one as it crumbled. Engineers
were intrigued. I didn't understand it.
My hotel's shadow brawled with the river's
flexing pewter currents as I photographed
melancholy barges pushing corn or coal.
Swaddling my fancy camera, again ignoring
posted rules, I handed dollar bills to every
homeless guy who asked. Which did I prefer,
dream or mountaintop? I'd seen videos
of each at the museum and I said something
stupid and true: Both choke me up. But I like
best his final speech, for the moment
he finishes the "if I had sneezed" litany,
allows the laughter—it's such a weird,
bathetic passage—then builds a new silence
inside the crumbling old silence: "Now
it doesn't matter now. It really doesn't
matter what happens now." He'd die
the next day. He knew it would be soon.
I'd rushed through most of the museum,
ignoring the old pictures and newspapers.
I thought I knew everything already. *Now
now now*. The present a pivot. He keeps
repeating it. "What are you waiting for?"

A girl in a tank top and shimmery orange
athletic shorts bicycled by, talking
to herself or the Bluetooth rig blinking
in her ear, and I thought I knew the other
dream of the man in the newspaper was
to marry the hooker he'd seen every week
for years and have her work for him instead.
Why did I think that? That and "melancholy
barges" and the dandelion? Maybe my eye's
not right. The homeless guy recited choice
selections, even mimicking the cadences.
"It's all right to talk about the new
Jerusalem, but one day, God's preachers must
talk about the new New York, the new Atlanta,
the new Philadelphia, the new Los Angeles,
the new Memphis, Tennessee." I gave him
a twenty and took his picture. In the film,
you can see Dr. King stumble as he takes
his seat, as if something's shoved him.
A shadow or current or choice. The girl
lay in the grass beside her bike, talking
up at the clouds. I took her picture too.

Taylor Byas

Geophagia

*"If Mike Espy and the liberal Democrats gain the Senate we will take that first step
into a thousand years of darkness."*
    —from a tweet by Phil Bryant, Governor of Mississippi, 1/2/2020

They say eating the soil might
be good for you. To have your pale
chiclet teeth redlined
by clay, your ocean-clear
mouthwash bloodied when you spit
in the sink. Mistake this for a split
lip, a back-alley beating
that has left the tongue fat enough
to rick your cries for help.
Your grandmother tells you to avoid
the clay cooling in the shade
of the taller trees, and you don't.
After rain, the clay goes garnet, clumps
of wine-dark up to your
elbows, smeared around your lips.
My God, you've gone

cannibal. They say eating the soil
might be good for you
with all its minerals, the blood
that wept from swollen
black toes and dried in the shape
of another country. In death,
someone fed this tree. After a few
mouthfuls tonight, you feel
a little madness creeping in. You watch
the sun set while sitting back
on your heels, its half-step into darkness
packing the world into red
clay. This is blood-warm, the heat
of night closing in like a mob. Bribe
the sun to set on you instead, let
it light you aflame.

The Black Girl Comes to Dinner

We drive into the belly of Alabama,
where God tweezed the highway's two lanes
down to one, where my stomach
bottoms out on each brakeless fall.

Where God tweezed the highway's two lanes
with heat, a mirage of water shimmers into view then
bottoms out. On each brakeless fall,
I almost tell you what I'm thinking, my mouth brimming

with heat. A mirage of water shimmers into view then
disappears beneath your tires.
I almost tell you what I'm thinking, my mouth brimming
with blues. Muddy Waters' croon

disappears beneath your tires.
I want to say *I'm nervous* beneath a sky brilliant
with blues. Muddy Waters' croon,
the only loving I'm willing to feel right now, the only loving

I want. To say *I'm nervous* beneath a sky brilliant
enough to keep me safe means to face what night brings.
The only loving I'm willing to feel right now, the only loving
that will calm me—I need you to tell me I am

enough. To keep me safe means to face what night brings
to the black girl in a sundown town—
that will calm me. I need you to tell me I am
safe. That they will love me, that the night will not gift fire

to the black girl in a sundown town.
Your grandmother folds me into her arms and I try to feel
safe. That they will love me, that the night will not gift fire
are mantras to repeat as

your grandmother folds me into her arms. And I try to feel
grateful. But *get home before it's too late* and *watch out for the flags*
are mantras to repeat as
we drive into the belly of Alabama.

A Grocery Store in Alabama

Over the apple bucket, I weigh a Granny
Smith in my hand and thumb the dents for rot.
I check for bruises like these shoppers check
for me—the blackened pit of a golden peach.

***

Another buggy's wheel comes screeching around
the corner, a mother peering through the shocks
of hair escaping from her bun, her toddler
pointing and poking price tags, palming fruits.

***

I wonder what it must be like, no pop
or sting on the hand, no preparation speech—
don't look, don't touch—from a mother trying to save
herself from the pop and sting of not-so-quiet

***

whispers, the manager's backhanded *ma'am*, the absence
of respect. Still—as I grab a pepper, garlic
paste—I can feel these shoppers slow around
me, as if someone paused this tape of my

***

black life, to point to me on screen and say
right there, we got her. I concentrate on the mist
of the veggie sprinkler, water sleeving my arm,
its hiss as soft as a mother's *shush*, or the chafe

***

of a handshake, sliding palms before the hollow
thump on the back, or even the mother bending
to cover her toddler's finger as she points
at me, her susurration—*don't point at that*.

I Don't Care if Mary Jane Gets Saved or Not

I can't lie, I tried to imagine myself
in Spiderman's grip—my damsel-in-distress
scream strung through the city like Christmas lights—
I really did. But my black ass would never be

in Spiderman's grip. My "damsel-in-distress"
don't look like Kirsten Dunst or Emma Stone—I looked,
I really did. But my black ass would never be
dainty enough to be rescued by a white hero. The movie villains

don't look like Kirsten Dunst or Emma Stone—I looked—
but the women who terrorize me in real life are
dainty enough to be rescued by a white hero. The movie villains
always come for the white heroine, and she will cry,

but the women who terrorize me in real life are
strategic, hammering out an axe with tears. The playbook goes:
always come for the white heroine and she will cry
wolf. Cry danger. Call the police. The 911 call

strategic, hammering out an axe with tears. The playbook goes—
there is an African-American woman threatening me; cry
wolf; cry danger; call the police. The 911 call
a masterclass on acting. Mary Jane would kill me if it was in the script—

There is an African-American woman threatening me—cry
until Spiderman dropped from the sky. The way I play dead,
a masterclass on acting. Mary Jane would kill me if it was in the script,
because what else could I be but the villain

until Spiderman dropped from the sky? The way I play dead
in the cocoon of Spiderman's web, you can tell I've practiced.
Because what else could I be but the villain?
I can't lie. I tried to imagine, myself.

My Twitter Feed Becomes Too Much

I come across pictures of two rubber bullets
nestled in a palm, their nose tips black
and rounded like a reporters' foam-covered
mic. The caption reads *These maim, break skin,
cause blindness.* Another photo—a hollow
caved into a woman's scalp, floating hands

in blue gloves dabbing at the spill. An offhand
comment in the replies—*are you sure that rubber bullet
caused that type of damage?*—the question hollowed
of genuine concern. The page refreshes. A black
man melts into a street curb from exhaustion, his skin
blotched with sweat and red. Protester's hands cover

his body, and this is church. A baptism—*cover
me with the blood.* And there are more. Hand-
drawn threats—*shoot the FUCK back.* Police cars skinned
of their lettering and paint from the bullet-
aim of Molotov cocktails in Budweiser bottles. *Black
Lives Matter* markered in thick letters below the hollow

outline of the black power fist. A gas mask's eye-hollows
glinting with tears. The page refreshes. Undercover
cops wearing matching armbands like a gang. A black
army tank crawling through city streets the way a hand
may tip-toe up a thigh. The page refreshes. A bullet
list of places to donate if I can't put my skin

in the game protesting in the streets. The snakeskin
pattern of fires from a bird's-eye view of DC. Hollowed
Target storefronts. The page refreshes. Rubber bullets
pinging a reporter and her crew as they run for cover,
a white woman's reply—*things are getting out of hand*—
punctuated with heart emojis. Protester's shadows blacking

the fiery backdrop of the riots. Badge numbers blacked
over with tape. The page refreshes. A man skinned
by the asphalt when pulled from his car with both hands
up. A police car plowing into a peaceful crowd. The hollow
promises from white friends to "do better"—a cover-
up for how quickly they will bullet

into our inboxes and ask us to hand them the answers. Black
rubber bullets—the page refreshes—a woman's forehead skin
split—page refreshes—a bloody hollow—refresh—take cover.

David Case

If I Could Rip

If I could rip the heart from a quintet
of Schumann's, could then step back
to see the arteries and tendons pull

it in to the place required by
Leonardo's famous sketch (displayed
by a pizza joint, then taken down

because of public scandal) or by
Mozart's balanced instincts, I would know
everything that poetry could teach us. I

realize that Mozart is not Brahms:
the ripping Brahms always demands
for his aged, masochistic flesh is

different in kind and kith from Mozart's
foreplay and caresses, the climax
spread throughout the movement so that

everything is touched with love. Both
things are love, and few can understand
two kinds of love, most never knowing one.

I can rip away the hostile mask over
my Mozart-loving face only in these ways:
devotion to these marks on scores and pages,

remembering kissing Anthony's eyes.

Tongue-Tied

Speechless, I drove north into the past,
crossing the Georgia line at Madison,
heading for the nation's ugliest
near-urban tangle, Albany, Georgia, then through
the hopeless sun and clouds of Columbus,
Phenix City, and Opelika. What difference
could crossing the Tallapoosa make? Still hours
before the wine lofts of Birmingham.
That city, following the journey, looked like
Atlanta, though not for long. The
brain-eating heat held sway over
Five Points South and its eateries full
of half-despairing clients drinking whole
afternoons away, with evenings
to follow, and no soul surviving in me,
flat on my back with wine to swallow.
I looked up at Sirius, king of stars,
king of the world too, for a long while,
and the rotted wood and clammy air
refused to yield their secrets,
mocking Agee's "Sure on This Shining Night"
("High summer holds the earth..."). Holds? No, crushes
in a bear-hug, an awful wet kiss.

Shelly Stewart Cato

Sonic Madonna, After the Storm

I sift
            for quarters,

order corndogs for the man

       heat steeps in air

downed wires,
             lank as sweated hair,

swoop overhead

        fresh off the street,
          a man devours tater tots

    when he reaches for his pup,
        when he cradles her like a babe

      the ulcer on her haunch seeps
              like the skies

        he offers foraged food

    to his balding cur,

       his thumb in chocolate shake,

      to suckle her

               a beaded curtain
               of gunmetal rain
               between us

               looks like chain

Maybe, Everything, Rewind, Reverse

—in response to a TED talk: "Your Kids Might Live on Mars"

Dear TED:

I need your help. You said in 20 years, our kids could live on Mars, and you said Mars is best, next to Earth. In 20 years, my kid will be—if he makes it—he'll be 39. I need to bring him sooner. If you could make Mars happen in five years, I'll do anything to get him there.

It'd be like carpool—only longer—you said 240 days to make the trip. That's about like being pregnant. I'd fill my belly up again, a spaceship warm with wool and chocolate milk, watch him drag beneath my skin like a bald-nosed baby mole.

You said you worry. I worry, too—we'll screw up Mars like we've screwed Earth. Dauphin Island's almost gone. A few red wolves are here or there. A garbage island big as France floats in our sea. For my kid to have a chance, I need to know ahead of time, it's better there. I need to know there are no needles. I figure not, because the atmosphere is thinner, and gravity is less, so I can't imagine needles—they're so slender and so little—can't imagine they'd be hiding in backpacks or in hoodies.

You said the seasons there are double—twice as long and twice as many. Maybe spring nods forward, then reverses. Fiddleheads frond open, then curl back into scrolls. Maybe, ash-cream petals fall to deadwood, whorl back into sepals, then deck the dogwoods out again. Maybe red-winged blackbirds flit the powerlines and skim his split-rail fence, then post real still and grow eggshells he can warm in cradled hands. Maybe he can have a hatchling of his own.

Maybe, everything.

You said years are double, too—we could use some extra time—like extra days on Leap Year. Good things happen when you get an extra day. It happened in my 5th grade year and 9th. Instead of flying men and busted shuttles on TV, my teacher showed us how a red-throat bird—its heart—would hum more beats on this, this extra day.

That's all I'm asking. Extra heartbeats.

Please TED talk, he's got a lot of friends in rehab. Some of them, their teeth are halved, and some are quartered. One guy, he's a sous-chef—he can't stop—even for his twins. Can he come, too? And can his kids? He wants to make his salted caramel galette and have his own café. And the guy who preaches Cowboy Church—him, too? And the brothers no one visits who pick ukulele strings. And the one who sings so that I'll notice.

And here's the very last. I had a vision. I saw my son's heart beating in Mars-time—1200 beats a minute. Pounding, pulsing fast in Starburst orange, atomic tangerine, and that red like Silly String. And all his friends held hands like paper dolls, their pupils, round and smiling. Someone played their bones like harpsichords and mandolins, and all of them could sing, and their bodies romped through sweetcorn, and they leapfrogged bales of hay, and their hair grew like liriope.

Please, TED talk, line my belly like a nest of twine and down and twigs. I'll keep him fed and safe and warm. Please, just get us there.

Anti-Ode to a Marriage: *"Why Antimatter Matters"*

I was listening to a TED Talk on the plane to San Diego, flying over snowy, Colorado Postcard ridges and thinking the ridges looked like mackerel clouds—meaning the earth looked like the sky, and the sky looked like the sky. TED said that for every particle of matter, there exists a particle of antimatter. For every particle of iridium, a particle of anti-iridium. For every electron, an anti-electron. And for the Milky Way, even an anti-Milky Way!

And I deduced that for every person a person happens to be married to—for every pink-eyed, stumbling fat ass that rolls over the bed's horizon and thwacks the snooze button three times—for every slack-jawed, twaddling, grizzled-face bunko of molecules that stumbles into the bathroom, drapes its dick (I wonder: Is *drape* too magnanimous a word here?) over the basin's rim so it can pee and not miss, checks its teeth for a fleck of last night's massaged kale (and finds two)—for every flash-fried, freeze-dried, molecular birth of a person, *there must be an anti-person.*

This would, of course, be me or if I'm the person, then my husband is the anti-person. So, if he is the one whose anti-matter is still lying in bed, then *I'm* the one at the mirror, showered and coffee'd and deriding his flaccid body when I slough a glance at the slump-hump of anti-partner lying in bed. If that's the case, then he could not be my anti-person. No, no, not the soul and reflection of me—he is more like that one red potato escaped from its Polypropylene bag and rolled to the back of the pantry, thinking it has been spared the roasting oven, the All-Clad pot. (Even as a potato, my husband is thinking he has superior genetics.) He withers there, bodily fluids leaking, and I, still a person and not yet a potato and normally a good housekeeper (If my husband were listening to this, he would say, *When did this become fiction???*)—I simply allow this to happen.

There! On the white laminate, sticky syrup puddles until the potato wears its skin like sackcloth, until the yellow-maggot-green-smush smell—not at first—no, no, at first, the kids all aquiver that it might be another dead owl in the attic; at first, the composite family nose recoiling as the smell weighs in silently like overnight snowfall. But there you have it, the weeping, rotten, once-a-potato—now anti-potato. I retrieve it with my yellow Playtex glove and to avoid the smell, swivel my neck around raptor-esque, and to distance myself, preen my scapulae like a roosting turkey hawk on a cold, cold night, and then walk that potato out to the curb;

and, of course, drop my potato—or rather, he sieves through the hole in my glove from Jacko's third-grade volcano project.

Hell, if it isn't snowing even harder now.

But wait, I'm saved!

Isn't that the snowplow over by Dollar General? Leave that mush on the sidewalk for the plow to sloosh down the neck of the sewer pipe. Because, no worries, my potato-husband will never cease to exist. Because his molecules have not altered, have only shifted from muscle to fat, bright-eyed to bulge-eyed, cream to butter bean. Potato, anti-potato, partner, anti-partner—it hardly matters. He's still here beside me—snoring on his king-size anti-snore pillow.

What I'm trying to tell you is I lost him. His molecules mutated beyond recognition. This is not an ode. It's an elegy. *I wasn't saved. He wasn't. We weren't.*

Snapchat at the Magical Arctic Puffin Exhibit

Maybe he has magic to keep himself
alive forever, says my little boy,

palms parallel to the floor,
elbows pulled in like a chubby T-Rex.

He grins and flaps and smoochy-lips
himself in the aqua glass.

A murder of teenagers captures it all.

Mega–

I got a big church. My church has got a big rock right in the middle of a big circle drive, and the rock's got a waterfall in it, and at night, the waterfall has big blue lights and big green lights that shoot all the way to the moon. My church has a TeeNZoNe and t-shirts that say, NOT TODAY, SATAN! We got deodorant in the bathrooms and neon vests for the traffic people and those orange sticks like airport people use to scoot everybody along. My church has got a bowling alley. My church's parking lot is bigger than the mall.

On the inside, we got a Starbucks and a basketball court. When Brother Wayne mashes the red button to lock the big doors, Chase and I know how to hide under the bleachers. My church has got big swings inside that shoot like hot-tub jets and squirt out preachers on 'em. And they all lock hands and arms and hang from their underknees like red and blue Monkeys in a Barrel from *Toy Story* because of the red and blue lights they shine on 'em. And sometimes, the preachers just pick up a little kid or two and dip 'em in the water and save 'em.

My church is safe. My church is dark. My church has got a life-sized cardboard Elvis at the Starbucks that says, *It's hip to tip.*

My church has lots and lots of people and a huge, fat, square swimming pool. My church has Jumbotrons and metal detectors like at Roll Tide football in T-town, and all the kids get to go through the fast lane.

My church has a band and a drummer inside an upside-down glass bowl, and he looks green (because the light they shine on him)—like when you catch a lizard and put him in an upside-down jar and slide cardboard under him and keep him for just one night. Lizards can see in the dark. In the dark, people can't see you cry. My church is safe.

Alyx Chandler

Curses

I try to be brave
in my body
but who can with

family like humidity
everyone sweating
out their egos

the neighbors commenting
on each other's figure, oh
how much they love

a barbecue of compliments
served up a little burnt
all of us made fake-sweet

in coated meat
dad says pick everyone
some tomatoes out back

throw in a few big ones
show them what a good
year it's been

I don't I grab
the skimpy limp-thin
ones contorted fists

weather-beaten bodies
pile them up in my t-shirt
this cloth bucket

I hold out
and underneath I let
my own belly hang holy

I hand them curses
little witch fingers
curled hot peppers, *c'mere*

Charley Horse

In Alabama I play defense

      buckle mid-game to calf spasms and

         call it what it really is—

the overworking of sore muscle   the shock of dehydration

      that shakes me into

         a sideline cradle

      let me tell you what

         nothing goes unnoticed here

     my gramma and her Lasik eyes like lasers on the field

         the coach who makes me

       tear mustard packets

     open with my teeth choke down quick electrolytes

to stifle a leg cramp its bitter sting

          a gag of yellow

I eat my teenage body good as

       an orange slice

       at halftime

     I let the citrus burn like an electric circuit

      on my open cuts

   this pain is a god

       I leave

          only to come back to

Off the Rails

I used to be one of those high-spirited women who run at night

lace up streetlights
tight like tennis shoes
into county darkness

let dirt roads knot lily-livered thoughts
pull them taut keep them tied in my throat

        I sought exhaustion—

owl screeches ringing like roll call
flimsy wooden fences rattling
single-family farms I passed silos

land so thick with pines no one would find me
I never carried a knife I just fantasized
the steel finger clasping my shorts
hard and sharp on my hip bone

like automatic porch lights   I detect movement
all my raw parts revving together
leading me to relics   the abandoned railway

the steel body made to move to haunt heavy
in the mad-bright tunnel of headlights

I run all the way into daybreak
to the freight train freed of resistance   but is anything

ever fully free of resistance when it's housed in a hurry
when I'm a flesh vehicle meant to carry a load   down a straight track

that doesn't deviate

until I do

Carrie Chappell

Windows

She is at her home in Bedford Village standing against a taupe drape,
While her petal eyes lunge up branches, heavens.
Night has come to fleece its witness, and she is a mistress
Of thought, a shape words dispute. *Star, waterfall, woman.*
She has always been too much speech to save herself,
But she can't stop the tilt of her head, the clearing of throat,
The impulse to streak through the uncharted quiet.
She admires the boney cheek of her berserk moon
And opens her robe, lets it fall, opens her mouth,
Lets it talk: *Didn't I tell you, as I told the congregations,*
The audiences, I'd never condone this martyrdom? Nobody but I
Can stand the truth of my exuberance, the principles of my misconduct.
Surely, an old satellite like you understands the morals of endurance.
At this, she turns to her living room, the darkened stage
Of a house, and sits to face the crystal ghost of a bottle.

From Paris, I stand at my *portes-fenêtres* against my onyx banister
As my eyes hunt February's grey requiem. Day has come
To coax its erotic hustle, and I am a mistress of here, a present
My past refutes. *Acolyte, ornament, girl.* I have always been
Too much courtesy to save myself, so I try to stop the pitch
Of my smile, the touching of neck, the impulse to smother the debris
Of my desires. I stare at the smothered sun in my berserk dawn
And open my nightshirt, let it fall, open my mouth, let it go:
Ta-lu-lah, Ta-lu-lah, Ta-lu-u-u-lah. I never wanted you martyr,
But I have held your name in the slag of my heart and dreamed you saint.
My darling, I will sing of you out windows as I will sing of you in books.
At this, Tallulah tucks herself in. At this, the berserk orbs of
Our berserk skies start their chronic traffic. At this, I turn
To the lit stage of my life to face the crystal spokes of now.

Lifeboat

Her arms splayed across the tank rims like masts.
Her legs churning, as bubbles wreathe her neck.
In the quiet, she skips a question like a rock to crash
Between my thighs. *What happened to your sexuality?*
Her lips fizzle with spit, turning the container
Into a deep fryer, my legs into milky potatoes.
I think of my past in the present tense, faintly
Drawing the bath waters where I once lowered
My body into a porcelain-enameled cistern.
Happened? I puff as if to make air consonantal,
As if I think I should continue throwing back out
What probes. With my left hand pulling the
Wet reeds of my hair, with my toes darning
The drain, I fix on her eyes, between the drapes
Of her hair. I swirl my tongue in the pool
Of plain speech, squint, lean forward. *Tallulah,*
I say, *when I was a young girl, I used to masturbate
In the bath with a Happy Meal toy.* She shivers,
As if a shawl has fallen down her back. I shiver
Too, and she whoops, *What in the hell
Is a Happy Meal?* My eyebrows droop with
The letdown: *It's hardly a double-entendre, not
Even a promise.* My tongue swirls again in
The pool of plain speech, then I say, *I used to
Run over my clit with a troop of monster wheels.
This is what happened.* And with that, I surge
Up and begin sloshing towards her. *Tallulah,
It was never mine. I was made to give it away
To plastic America. And, later, when the guilt
Of touching myself was drowning me, I prayed
To be saved.* Here, Tallulah stands herself.
And? she says, voice rising like a cresting wave.
God did not hear me, I tell her. *Instead,* that night,
In my dreams, *a gang of women came chanting,
"Only for a man."* As I finished my confession,
I began to fall, but Tallulah swam up close,
Drove my head into the deep, then flung me
Up, like a conch, to meet the brine of her lips.

Robert Collins

At My 50th Class Reunion

When my former classmates learn
I've been living all these years
in Alabama, they label me most likely
to secede, which suits me fine
since, like most teenagers, I never felt
that I belonged. I hear of hoarders,
gamblers, homeless drunks, some dead,
some ailing, some with whereabouts
unknown. The famous physicist
who gave the valediction hasn't deigned
to grace us with his presence.
Why would he? Predictably,
the prom queen, now a struggling
artist, still needs to be the center
of attention, and the TV star,
her best roles receding in the mirror,
has had some major work done
though no one's cruel or brave enough
to say so in her presence. Scanning
the class photo on display, I'm stricken
by how few faces I remember
and actually knew in any way at all,
being shy, aloof, and terminally
self-centered. I find myself
and several more with asterisks
beside our names denoting our induction
into the Academic Hall of Fame,
still singled out for our achievements
half-a-century before. Despite the likely
tilting to the right, and further,
of the vast majority here to reunite,
age proves the ultimate democrat—
liberal and progressive—as I realize
when I peruse the lengthening roster
of the names of the deceased, 15%
according to my hasty calculations,
and growing even as we gather. Before

the last song plays and the evening's over,
we stand en masse for one final photo
we've earned our rightful places in
merely by surviving, and I can't help
but feel compassion for this group
of total strangers I've now become a part
of and have known most all my life.

Holding My Hospital Birth Certificate Seventy-two Years Later

My older brother finds it
sorting through some papers
for Ancestry.com and posts it.

It doesn't even give a name
nor the physician who attended,
just my mother's signature,

sex of child, date of birth,
and one tiny, blotted footprint
(perhaps all I'll leave behind),

with the endorsement of the nursery
supervisor long dead now. In her hand
near the bottom, the word *Save.*

H. M. Cotton

Library: the week after my father's death

Halfway between Flagg and Lee, I find
the spine my daddy checked out once
a year since 1943. Gap-toothing the row
of balustrading books, I pluck it
from the others: brothers diving spikes

along the mineral rail line. Winding through green
and red, coal mines and soot, these words etch
the history of my father's side. Birdsmouthing
its hardback binding, the book swallow nests
lightly in my hands. A page shudders

as a man with Capote passes by while, outside,
bricklayers kneeling by a broken wythe
butter culls for a Dutchman's repair
with clinkers darker than the rest. Now, alone
I cosset the due-date card from its front flap

fold. The numerals line up like mantrip cars
battening down the page, the first half-
handwritten with curly 2s and 5s. The latter
stamped in iron red. I slip it in my pocket
to shadow box with his marriage license

and engineer's watch, then fingering the book's
corner between its mates, buttoning it back
till it fits like a steel tongue in its striker plate.

Play the Line

Our empty boat slip needles toward Panama.
Across the bay, embalmed in brackish
backwash and sand, pilings finger up like broken
masts. At low tide, a heron high-steps

among them, looking to gullet a speckled trout.
Clutched against the breeze, I see you and our
last day on the water, back when colors
came in brighter hues. We kayaked the cypress knees

and when I cast my line, I caught nothing
but the flesh along my upper arm. You kneaded
the kahle through, nipped the barb, and pinched me free.
Now your hooks are big as hands and you have moved

on to blue water and bigger fish. Maybe you will return
with the pitcher plants' bloom. Tonight, the sun sets in layers
of annealed steel. Minnows whirligig in the shallows,
the heron still stalking their wakes. I have learned to wait.

Honeysuckle

Bines twine clockwise. Spring has
clapped the dust from her skirt
and paper-mâchéd a thousand
milk and butter twists.

The bees have come to cull
and found their offices closed:
petals turgored tight as a spun
maypole. Sugar ants jaw

to cleave a cream nub, but
cornucopial buds kernel unto
their own, shut up like I am,
unwilling to be the first to share.

Asterism

Winter waxes full. At eight and ten
we used to gather stars into our own
constellations, set them to names
and Pollocked them on butcher paper
from momma's sewing room. Later,
we hung our history on a clothesline
between a pine and gutter spout,
our timeline rippled like a sheet
set out to dry. And when
Daddy's favorite redbone took
with distemper, we stippled him
into a canter so he could race
around the heavens. We were gazers,
you and I, star-wheeling with crayons.
Now, Orion stretches out flat
on his back, breaking the horizon,
and you recast his myth with ours,
ending with an apple blossom altar
and a ring, instead of the scorpion's sting.

Chella Courington

Lynette's War

Cousin Lynette says she's tired
of cleaning houses of rich bitches.
They don't even shit like us
got toilet seats that float to the bowl
never make a sound.
She hands me the baby
over the front seat.

I'm tired too
tired of babysitting Leah
who grabs my earrings
covers me in crumbs
bites off the heads of animal crackers.
Only eats heads.

Lynette says she's sexy, I'm not.
Freshman year she called me a *mutant.*
Raisin boobs on a fifteen-year-old's wrong.
Mama took me to the doctor
and he shook his head.

Don't know why I hang with Lynette.
She's like the girl who cut my hair
at Cinderella's. Said I had
the ugliest strands she'd ever seen.
I kept going back for more till
Lynette blurted
you don't need to pay for that crap.

Yet she's a good mother.
If Leah has fever, Lynette won't go
to work. *I'd rather lose my job*
than leave a sick baby in daycare.

She might call me names, but
let somebody else do it
she'd scratch their eyes out.

At the Sonic, some boy from Crossville
leaned in the window, *drop the fat chick*
let's go driving.
She clawed his left cheek
screeched away
tray still on the car, cokes and fries flying.
Son of a bitch thinks he can dump on you
and get lucky with me.
Stupid bastard.

I thought Lynette would be the one to leave.
Never let anybody walk on her
or me though she did what Johnson girls do
after turning sixteen—she got knocked up.
Wouldn't tell a soul who the father was.
We all thought Sonny Cruz.

He went to Afghanistan in August
emailed Lynette every week.
Like they were junk, she'd hit delete.
He started writing letters she stacked
on her dresser—unopened.
Staying in touch with soldiers
is talking to the dead.
I tell her lots of boys make it
and Sonny could come back.

Lynette turns away
he won't be the Sonny I knew.

Before the homecoming game she
carries his letters out to our grill.
They catch on the third match.

Every last word.

Flying South

The first thing I heard of Winston Walker
is that Friday afternoon he shot me
in the eye. BB the size of a mockingbird
iris and about as yellow. Arm draped
over the fence, I watched him walk
toward me. Cock. Pop.
Wasps nested. Screams covered me.

Ice cubes froze the sting blue. Weeks later
my sight, sharp as ever. But the pasty scar tissue
turned my head down, hid the eye behind
cloud cover. No meteor showers
visible. Just an ugly white
glob Winston Walker called an accident
no doctor could erase till I was sixteen

and moved to Birmingham. Doctors scraped clouds
off blue iris—ashen crater in their place.
When I raised my lid, the sky appeared.
After thirty years Winston Walker telephoned.
Honest to God, I just wanted to scare you.
He dreamed I shot him full
of Adriamycin exploding under his skin

infrared starbursts burning every breathing cell.
Come November I expected him at New Hope
to be cremated, ashes scattered where he hunted
whitetail deer. In a simple casket he
was lowered near his mother as shadows
passed through us.

T. Crunk

Visiting the Site of One of the First Churches My Grandfather Pastored

My mother said later that, to the shovel operators, we must have looked like some delegation from out of town that couldn't find the picnic. Or else the funeral. Not so bad my brother and me jumping the fence, and my father, but then my mother, and all of us helping my grandfather over, and finally my grandmother deciding she wanted to see, too.

Then all of us standing together at the rim of the pit in our Sunday clothes, sun reflecting off my grandmother's black patent purse, a few trees still hanging on nearby, roots exposed, like tentacles, like the earth is shrinking under them. The smell of sulphur.

The giant bucket scoops up through the rocks and dirt, the shovel swings around, the bucket empties, and the whole thing swings back, the noise taking an extra second to reach us. I am watching the two men inside, expecting them to notice us, to wave us away because we don't belong there, but they don't. They must be used to it.

Years later I will remember my grandfather saying that they strip away the land but all they put back is the dirt. Maybe plant a few scrub pine. "Good for nothing any more," he says now, turning to go back to the car, "good for nothing except holding the rest of the world together."

It looks almost blue in the sun, the piece of coal I have picked up to take home for a souvenir.

Redemption

1.

Driving through the mining counties
Green River to Central City
light of dawn like water
shadows rising to the surface

going back for my grandmother's funeral:
in Muhlenberg
a raised welt of railroad tracks
bitter porches emptying to morning

and beneath the skewed abandoned
cross of a telephone pole
a woman with a tin scuttle

gathering coal that had fallen from the trains
dried clots of earth's blood.

2.

Afternoon at my father's house
sun filling empty flower pots by the coal shed

watching the holly-hocks the roses and mimosa
recalling one of my grandfather's sermons:

how the souls will one day set out
to find their new bodies

how they will leave behind this hollow earth
swirling with ice and rags

I imagine them rising above the blistering corn
above the dust of the dry rows the chaff settling

and all they can see from the air
is the smallest thing: a piece of straw

caught in the planks of the barn door
a black wasp clinging to the kitchen screen.

3.

Awake that night in the spare room
which once was mine

streetlamp through the curtains
lit sparkler of moths
radio from an upstairs window

fear of nakedness of insignificance
the corridors of my narrow life

the viewing room was carpeted and modern

counting sadly backward to myself.

4.

Moon in the spines of the hawthorn
clouds amethyst and omniscient
hands of the clock again moving
toward morning and I picture headlights
tracing through the cemetery as through a maze:

when our souls lie waiting in their beds
our bodies
awaiting the end of baptism by earth

and we picture somewhere above us
the house we were born in
can see the hydrangeas and impatiens by the steps
a crown of gnats hovering above the four o'clocks
a red bee bowing into one of the yellow blossoms
and through an open window a lamp
curtains reaching up into the room

what peace will lift us
whispering what hope
who want only to rise to the surface
as through water

what peace when we want to return
not set out
when we want only to step up onto that windy porch
to step back through that fiery door?

from Summons

There's two ways to ring a church bell. One way, you pull the rope and let go, so the two claps come one right after the other. That's the way they ring it for church service or a camp meeting. They call that the meeting bell.

The other way, you pull the rope and hold it, then let go, so there's a little wait between the first clap and the second. And when you hear that, you drop what you're doing and come running, because that's the way they ring it when there's a fire or an accident, or someone has taken sick or has died. It means someone is in need of help. And they call that the mourning bell.

They called the big meeting at the Bethel Church to tell people what they were going to do about building this dam. Everybody from that end of the county was there. Me and your grandfather were there, along with everybody else from that end of the county. Trucks and wagons were pulled in everywhere, all around the churchyard, all up and down the road.

Before it started, you'd have thought it was a Fourth of July picnic. People gathered around in little groups, visiting and laughing and talking. Children running and shouting everywhere.

They all thought they had something to celebrate. Thought they were going to get rich off this dam project. Thought that if they *had* to sell their land, they'd just hold the government to whatever price *they* wanted.

There were three TVA men there. When it came time to start, they asked the preacher to go inside and ring the church bell to call the meeting to order. The preacher had already spent that morning with them, showing them around the countryside. He knew what was about to be said that afternoon.

He went into the church vestibule, and he rung the bell, all right. We all heard the first clap, but then there was that little wait before we heard the second clap. And right away it struck people, clear as a gunshot.

He rung that bell that way three times.

71

By the third time, there was hardly a word being said by anybody. And there wasn't a soul laughing anymore.

Those three TVA men were city people. They had no idea what they'd just heard.

But everybody else knew. And they were all gathered up close around the churchhouse steps, looking at those men, listening and waiting, solemn as a funeral.

Prayer

There where my breath enters the darkness
and I cannot yet follow

you who are lost
await me

with your signal lanterns your pitchers of milk
on the opposite shore

where you gather thorns
to feed your watchfires

scattered across the snowy fields
where you kneel at the water

washing the clay from your hands.
You who are nothing

nothing but the earth once touched
and made holy

children of dust
once raised to the light—

there you have done my starving for me
there you eat the salt crust

of your longing and are filled.
And what news of my journey

will I bring you in return
what scarred memory

of the last hour
before I cross over to you—

a rain crow lighting on a gate
October wind

harping on the fencewire?
blue dragonfly

the delicate
stained glass webs of its wings

lifting from the footprint
I leave

as I step into my boat?
Until that day

the earth shall free me
and you gather me there to you

beneath the witness tree
to shelter me against the wilderness

you who have suffered the wanderings
of your children

watch over me
here where I seek my comfort

on this stony ground
covering myself with darkness

here
where I wait for the light

to open and receive me
here where I pray—

come down
now to lie near me

to warm yourselves
at my fire.

Ars Poetica

for H.J.G. (d. 1994)

> *Poetry is the slowest form of nonexistence.*
> —Augustin Pop

1.

Time
steps out of

the hallway clock
quietly

so as not
to wake the mirrors

drifts through
the upstairs rooms

closed off
for winter

filling slowly now
with memory

this house
whose children

were once
its promises

whose roof was once
its wings

night
now hung

at the windows
moonlight

ghosting the trees
now

even the fire
is weary—

smoke
across the hillside

an angel
yearning

to be
heavier than air.

2.

There
the road is

a gray
water of time

where I
would set out

to climb
the holy

mountain of bells
nightbirds

taken
to their nests

world-spent
and quieted

net of fireflies
unwinging

like sleep
about me

surface of the dark
giving way

revealing
lost kingdoms

where the snowstorm
rests

in its cave
and the spider

sings out
her web

and I
like a word

released
from the tongue

find a path
through the air

become smoke
become nothing

and thus
like a shadow

at evening
I am gone—

3.

Here
leaning over

this page
into the circle

of lamplight
I thought I

saw you
little stranger

little
ghost orphan

stillborn
other

of my life
thought I saw

what grave
distance

you had come
carrier of light

through all salt
and its bitterness

climbing
the steep stair

up through water
drawn

by the sound
of oars—

but no

—again
it was only

the dry mote
fine grain

of time
setting off

across the
unexplored

ocean
of my eye.

Laura Davenport

I Have Found Joy Again and So Will You

Begin in the mouth of birdsong,
the cardinal's incessant note. Begin
with the garden's green work:
some flower early, some linger in the bud.
Some creep, send tendrils. Some
gather sap. Those with much to give,
give again. Flower for your own
sustenance, propagate future selves.
Like the fig, the wasp that devils you
feeds you, and feeds from you. Begin there.

Love Poem as a Snake

Each day that year you left before the sun
like some cursed prince, drove to work in darkness.
Long nights we never spoke, passing between us
the damp weight of the baby, paced and rocked her
until the next hour struck. The baby, too,
as if under some spell, would doze in my arms
until lowered to crib, lids half-closed and searching,
then jolt awake as if bitten—until the sun's
first rays spun gold across the neighbor's azaleas.
Then she sank into infant sleep
like a small stone in a field, the little pearl
mouth opened in an O on the crib sheet
patterned with clouds. So out of place, that snake
winding along the porch, seeking warmth
under the house, you called me out to see it.
I checked its head, declared it neutral,
showed you the rounded snout, and for a while
we watched its scales pulse in the early light.
Your aftershave, your pressed work shirt grazing
my arm, the hard pink scar of the silence
between us—I've tried to start this poem
hundreds of times. I'm still afraid of the darkness

that coiled inside me for months, seemed without end.
How I writhed in silence, slipped your grasp,
slick and cool to touch, whenever you tried
to try again. Late enough, already, for work,
we studied it a while, side by side, called it a poem:
How these gifts spring before us,
winding up from wherever winter keeps them,
to seek the warmth that is coming.

Quitting

Every cigarette I smoked was sorrowful and so
I gave them up. I didn't inhale, had to lean
against a porch rail
with one floodlight behind me
and the yard below had to be dark.
In the car I was afraid
the ash would set aflame the back seat,
the fire would spread to the gas tank
and the open bottles
of Zima. And the shame of drinking Zima
stays with me whenever I hear that song
we played which meant everything
as if our lives could be summed up, just like that,
beautiful and full of longing.
Could be charted, verse and chorus,
like the staggered Tarot lines we read the future in,
a few short weeks in summer.
Had I known I would not miss them,
the boys whose faces I traced in sleep
and in the day could not raise my eyes to,
I would have asked the cards
something else: What will I say to my daughter
of memory? That it is like the bright nail
I picked up in the street, carried for a block
and hid, out of sight, in the sewage drain
and this gutter is not the one
I floated boats in, and the boats you will make
from paper are not like mine
at all. And there will be a woman
or man someday you would like to forget
existed, and you will be alone then,

the last one riding in the car at night.
It's easy—all you have to do:
don't listen to that song again.
And once you are alone in the dark
you must not lean into it.

Why We Don't Write About Kudzu

As if it's not enough that the twelve-fifteen
with its mile of coal cars comes to rest
fifty yards from the porch, idling awhile
before it resumes a slow, northward shuffle,
and the halting clank of car meeting car
echoes through our sleep, a line snaking back
along the lip of the river like a slow tune
we cross, re-cross in creams
as the refinery lights' slow blink powders the room,
and the headlights on the county road
slice through the trees like the brakeman's ghost
still checking the rails as high schoolers parked
in the parallel fields keep watch
for his slow, hovering lamp.
If the night is warm enough and wet,
salamanders cross the dark, slick roadways,
seeking still pools in the ditches,
the shallows beneath a bridge where the lone
dawn heron stands loose and alert,
a spark of aluminum in the reeds.
After years, still new to this place,
you try to give meaning to these visitations,
as if a pine's particular notch
or the sudden shift of sparrows in flight
were blessings, as if blessings were the same
as touch. Once, you felt it, what is whispered
by the highway markers wrapped in weeds.
You were photographing dusty boilers
of the iron works closed since '71,
and you could almost name it
as you paused atop a hill of slag,
rubbed rust from your palms:
an old dog licked the shine from a potato chip bag
and you felt the weight of a hand on your back,

remembered the boy falling into that furnace,
retreating men, the hot ore emptied out
on the ground. The next day,
they had been turned away at the gate,
those same men who watch you in silence
from the bridge, raise their eyes to follow you past—
lazy, afloat on an inner tube, pale skin
and bikini. They hate you, you know,
your bare skin reddening in the light. Still,
you feel chosen, as if the river curls
around you, presses you forward,
and at your passing the woods begin to unfurl
heavy, delicate blossoms: pink lady's
slipper, low stalks of jack-in-the-pulpit gleaming
white through the undergrowth, a telephone pole
enmeshed, great jade vines throttling the wires.

Reconsider the Western

How the whore stands wordless on the balcony,
her window one light in a black well, the alley
where the hero's bobbing Stetson disappears—
the hat he crushed or twirled
between his hands as he sat dumbstruck
on the bed. Not taking her, no, but having
been moved, he left a few coins
anyway. Easy sex must have impediments—
buck teeth or scars, a child tucked away
who is, in the end, revealed—some outward
semblance of shame. But this one: she's frail,
consumptive, the pitiful ward
of the madam, and the hundreds of men
that pass through the territory
are like clouds passing over the still plain
of her body, the field our hero stumbles onto,
drunk on whiskey and the morning glow,
wheat-colored like her hair.
It's like this: afraid, but drawn to her,
he wants her but not here, not now.
As he rides past the double-forked cottonwood,
a branch bends to the water as she is bending,
dips fresh cloth to wipe the dust of travel
from each new face, each rough and heavy customer.

Porpoises

In college I spent whole days by the river
watching yachts drift, toward dusk
finding a bench on the white gravel path
to catch the harbor breeze. I filled page
after page in notebooks or sketched the palms
outlined against the sky. And once,
deep in a story I was writing about seeing myself
as a twin—the twin and I were talking—
a man approached in a half-hearted jog
and stopped to say something about the weather.
Yes, I said, *it's nice*, and he asked my name
and whether I went to the college. *Yes*, I said.
I did not know what to say to a man that old,
so I pointed to the river, said *look*,
where the sleek fins lifted in rhythm,
my favorite thing about that place
and, still, about those days. Though I could calculate
their speed, the current, where they'd surface
was always a surprise. The man sighed,
and now I am not sure whether he sat or only
stood there, but I believe he sat,
and the sigh was like dropping a heavy load
with the knowledge that soon he would lift it
again. *Actually*, he began, the words far off
as if I had retreated into myself—
those are porpoises. I stared ahead as he explained
the size of fins, blowholes, their gray flanks lost
in the dazzle of ripples from a boat.
I couldn't tell you why, even now,
but I am certain they were dolphins
as I was certain then that something had begun—
in airport lounges, polished bars, a corner table—
I would never again be allowed to sit alone
with a book, or keep my own counsel,
or stare off in silence. Either you are nodding now,
or you are shaking your head,
putting down this book to tell me I am wrong,
that no one sees a woman alone
like a coin to pocket, a sunset
to photograph and keep. I don't remember
how I got the man to leave,
unless it was to become so small and still
I blended with the bench, the stones, the water.

Daniel DeVaughn

Reverie on Debbie Drive

Deep in her stories
and conditioned breeze
my mother sees her son
in his loop, considers each
heaven she's relinquished
to me, the promise, the dream,
a little crown or ring.
Bluegrass. Bermuda. St. Augustine.
I add up the silly grasses
I've nicked from earth's
patchwork in strips, imagine
the world I would make
of them, the road I would take
to anywhere but this place,
riding my spiral of grass,
ending at a center that is
no longer mine, the fading
name on a mailbox agape.
I kill the time, those thoughts,
in song, trying to compose
to the two-stroke's two-step,
knowing that none will come
to light. Here, I have learned
that dawn is no arrival, no white
horse of breath, and words
will dry like the Russian empress'
delicate spores, rupturing open
to air. Still, I gun the mower
once more, turn back into the one
world and no other—right, right,
left sometimes, August
balling its fists around the hair
she gave me, insistent helix
I brush back from the eye.
Days like this one, the hour
still will expand in great chambers
of green, over the lineless road,

beyond the empty field, its suspended
gourds, the robin's world,
spilling like kudzu
beyond cashiers of checks,
stickered, roadside wrecks,
till farther, the Spanish
fort town in Florida
we once visited, she and I,
with the unaddressed
postcards to prove it,
icons of graying mosses
stooping to gravel paths,
the breakers' that laced
jeweled highways to horizons
of blush and citrus, ancient
battered parapets, and dark
disused magazines like coastal
caves. Then whole oceans
of what I will never know.
We breathe the air of Jesus,
she once told me. The same.
I pull a dusk into my empty
lungs, remember the lines
I have read, centering
within the Bishop's *three times*:
a trillium bloom in the palm.
The others nod in the side yard
with me, ripe for cutting.
Aren't the seconds a chain
of arrivals? My grass shadow
knifes into the rose light,
tomorrow as good as here.

Bros

—Devil's Den, Delta, Alabama

The river, blue vein, splits in flumes
through muscled boulders, mica flecked
as, above us, a hawk homes a comm tower
masquerading as a pine. The small late life,
pale pink, inside its curve of beak
expiring, as the feathers rush, splaying to fold
in neurotic wind.
                    I turn, watch you in the sun,
its massless body dropping like a palm to end
atop your open length, alabaster slick,
unbroken yet, in each now as it comes
—*this* and *this*—sandstone nudging, imprinting skin.
The hawk shifts and grows small as heaven.

New, this sensing omnipresence, even
today, descending the mountain, through cells,
thresholds of warmth long after the sun
has passed, the slow accumulations of a day
nothing for what we leave, which surely, it seems,
goes on as someone, somewhere. I settle
for the river, what lives wait in its yoke,

like your own, lids lashed and rolling in a dream
I will not see. So I push my fingers through this hip
of pouring glass, bone-cold to the wrist,
watch as the water has its way with the light,
my fingers opal, amethyst, sapphire, till a part
of me, small and durable stone, softens
and, burning, settles as water singing over
and against its own falling body.

What sees me see your veins of sky, or shelf
on which we lie, the thread of a river that is one
going and the same, here or behind the school,
where rapids once rose to hush on brick,
the soles that kick in shifted light, treading beyond
the bend? Let it. All come to me, utterly clear,
and I can feel nothing. *But wake up.*

Kindling

An old-growth oak has fallen across the trail,
its angular wreck of shattered fractals filling,

spilling the wordless mind. It points toward the valley floor,
brought low in the night by another summer storm,

Gulf-harried, roots slipping again through clay-silt
and pack to collapse in borderland, these fingers

of green we breach to call home for such bliss to follow.
This day-laborer and I mutter and circle the difficult bulk,

survey its fragrant wreckage, the bright sap, the bitter resin,
flayed and splaying heartwood like a big cat's bristles.

I finger a furrow charred at the edges, a little warmth
lingering on. Had this been another deadfall found

in childhood, my friends and I, surely the ruins were
of a better people, their power in their quiet under

high canopies, a soft cathedral, intoning the holy thrill
of an endless day we would have forever to remember.

Doubtless all of it was ours—a cache of nuts, a nest—
impossibly intricate—now my crown. *See?* Such small signs

that any life at all had grown and passed in the seething
green, islanded amidst our lighted humming streets.

We lived out our days till there were no more of them,
blurring, like the hurled stone at twilight, behind the vinework,

privet and kudzu, the yellowing paper of our faded now.
Here, in this little fire lane, a little mystery, if you listen,

might pulse in time to the left and right-hand sides.
Already spent, we spill the petroleum's gold, our sweat

its poor prefiguration between the chain and growl,
limb by limb dismantling the vastness between us,

always the thing we claim as our own. And we are
sure to keep our eyes where life in every form flees

from the trunk and toppled canopy, on those bodies,
the overstory brought low, the nonnarrative, the work.

Still, only a week ago, a local boy, good as home
in the night driving, knew light by a sudden turning

of the earth against him, the longleaf pine settling where later
we took it apart. Covered a while by the nearer violence

we do not hear the woods in uproar, trees doubled
like grieving mothers, hands skyward and wild

on the wind, nor even our own uncertain thoughts
as they branch and fork toward a horizon that more

and more for us seems the ultimate cul-de-sac.
Small blessings, in time. Like confetti,

a gingko rains its gilt fans across our path back down
the mountain, ours the only movement in a brush tableau.

Save this family of toadstools that has risen,
is rising, up from blackened earth.

Flying South

Suspended in memory's sheer amniosis
you slide through a cloudless present,
orbs of light like ghosts having dropped
the thread sailing, searching the seamless
eggs of closed luggage holds.
A baby screams, a digital bell swings
and reverberates along the fretted nerve,
elongating the wait to be alone
with your regret, the coming future, now
and increasingly a place you thought past
for good. Still, there is the light,
a sunrise that comes quicker with the twin
jet engines' frostbound lift,
the shuddering roar in blue light
set to sooth, and the glow of not-home
like a souvenir, memento of marble,
or alien bulb, near split by the radiance
it makes and that you hope in stowing away,
somewhere behind your heart, will spell
or stay you for the coming year, the rising
earth, the landing fear that nests with a hush
of braking wings. Beat, you push and
pierce and break back inside a life
you find is yours, always was, the house
dark, hallways wired and tacked
in moted curios set just so
for this finally arrived iteration of the being
that looks back on what is coming,
like the dog on whom your presence dawns
as shade, halfmoon opal and gray,
the thatched irises seeing a thief,
but sniffing out each piece of what is,
is not, might be, its you at last come home.

Family Bible

On or under issues of *Southern Living*,
piled atop the coffee table, altar
of the one t.v., it abided, a pit in the seasons'
by-and-by, wind scouring branches

for the word beyond the window,
or creek stone silence for a song.
Though I learned, in time, it is a cry.
After Daddy laid on a switch, my still small

voice would wilt to root again,
feeding on that music, striking like Mama's
hydrangea cutting, far into invisible
earth, held hard by a brick to what is

good for it. Most mornings I've lost, but one
I remember; how I toppled my mug of milk,
the one printed with an image of a dog
paddling blue chop. I watched the white

wash the black leather, drip to shadow
the gilding edge, then enter the book, mute
before the History channel coursing on the wall.
All mouth emerging to lick me clean,

my father, towering, boomed, *This
is the most important thing.* Then, like a newborn
fished up and held near his heart, it dripped,
and in this silence we stopped. My mother

says what is brought into the world cannot be
taken from it. Of course, I agree. We sit
now, and we eat, he and I, practicing
the lesson of listening, holding one's tongue,

which is not the same, I have learned,
as silence. Sitting near him, face to face,
the story is there in skin—furrow and crease,
the deepening line. And we read.

Will Justice Drake

Heading In

Never could I have imagined that round was our last, but they
sliced with the scalpel along his bare breastbone and abdomen
seeking an answer between his unfinished extremities.

He was my son. And I have unloaded the last of my
burdens. Not this unblemished boy bathed in the water and
infant-like, limitless, now only infinitesimal

except in the eyes of his father, more than a fragment of
data now added to charts and now added to schema still
lost in the roughest of estimates, guesses, and tosses of

grass in the wind—yes *we* had undying affection for
grass as it spun to the ground in the wind; it foretold every
lie, every bounce of the ball and its arc in the air, every

echo colliding through pines as the clubface connected and
struck to the sky something crisp and sent clear, and
compressed in unfaltering flicker of fingers and earth every

swing he had taken since birth. No, it's that our one ritual
might have done nearly the same, or more—my God—and how?
How can we miss the ball drift in the sky, its blackening?

Intercession

for WHD

The only hay baler was me and Euel
in the barn catching what our father threw
from the truck bed, hearing him shout, "You'll
have to hold your breath if it bothers you."

My lungs burned in the dust either way,
a hundred pounds of hay through the loft,
cheeks puffed tight with a breath I'd saved
to keep from collapsing in asthmatic cough.

I'd squint before tossing the hay in a heap,
and the golden dust would billow in the slats of light.
Each mote moved its way. I breathed.
They moved together. I breathed the light.

If I called out now, I would crow
like a rooster, like the bronze bird in the floor
of the car in town. The man always showed
up with the fowl in the front, his greens and gourds

in the back. The bird would cluck and squat on the news.
Its litter splotched out words, and its bright,
amber eye cocked upward and true
like a scope looking past the sun at the night.

Four years later, I lay in France,
cold, disarming mines, pressed to the ground
like a creature scratching food from the sand.
A mortar fell. *Ventre à terre.* No one around

except the girl turning round and round
on her doorstep. Her dress flared out
like a parasol twirled around
in the rain. The child beneath it wondered how

to keep us dry in the squall, became a mother
calling to come home, to look in the cupboard
for the pressure plates stacked like saucers,
and something—I've forgotten—about being discovered.

Back home, up on the water tower
near that abbey of German monks,
someone kept shooting rivets at an hour
when we were all sleeping. So I jumped

out of bed to find him in the dark,
but instead I heard flapping wings,
the woodpecker pecking at the metal bark
of the antenna, the *tap-tap* perhaps her flinging

a coded message into space, like a prayer.
Or maybe she was receiving one for me.
After a while, it suited me to hear
the rhythm, a kind of peace
                    like a volley of mortars,
                                    like a cough.

Ansel Elkins

Native Memory

River was my first word
after *mama.*
I grew up with the names of rivers
on my tongue: the Coosa,
the Tallapoosa, the Black Warrior;
the sound of their names
as native to me as my own.

I walked barefoot along the brow of Lookout Mountain
with my father, where the Little River
carves its name through the canyons
of sandstone and shale
above Shinbone Valley;
where the Cherokee
stood on these same stones
and cast their voices into the canyon below.

You are here, a red arrow
on the atlas tells me
at the edge of the bluff
where young fools have carved their initials
into giant oaks
and spray painted their names and dates
on the canyon rocks,
where human history is no more
than a layer of stardust, thin
as the fingernail of god.

What the canyon holds in its hands:
an old language spoken into the pines
and carried downstream
on wind and time, vanishing
like footprints in ash.
The mountain holds their sorrow
in the marrow of its bones.
The body remembers
the scars of massacres,

how the hawk ached to see
family after family
dragged by the roots
from the land of their fathers.

Someone survived to remember
beyond the weight of wagons and their thousands
of feet cutting a deep trail of grief.
Someone survived to tell the story of this
sorrow and where they left their homes
and how the trees wept to see them go
and where they crossed the river
and where they whispered a prayer into their grandmother's eyes
before she died
and where it was along the road they buried her
and where the oak stood whose roots
grew around her bones
and where it was that the wild persimmons grow
and what it was she last said to her children
and which child was to keep her memory alive
and which child was to keep the language alive
and weave the stories of this journey into song
and when were the seasons of singing
and what were the stories that go with the seasons
that tell how to work and when to pray
that tell when to dance and who made the day.

You are here
where bloodlines and rivers
are woven together.
I followed the river until I forgot my name
and came here to the mouth of the canyon
to swim in the rain and remember
this, the most indigenous joy I know:
to wade into the river naked
among the moss and stones,
to drink water from my hands
and be alive in the river, the river saying,
You are here,
a daughter of stardust and time.

Blood on Your Saddle

Jericho.   I return in winter
to the cruelest acreage I know in Alabama.

Mama   I say.   Speak his name.
                                        Robert.
Your twin   the other half of   the bivalve shell of your heart.

Tell me about that winter
when his eyes changed to gray.

> At Jericho the lake was almost frozen.
> In a ditch by the highway we found a litter of stray puppies
> —eight, like us.   To die from hunger   was too cruel.
> We agreed to give them the gift of   a quick death.
> It was the bone stump of winter.   Night rushing in.
> We tied them in a potato sack   to drown them.
> But we had no gloves   and the knot I tied
> wasn't strong enough.   They cried   they clawed wildly
> at the icy brim.   We watched
> until the last one   then walked home
> down the lane into   the freezing slash pines
> not meeting the other's mirrored face.
> Neither of us was strong enough to console the other.

Speak his name.
            Robert
shot himself at Jericho
the following November. The blackbirds flew
from the branches where they roosted
in the winter tree of his heart.

Hours later you came like an archeologist
to clean up the remains.   Shard of bone.
A fine mist of blood on fallen leaves.
Empty styrofoam coffee cup from Hardee's
drive-thru, its bitten rim where his teeth had been.

Out of eight children   you alone survived
the ghost of childhood.   Haunted still
a black mare in solitary pasture
burning across the hunger fields
of winter   your coal-black mane in flames
setting fire to the land as you leave.

Tornado

When the sky threw down hail, I knew
    our world was sudden, changing. In the violence of rains
        we ran, I held my daughter with her water-soaked braids.
She covered her ears and counted
    one Mississippi, two Mississippi
        the space between lightning and thunder.
We heard sirens. Birds fled the sky. Soon
    the wick of the world smelled matchstick blue.
        three Mississippi, four
When the winds had blown off all the doors
    we were soldered only by a handhold.
        I'm not a believer
but I took shelter inside a prayer
    when I saw a white horse
        fly across the sky.
one Mississippi, two
    I tried to tether you
        to me. Through sweeping winds
of glass and debris
    I struggled to see.
        one—
I watched my daughter fly away
    from the grapnel of my arms. Unmoored
        like a skiff, she sailed alone out the window.
I awoke into the fingertips of rain
    light against my face. Wreckage
        of a new world greeted me—
a baby blue bicycle lodged in an oak tree,
    bright spoke beads in the shape of stars
        on a wheel still spinning.

Kristin Entler

Injection Training

On the overbed table: a pile of ketchup
packets, a baker's dozen of straws

brought with each new Styrofoam cup
of ice water or juice or sprite, cannulas still coiled,

open pouch of syringes, cyan stressball,
alcohol wipes in foil houses. The nurse's hair

shimmies like late October leaves. *Practice.*
Hold the syringe like this, she instructs,

pinching one of them between first knuckle
and thumb flesh. In her other hand, the ball.

Me and Mom mime her squeezing blue foam fat.
This is your stomach, she tells us what we see

on TV is wrong—not to ready thumb on plunger,
use our index finger. No sensationalism. No dramatic flair.

After, a dewdrop of insulin leaks from the hollow.
Plastic clicks on walnut laminate.

A Tickle in Her Throat

and this almost-girl learns to swirl a spoon

                      through a brew she's thinned to last her through thaw

as if she can hold a bowl of health in her hands again,

                      for the first time since some other life she just knows

from dreams. mid-night growls in the rose bush

                      on the out side of her blinds. trouble in this place

she once called home. this body she once knew

                      could out-run any bear now a cage of scared bees.

she sees his brown paws shake last night's trash

                      out on the porch from her spot by the sink

where she hopes to fend them off

                      with the bone broth that blooms

on the stove. more magic

                      than the meds when this type

of rage stings her lungs

                      and she senses wolves

stalk the woods'

                      for their own share

of what

                      might be

left

                      over

Night Coyote at the Ocean's Edge

with moongone sky
with endless sea
with sightblind fog:

sepia eyeshine

a wolfhound god
a cloudbound blur
a shadow's shade:

hazy hirsute pepper coat

the footfall hush
the luckstruck view
the lunghold gaze:

battlebound & beastbred mist

then pawprint coast
then southern breeze
then cloudless sky:

ceramic starshine

and salttrimmed crabs
and spearblade light
and gulfpink fins:

sunrise of another kin

In the Guest Bedroom of My Parent's House, I Rummage a Photo of a
Version of Myself I Thought I'd Lost and I Need to Say, Dear Girl:

All the time, you believe you're telling
a sad story as opposed to a safe one

& a mind possessed by evil notions
must begin stocking up with images:

& a southern sun where the milk
of a mountain laurel is toxic

& synchronous fireflies flash
an eye-blink of splendor

& spicebush swallowtails beeline
to turk cap lilies for their orange

& autumn is nothing more
than a cup of tea gone cold.

& you will not die because you are
sick but because you are alive.

& the worst thing about therapy
is the juvenile metaphors.

& not all fears are rooted
in the darkness.

& pretending the hospitals are empty
does not actually make them empty.

& a sheltered life is a daring life
when even the smoke is out to get you.

& somewhere the 52 Hertz Whale's sound
signature is plated on a scientist's wall

& hope, goddamn, that tiny sliver of light
you believed could fill your heart? You hate it now.

& an essential pre-requisite of a good researcher
is the willingness to be wrong

& the invitation of constructive critique.
But when you can't see something

& the doctor tells you...
you can't understand the severity.

& just because your life is a mess
doesn't mean your kitchen has to be.

& accumulation is the result
of obsession. It's Wednesday

& even mushrooms pray
to the stars. Lesson one is survival.

& you're supposed to be leaving soon,
so forgive the spring ephemerals

& the canopy that starves
them of sunshine

& alchemy rising out of the mud
of the river that sings

& save all your ghosts
for a ritual of remembrance:

your body hovering delicately
on the last edge of childhood.

*Composed of language scavenged from the works of: Emily Cinquemani, Chris Stapleton, Frances Ponge (trans. Joshua Corey & Jean-Luc Garneau), Eudora Welty, Kevin Wilson, Alex Ibe-Cumba, Yayoi Kusama, Taylor Swift, and F. Scott Fitzgerald along with several documentaries about the earth, whales, mushrooms, and Muscle Shoals, AL.

Another Type of Hospital Room

in my bed surrounded
with buzzers

with wires with tubes
with—

a symphony of carrion
swooning

over the distant tree line
of sweetgum

of sycamore of oak of ash:
invisible—

what breathes through kudzu,
ivy, spanish moss.

William Fargason

Sugar

The summer my father swallowed bees
the honeysuckle outside our house bloomed

longer, larger even than usual. In the heat of June,
he pushed the mower back and forth,

always matching the lines the wheels made
in the grass to the edge of the next row

as he came back, his dirty white t-shirt draping
only where it wasn't stuck to the sweat, his arms

powdered with clippings. My father wiping his
brow. My father saying the varmints are back at it again.

My father saying we could use the rain,
saying I should go outside more.

My father saying a lot of things. As he
worked, he left his open can of sweet tea

on the porch railing. Sugar is sugar to any insect.
He took a break for a drink, didn't stop

until the can was empty. Later, he said
he could feel them inside stinging all the way down.

When My Father Tells Me My Great-Grandfather was in the KKK

he tells me in a hushed voice   as if someone could
overhear him   as if those sins could come back

into that living room   lined with animal heads

and gun cabinets   a fallow deer   a mountain goat

two largemouth bass   a red fox at full alert   listening in

he leans in when he tells me   as if anything could change

where we are   no one can change   where they are
only where they are going   we share a family name

my father   my grandfather   my great-grandfather

I'm the fourth   and the last   of that lineage
that system of blood   my father's hand

runs through   the dense fur of the moose head

on the wall   he says one day   all of this will be mine
it makes sense now   why he said for me to always keep

the pistol he gave me   in my glovebox   when driving

through a   bad   part of town   what he meant was
a   Black   part of town   I remember as a kid

driving with him   to his hunting club in a small town

south of Selma   we stopped for gas   my father's tense
shoulders as he left me alone   he showed me where

his snubnose .357 was   in the center console   *just in case*

I was taught to be afraid   I grew up being told
to shoot   at the first sign of movement

no matter the fog in the woods   I left that state

with more than a century of sins inherited   the pine trees
in my backyard no longer innocent   the very grass

sang everything I didn't know   I knew was wrong   I must be

different   I can't let what I was taught   be what I teach
if I leave this place   or don't   I carry those pines

those sins   in me   like sod carries the soil it was cut from

When the Cop Tells Us

to call our parents we do: we had been caught
drinking Smirnoff Green Apple behind

the Hoover Met. Then the cop tells us
he would've taken us in, my friend and I,

if we looked more scummy. At seventeen,
I believed this to be luck, as one might

believe the rain stopping right when you walk
to your car, or a string of green lights, I believed

that where we parked my friend's truck
in the dark of that parking lot was a safe place

to drink on a Wednesday night, our two outlines
slumped against the truck bed throwing

the empty bottles into the edge of the woods.
Now, I see there is no luck in these situations:

we were white, and so was the cop
with his shining bald white head. If we'd been

Black we wouldn't have been given the chance
to call our parents, we wouldn't have been given

anything at all. And so we walked free. For almost
a decade later I believed in luck, in what

I thought we got ourselves out of, not realizing
our skin had opened an escape hatch

and would again and again and again.

My Father's College Roommate

Auburn, 1978

He would watch my father from across
their dorm room, each step and turn made, the outline
of each leg and curve. After a tough workout,

my father would peel off his sweat-soaked gym shorts
and shower in their tiny dorm shower, so close
to their bedroom that the steam would cloud

the light fixture on the ceiling. My father would
emerge, towel draped in all the right places,
half-dry, water beaded on his taut skin. How young

he must have looked, a colt penned in a stall.
Sore, my father would ask his roommate to rub a knot
in his back, loosen the muscles. This should have been

a scene in an old romance film, slow pan
from him to him, but it isn't. There should be
a kind of cello suite playing softly. But there isn't

and never was. My father didn't know his roommate
liked to touch him—so when his roommate paused
in his massage for a second too long, laid his head

on my father's back, my father jumped up, clocked
him in the jaw, sent his body to the floor. In his
confusion my father lashed out—scared at what

he didn't know, he had never been shown tenderness
before. The sound must have been soft, as touch
can be, a kiss or a handshake or a fist in the teeth.

Kate Gaskin

A Small Sample of Snakes I Have Known

Cottonmouth

That summer, from your nest
beneath my grandparents' dock, you cut

delicate wakes through the lake
in the damp morning heat, the air clinging

as close to us as wet cotton. We were not
afraid, though we should have been, my siblings

and I. We cut flips from the end
of the dock while the snakes dropped

from the pines. What did we know,
then, of omens?

Garter Snake

Oh black tangle
of smooth bellies,

oh stripe on strip, garter
of trunkless legs, patron saint

of the limbless: slick, strong,
and adapted. Oh garden

nester, pampas grass lover, all
the mating balls of you

we discover in the bushes
in your tight and pulsing

weave. When my husband
severs a yucca at its roots,

a whole quivering clot
of you slides out from the stump

as if just born. I watch
your slender bodies glide over

his boots as he startles back.
In his throat he holds

a scream like a swallowed egg.

Copperhead

You, storied viper
of the forest, bugaboo to children

running barefoot through the woods,
second only to cottonmouths

in the fear you strike
at bedtime. You, of heat-sensing pits

and live birth, of the cool, dry
den, field mouse in your throat,

head like a worn penny, no warning
shots to fire. How you keep

your secrets secret, will nest
even in suburbs while a baby plays

in the Bahia grass just a few paces away.

Timber Rattlesnake

Well, aren't you bold,
heavy-bodied god of rough

boulders, guard of our rocky
outcrops, of the gates

to bottomland hardwoods,
pine flats, cane thickets dense

and knife-sharp. Your fangs
in repose, your crossbands

that cut along the length
of your dorsal, your fat, slow

heft in the path, your sudden
rattle. You could be anywhere

gathering the sun
into the dusty bag of your

body. I could be anywhere
walking toward you,

a heartbeat
from hearing you rise.

Hognose

I am so naturally repulsed
by you, my sweet,

startled nightmare of a pet,
your delicate, upturned

snout, your terror to see me
on the shoulder

of the road, running
past saw palmettos and lyreleaf

sage. Of all snakes
you are my favorite, my small

dramatic talisman
lying belly up and coiled

limply as if dead. We're not far
into an endless summer,

the salt bay whetting our dread
in this age of inconsolable tides

and bombs that never stop
falling, but, oh, little hognose,

even now you are shedding
free any memory of me.

Postpartum

Springtime, the azaleas
in bright flare, the baby there

beside the rocking chair
on my parents' front porch.

And you are where?
Here is a monotony

of baby gear, the swing
that clicks him side to side

a small origami
of laundry, loose bottles

frozen rings for his teeth
one breast that gives

its milk, and the other
that gives up in grief.

*

He is rolling over
front to back, back to front

as you crouch
in the desert and cradle

your phone. A miracle

to see it at all

from so many miles, the planes
that drone, the wind

that scabs the brush, your face
the crust of salt and dust

you wear like skin.
Again, you say. Again.

*

And tease me, my boots
my kin, the wind

in my hair down Elkahatchee
Creek, the shed skin

of ribbon snakes
in the summer when

we chased the low jewel
of Hale-Bopp

down our neighborhood streets.
I did not want to come home

to this, you gone, the ghost
of my legs whitening in the lake

you kissing me
you kissing me and then—

*

When you left
I dug myself up

like a bulb and moved
back home while you flew

off to war. Now I nurse
from my right side

as the catalpa trees
flush white

and the yard weeds over
in bright green.

Ghazal for Alabama

And what of the river Alabama?
It is deep as the Coosa, the Cahaba, green as an Alabama

field—tall wiregrass, jade and then golden. In winter
the rye is green as the eyes of the first boy I loved in Alabama.

And in the pasture the hot tangle of pigweed is red
as a gummy smile, and the copperheads of Alabama

coil neatly in their soft nests of dead
leaves beneath the airy sycamores of Alabama.

And in the field there are bonfires and grain
alcohol and a pickup truck that peeled away into an Alabama

night—1995—a girl flung from the bed and paralyzed.
She never played her clarinet again in Alabama.

And later, two sisters in a rolled car in a peanut field
one calling her mother, the other lying in the soft Alabama

dirt, her leg wrong, her head wrong. She'll become so thin
and restless during the next decade in trailers across Alabama

like the trailer where Lacey lived with her two daughters
and husband. Where they smoked made-in-Alabama

meth and then left the girls alone to pick fields for stones
quartz and mica, anything with a little Alabama

shine until one day she wanted to stop, but her husband
didn't. He wanted to smoke all the meth in Alabama

beneath its simmering star-hot sky. This was before I left Alabama for good. Some nights the moon was ripe as an Alabama

peach. Some nights I ate Chilton County peaches
over the sink in our first home in Alabama

as you pulled me closer, whispering Kate, and I knew you
loved me, you loved me, you loved me even more in Alabama.

Bad Fruit

Say I come to you with an apple
for a palm. Would you eat it?

Perhaps the word etiquette
translated across a body of tenderness

becomes madness. If it is true
our bodies ripen and spoil

like fruit, then to capture the sweetest
bite is a trick. Say we marry

and our bodies become a road.
Day in and day out, we wind

past beautyberry, red basil, trees
with oranges like heavy yellow lungs.

In the yard is another fish-kill
and everywhere the oaks wear moss

for hair. I have heard
an unusual bounty of sharks

has been photographed beyond
the lip of the shore

and I have seen
the rough feast of dolphins

the brown curl of the tide
like a tendril of hair fallen

across the mouth of the sea.
We lost the hibiscus in the freeze

last winter. So many palm trees
have died on our watch.

Say I come to you with shoulders
like prickly pear and forearms

slick with pokeweed. For years I beg
you to eat. In the air ospreys sail

like a killing over small castles of fish.
When the sea rushes in

we pucker back our mouths and sputter.
What is saltier than two bodies in love?

Landscape with Logging Trucks and Invasive Species

Alexander City, Alabama

Lucy says she doesn't know what to do
with the 50 acres of longleaf pines
she inherited with her husband. She doesn't

want to clear-cut them, reseed
with squat, fast-growing loblollies
or ragged slash pine, but the money

is so good—all that tall, sturdy wood
so strong and hearty that whole forests of it
were gone by the 20th century, sold mostly

to England, the almshouses and malt
houses, churches and warehouses
of London constructed from Alabama,

Georgia, Mississippi pines. She's a forester
by trade. She lives deep in the shade
of all those tall trees. She loves the water

too, said when she was clearing the Gulf
of tar balls after the oil spill that there
was nothing sadder, and when I asked her

are there really alligators this far north,
she shook her head, said, I've never
seen a live one, but there are nests beaten

into the cordgrass along the rivers. Whenever
I go home I pass a stretch of longleaf pines
rehabilitated for pheasant hunting, pass

their slender branches, green needles
clean and sharp as new fishhooks.
But in my parents' backyard, the loblollies

choke with vines—mostly kudzu—
and wisteria rides the whole neighborhood
hard, its tired '70s ranch houses, sagging

telephone lines, trusty hard-chugging
air conditioning units. Lucy says she's going
to do it, give up, the money is just

that good. And I agree you can accept
almost anything. Even ruin itself
blossoms each spring, the river suddenly violet

with invasive water hyacinth.
Who can thrive
this long and still be good?

Juliana Gray

In Andalusia

Say it to rhyme with "can't stand to lose ya," the ugly town
with a pretty name, Alabama's Andalusia.

Find it in the Wiregrass, poor and parched, a blot
on the maps of three Southern states, covering Andalusia.

Aristida stricta, wiregrass, can only thrive
when regularly burned by summer fires in Andalusia.

The locals tell of skunk apes and wampus cats
lurking within piney woods and scrub near Andalusia.

Maimed cattle, claw-scribbled pine bark, methane stench.
Imagine the monsters walking free in Andalusia.

At my grandmother's house, there were horses, cows,
and a collie named Cokie who tried to herd me in Andalusia.

A vase of seashells painted pink and glued to wire stems
captivated me in her parlor in Andalusia.

I wasn't allowed to play in that room, to climb the velvet sofa—
but oh, the shells! Such perfect roses in Andalusia!

They burned, those roses, and did not grow again
after her husband torched the house in Andalusia.

That was the first time she tried to leave him.
Arson is one way to bring a wife home to Andalusia.

The second time, she fled the double-wide they'd raised
upon the scorched foundation in Andalusia.

He killed her, shot the neighbors who sheltered her,
then calmly turned himself in to the sheriff of Andalusia.

Sift gray ash for lacquered petals. Pluck shotgun shells
from bloodstained shag. Souvenirs of Andalusia.

A Trick of the Light

This aberration, sun refracted through
illogical beads of falling rain, up north
they give a pretty name—sunshower—

as if a freak could thus become a flower.
Our Alabama exegesis says
the devil must be beating his wife, enraged

that God created such a beautiful day.
And who is she? Not Persephone—
no, a woman like us, more like to eat

blackberries than pomegranate seeds,
a woman who shops at Wal-Mart (yes, in hell),
a woman with crooked teeth and blond hair

parted brown, who cheers for Auburn though
her parents couldn't afford to send her there,
a woman who loves her man even when

he reels on her, who screams apologies
for whatever she must have done, anything
to make him stop, a woman who tells the cops

(of course, there are many cops in hell)
that it was a mistake, the neighbors heard
the TV turned up loud, she doesn't need

their help or shelter, won't be pressing charges,
and the golden light of heaven burns down
and sparkles through her tears, and the devil swears

it'll never happen again, and he buys her a present,
a pretty ribbon in seven colors to wear
around her neck, his promise, his solemn bond.

Nobody's Mother

"Can't you see from my really thick black eyeliner that I'm nobody's mother?"
—Karen Kilgariff

Can't you see I've trimmed my home
in sharp corners and glass?

Don't you hear me saying *fuck*
in every fucking sentence?

Can't you see these cracks and lines
around my sideways mouth

were not inscribed by laughter?
No locks on the stove,

no controls on online porn;
electric outlets gape

for exploratory fork or finger.
What the fuck is Gogurt?

Here are my rickety stairs, here
my long-deferred roof,

bucking up rusty nails.
Here is my liquor cabinet,

a proudly shining congregation
beside the household poisons.

Here is my standard, human heart,
beating only for itself.

Honeymoon Palsy

After fumblings they call "making love,"
the newlywed couple spoons, a pose
they've seen in movies: hand on breast, his nose
buried in her hair, his arm shoved
beneath her head. The tender weight above
his arm seems nothing, so he sleeps, enclosed
in bliss, the afterglow's sweet repose.
He wakes to a hand dead as a pitcher's glove.

Usually, the damaged nerve recovers.
Throughout the long, oblivious nights, they lie,
seemingly aligned, heart to heart.
Already, they've learned so much, these new lovers:
touching without meeting the other's eye,
going numb to each other, part by part.

Regan Green

Dove Poem

My father is moving again. We go to Lowe's,
which smells of my childhood, to purchase
a utensil holder, a plank for the bottom lip
of the bookshelf because the floors are so uneven.
Looking at the price of mattresses,
he says, *hard to squeeze blood from a turnip,*
which means it is not impossible.
A mourning dove is cooing in the lumber aisle.
One high trill, then three cries like the glass slivers
still in the curve of my mother's foot,
the shards so dull, her body doesn't know
they are not the body. By now
tissue has formed around them.
It would not be impossible to squeeze them out.

Grey Heron

We watched him swallow the fish,
that egg-shaped lump swelling
the gullet, somehow scaling up
just for the neck to crook again.
It took half an hour. We ate
cheese and crackers from a paper
towel. You accidentally called me by her name.

Sharony Green

Wide open

Brown ashy legs
Hung over a wall
Salt water under our feet.
How Grandma know we wouldn't fall?
Or maybe she did
cuz we spent more time on canals snaking through Dade
Give the fish bread now.
We hoped for speckled perch
No mullets
For the sport, she did it
"Slice it like this here. scrape it like that."
This before the labored breathin
and the spins around buckets in shallow water
They knew they was bout to die
like the fruit hanging
with eyes wide open.

place 2

We also fished on the lake where eyes watched God
A big button in Florida's belly
                    Get in that sleeping bag. Stop scarin my fish
And then a wrinkled twenty
                    Get a room
This was back when you could send kids
to a motel cause they grandma needed a break from expectation
An unlocked adjoining door
spent bodies
but no one touched her grands
with they pink cookies and peach Nehi
A map on my lap said what they signs said
Like Zora, I looked in wonder

The dutiful

A lil house in Eau Gallie in '29
when things were still humming for a brown Barnard girl
Fannie Hurst, Mason and Hughes
Don't bother. Who could understand it all?
Back to Eau Gallie in '51
Butterflies around ornamental water
Pink verbena there, too
Indian two blocks to the west
It is sliced with sandbars
But the Atlantic sends a breeze
Fish, crab, shrimp in a phosphorous glow
The blue jays, cardinals, mockin birds cheer
cause a snake released
She try to buy this dwelling on Dixie
Mules and Men written here
White Man say no
On to Fort Pierce
Stood in the gap for Miss Ruby
between voodoo columns
fruit crates, a typewriter
But that bacteria-tainted water in Honduras has her in a way
Hypertension and stomach have her in a way
The dutiful lit the match
The good policeman say wait!
The edges of her papers curl into themselves like countries on a map
An ant might decide these were no different
twenty years stood between her and the coaches
on the backroads lookin for ballers
But Ah'm getting ahead of m'self

Theodore Haddin

Grandpa Wears Neckties

(For Jeffrey Meyers)

He stood his usual grinning self
before the mirror with his new bowtie.
'I can do this easy,' he says, and begins
to wrap two ends tight about his collar.
Then whatever slipped stuck in knot.
He looked at it and went right on
as if to finish the job. But it twisted,
it didn't turn, it caught his finger.
He was struggling with a snake.
He gritted his teeth.
At last he had to admit he couldn't
do it. He hated what to do next.
He sought the scissors in the kitchen
and held one end of the rascal till he
could cut it all off, blue Blenheim
it was, Churchill's favorite, shredded
to the floor, as if old buildings had
fallen in London. But he was so far
from the London streets now he'd
never go back. Then off for a necktie,
black, and carefully wrapped it,
pulled it back. He couldn't be seen
doing this. With his foot he kicked
at the scraps.

Greatest

He pauses along the walkway
of the rotunda with a torch
to what he and others have been
and to what flourishes now
at the turn of his hand.
We stand to watch the glow
of the future that started
with his words when he stepped
into the ring. We laughed with
disbelief till Sonny Liston lay
flat on the floor, and Patterson
later touched hands with him
who had easily done *him* in.
Still outdistance-dancing war
and his opponent, he spoke
before the truth was known.
War was not in the ring, where
fighting was done with fists,
and it was legal to knock
somebody out. Something under
this man's skin was greater than
any boast begins, or the speed
of his feet or a swift blow to
the chin. When he retired,
the spiritual life he had nurtured
through all the fights emerged
the real winner. More acts of
kindness and generosity came
as the world welcomed the
champion of peace, just as
the light he lights tonight
illumines the darkness around us.

Leaf and Bird

A leaf passing for a bird
has been on the roof
for months now, no
move, no wing, no flight,
stands rain and hot sun,
the inquisitive squirrel,
and no mate ever in sight.
If it could fly, it might
decide to glide toward my window,
like the wax-wing that thought
I was the welcomer, straight
into my kitchen, but wasn't.
How interest in me could
so overcome a bird to crash
against invisible glass
could only be caused by
craziness in spring.
If I imagined something
about a leaf, I suppose
a bird could imagine something
about a man. Maybe the bird
just wanted to be in. And
maybe I just wanted to be out.

Thoughts on the Mona Lisa

She's the most famous portrait in the world,
we know; we were not ready for her turn to us,
and now we can never stop looking at her.
No side view of yellow and rich red brocade,
nor the plain tunic and open eyes of youth
testing the question mark of the world before him.
We might call up the later scowling faces
of Rembrandt that emerge from darkness
as if to tell us they are there; or even the later
full and three-quarter faces of Van Gogh,
a postman Roulin or a peasant woman in
a wheat field, all color and bright.

But the puzzle in the Mona Lisa is in
the character we meet for the first time.
We know about her lips, eyes and hands
(opaque of pearl). Much has been made
of her smile. Her body rises up before
a *campagna*, light behind her hair. She
is not the *Madonna of the Rocks*, or any
other Madonna we might remember.
She's the Mona Lisa without fanfare,
simply dressed, making the woman,
in light and shadow as she was, unadorned.
Not so much the secret knower, as the
woman celebrating her self. Something
in her belongs to us. Her smile, not wide
at all, not generous, suggests an inner
life kept, as we might keep ourselves.
She knows more than we do, as if
Da Vinci himself saw in her eyes
what everyone wants to know. And,
looking at your hands, your neighbor's
  eyes, you don't resist looking at hers again.

Van Gogh's Poem

It could have been a bud of green he saw
one troubling day beside an ash heap.
In the only painting of "The Sower"
with a tree in it, Van Gogh darkens
the human as dark as the large tree
trunk that dominates the scene, in
a field just becoming green. A spot
of brighter green appears beside
the sower as if a light has gone on
in the dark of body and tree. Where
limbs have been cut off, the trunk
has sprouted strong shoots that
pierce the air. It's fair to ask what
Van Gogh is planting in this scene.
A poem how earth in the spring,
the human, the dominating trunk
and the round evening sun are
the hope of things that get planted
and have already begun. We are
waiting for things to emerge, and
the poem is the emergence of spring,
just as perception and thought converge
in a metaphor in the making, and
we, the observer, are urged to feel
the change. For Van Gogh, nothing
could better depict the hope of man
and earth. In this poem the sower is
not merely planting seeds, as in the
other sower poems, but with powerful
colors and some clever restraints, Van
Gogh creates his poem in paint.

Audrey Hall

Downhill

The busman has rectangular pupils
when he holds his hand out for this trip's dime.
Today my wallet's too light for scruples;
I borrowed my fare. Charon leaves on time
to take me past the neon dive bar sign
through the concrete tunnel into shadow.
In my bookbag is the downy brie rind
for Death's dog, a bottle of red Merlot
for Death, and my high school flute, unshining,
closed-hole, to play for him and his wife.
What does Orpheus do when he can't sing?
When he's on stipend? Has no lyre or fife?
I write on my knee a hasty sonnet:
let her return, hand in my back pocket.

Mannsdale Road

Grass rushes into the scar of cleaved land
near the new subdivision: a single stag drifts
and looks around as I drive by.

More tornadoes in the evening forecast,
the clouds purpled vertebrae.
I think about crying and decide against it.

Who has time to mourn
a hill's worth of pines in Alabama
when the Sargasso sea endlessly gorges on

cigarettes, sun-dried seaweed, and milk cartons?
An hour ago, I watched a businessman
miss the bin with his smoothie cup,

electric green spatters on the concrete;
he considered picking it up, decided against it.
The green repeats, an afterimage

through my windshield, blurring
into the roadside Bradford pears.
Who has time to mourn

the pond filled in with dirt,
the turtles pilgrimaging
as the wind picks up,

when somewhere a white rhino
lies on his side, kicks out a foot,
thinks about rising and decides against it.

Kathryn Hargett-Hsu

Bopomofo Abecedarian

[of miscegenation]

Between the rose house & the house
            burned open: between
pokeweed berries stolen by thrashers:
            July sharpens the beige

magnolia blooms. Decadent,
                        the turkey vulture arrives
for its ritual of tearing. Its beak:
            red blister stripping red blister.
                    We ride into

decomposing heat with no A/C.
            In the blood-
town of my father: *He thinks you'se one of his kind.*

Insatiable & everywhere,
history drags its wet hair across the county.
                    It chases down the pickup trucks

& guinea fowl, furious artifacts.
            O
Country road, ballad never mine,
            I know you'd like to wind that birth
                        cord around my throat.
            Do you see me, little girl

half-breed basted in the blueberry fields—
            I chewed young cattails &
juiced oranges with my hands.
            These

quiet roads run me down,
            daughter of no mother of theirs.
My blood points to four different poles

only to corner itself in the same
chickadee's song. Say it: I was born
            contraband, my veins

shuddering alive beneath the Alabama moon.
            Unseasonable mongrel, I came of no frost,
                        gold-haired runt of no mountain.
            O
Russellville, I rounded my vowels,
            guided them over the hills—

zealous for recognition
            with a hook in my lip.
                        & yet
still I wait for that
yes—that terrible glimmer of likeness—
                        while, in the backyard,

a wasp trapped in a fig releases
            its wings & dissolves into fruit.
                        Say it:
I was a felony here.
                        You don't forget a thing like that.

Internal Dissident

I was born with a cudgel & a mole on my cheek.
When the fog told my mother her name
was dead, I crushed the fog with my milk teeth.
I knew the blister of annihilation

before I scraped soot from my gums.
I was born so I belly-crawl. I was born to refuse
to be the proliferation of another's erasure.
To be unmeasurable is to be anti-imperial.

To slither. To refuse the debt
they made of your blood. It was a state tactic
to burn *Hsu* from my birth certificate,
they said they'd scorch that yellow undergrowth

for a new forest to drum. But I know
I was born with wild pigs fleeing brushfire
& provinces obliterated in air raids,
that from the commas of immigrant desire

I tore into feral territory. I'm a beastly child.
My mother gave me a heart that beats me
through finite revolutions of moons.
She birthed me into a verb, an action to perform.

Hsu Gai-ti. Remove the radical & my name is ember.
Xu Kai-di. Change the tone & I am the sound of flaying.

I was born with this fire & I was born
to cut it out of my own throat.

At the Center of the Laogai: 余烬

Before Mom was spit from the spigot
of a detention center, a dragon
sucked the red out of a koi's pride
& 阿公 boiled a koi to spite the Japanese.

Before 姨婆 spat in the foreman's
mouth, shame starved the foxes
out of your stomach. You low-tailed shadow
humming with the dusk of paws:

to you melancholy is brimming
& delicious. Your hip brushes diaspora's tablecloth
before you knock its vase from the table.
The army drags 姨婆 back into the forest

& buttons her name onto the mast
of a prison letter. Daughter,
memories do not spawn without first touching
the thorax of longing. If you believe them,

a name can wrench itself free from everything
but its geography, like the dream of ripe longan
drilled through a prisoner's throat.
Guilt cauterizes the air around it,

but sooner or later, the foxes come stitching home.
In the Strait, the naval brigades follow
a wild thread back to shore. In the Strait, the dragons
tusk off their feet for the rest of the refugees.

It was war, Mom said. 就是家.
& here come the foxes. In the dark room,
阿公 binds the sympathizers' wrists
& whistles to those thousand-pawed beasts.

Dark Peak

Peak District, 2018

November will pummel you if you let it.
        Beneath it: a stain you can't scrub off
        & gales extorting the moors. You wear
your thickest socks. On walks to the clinic,

        you stomp your reflection in crowns of rainwater.
                You arrive alone & without your shadow,
                that wet animal still pinned to a mattress in Lenton.
        When you're sober, you feel it wrest, claw-&-knee

        home to you. You don't want it anymore.
                It bleeds when swabbed. You prefer the loneliness
                hat arrives in the wide expanse of days
        & piles from one appointment to the next—

it squints at every mild face & sustains the husk
        growing around you. When asked, you answer.
        You flat mood. You deny your scent. Early on
you vowed not to spar for a stranger's last lock

of empathy, though you often mistake compassion for pity.
        On non-clinic days, you buy a ticket to Hope.
        Spray-painted sheep wander as expected.
They eat what they eat. No one expects much

        of you, dark-eyed foreigner, & how you indulge
                in their erasure of you. Wind bristles

your cheeks' fine fur. Rain darkens the gritstone—
the moors mud. You walk slowly to avoid the cut.

But the cut isn't a cut—it's a hymenal laceration,
                & it will not abandon you just because
                you've fled to higher ground. Again,
        the slitting weight of it wrings out

that photonegative self—not your shadow,
        but the anterior record of your shadow.
        She wears exhibits 15-19 & an olive coat.
She trails beside you in the gusting

peat moss, at times silent, at times whispering
        in a tongue you hardly know. You would like
        to discredit this self. You would like
to indulge in the lashing & tonsure,

        to braid a jute rope & petrify her beneath brutal peat.
                Be kind to her. Like other evidence, she will
                be destroyed in seven years. She appears to you
        because something inside you wants her

                to appear—to say: yes, the ladybeetle did meander
                        across the frosted window—& yes, the nurse's name
                        was Natalia—& perhaps the world is kinder
                than its inscription upon your back.

        After a while, she stops whispering. Again, the glazing wind.
                Again, jute rope's open question. You continue
                to walk through misting rain—the self follows
        the rain—turn your head. Tomorrow,

she will sit beside you at the back
        of the waiting room. Together, you'll wait for a nurse
        to mispronounce your name—a woman
who believes you, & who you will never see again.

Petition for Naturalization

ALWAYS GIVE YOUR ALIEN REGISTRATION NUMBER WHEN COMMUNICATING WITH THIS SERVICE

ALWAYS the immigration officer's confident pen,
a black blister, to GIVE us a new body.

Three hundred petitions:
      yellow to medium brown to medium
      Mongoloid to medium fair to medium
      white to medium:

            YOUR revision logged in a wide folder
            of ALIENs lapping at the harbor.

From 1882-1965, America federally slammed its door
on Chinese immigrants' toes.
Weeks confined to isolation wards.
Their names skewered on REGISTRATION forms
      (or returned to the wine-dark sea).

                It is impossible to know the NUMBER of Chinese laborers
                maimed in pursuit of the ocean.
                    (That is: the Central Pacific Railroad kept no record of their deaths.)

         WHEN nineteen Chinese were lynched
         on a single night in 1871, a fair man
         cut off a medium man's finger in pursuit of a ring.

                1970s: first Chinese restaurant in North Alabama.
                My grandparents spoke little English.
                    The fluent daughter was tasked
                        with COMMUNICATING WITH the fair customers.
                Nonthreatening vocabulary & nonthreatening chop suey smiles.

                When the general died of tuberculosis,
                    four generations were quarantined in THIS small house.
                    The smallest of them slept in drawers.

                Some labored in the SERVICE of nationhood.
                Some died before they could return.

            When the Tennessee River flooded,
                they collected the exiled carp no fair people
                would harvest.

    (I?)   the ungrateful progeny go for the eyes.

UNITED STATES DEPARTMENT OF JUSTICE
Immigration and Naturalization Service

UNITED STATES OF AMERICA

PETITION FOR NATURALIZATION

No. *13024*

A.R. No. A35 135 165

To the Honorable

The ....*District*........ Court for the ....United States........ at ....Birmingham, Alabama........

This petition for naturalization, hereby made and filed under section ....316(a)........ ,
Immigration and Nationality Act, respectfully shows:

(1)

Hang an American flag from your window.

TRUE & CORRECT, the angel will pass over you.

(2)

In my classroom, the PRESENT PLACE OF fair:

Blonde hair braided with dandelions.
Lunchables & crustless sandwiches & mini muffins.

My fair classmate trying my own afternoon snack,
then retching nothing on the floor.

After school,

I lit a candle in my bathroom
& cast a spell for green eyes.

I stared at my reflection, willing flora
to take RESIDENCE
in dirt iris.

(3)

Fair people do not own nature stories.

Who said they could take it from us?

We were all BORN IN the trees,
slept in the canopy before we had language
to describe it.

Write about flowers.

Bloody your hands with a blueberry bush.

(4)

I REQUEST THAT MY NAME
    BE CHANGED TO   dirt eye.

(5)

Humid summers in unceded land.
Two radio stations.

                Pawpaw could still drive.

In the back seat, I drank fresh orange juice
with my medium sister.

                Around us,

        wide acres of unceded lumber,
        guinea fowl chasing cars down dirt roads.

The hawks HAVE NOT ABANDONED
        SUCH RESIDENCE of their inheritance.

        We invade.

(6)

Nana dotting Country Lily 01 foundation on my cheeks,
smearing it into fair ash on my medium face.

Our difference cast in no shadow
            & CONTINUOUSLY IN THE STATE.

Form N–405 (Rev. 11–27–78)N

137

(7)

How she once touched the UNION of my eyelids
& wondered aloud,   *Where's the crease?*

(8)

After a few generations, you, too, can become fair,
if blended with fair people.

Trade bok choy for green peas
& oyster sauce for ketchup.

It comes not IMMEDIATELY UPON TERMINATION
but like a fissure in plaster,

the tectonic plates
BY TREATY OR STATUTE

pulling apart the ground.

(9)

Assimilation is a bureaucratic practice.

Complexion is an OTHER THAN HONORABLE euphemism,
which can be scratched out
in black pen, corrected.

Fair, medium, dark.

That is: you are between states.

That is: subject or accomplice.

I cross the unceded stream again & again.

Medium daughters of fair father,
fair daughters of medium mother—

                    I HAVE NEVER BEEN SEPARATED FROM
                 this riverbed, that bisection AGGREGATING
                      the conditions of medium containment.

                    That is: do what you're told.

                    That is: fair violence & SERVICE TERMINATED.

(10)

        A pen can waterboard or LAWFULLY ADMIT.

            The wisdom, once:

                to be counted is to be subject
                        to the (neo)colonial enterprise.

                    So: decategorize.

                    So: become unmeasurable.

                REFUSE TO WEAR THE UNIFORM of empire.

(11)

(12)

But the instructions are unclear.
                        For so long
        I BELIEVED IN,
                        ADVOCATED,
        ENGAGED IN
                        my own vanishing.

I compass my yearning
                out the window,
                        to the oak trees,

        thinking of Mitsuye Yamada.
                How invisibility is an unnatural disaster.

                To become uncountable,
                                debureaucratic,
                without disappearing altogether,

                        is an impossible proposition.

(13)

        In the nineteenth and twentieth centuries,

        the United States did not consider Chinese women
                GOOD MORAL CHARACTER, slits

                        DISPOSED TO THE GOOD ORDER
                        of an infiltrating snake.

                        Inscribed into law:

                        Medium & lewd & immoral.
                        Medium & where is your decency?

                In 1875,
        Ulysses S. Grant invited Congress to consider

                "perhaps no less an evil—the importation of Chinese women, but
                few of whom are brought to our shores to pursue honorable or useful
                occupations."

Inscribed into the archive:

Medium deviant.
Medium & venomous to the national bloodstream.

Sign along the dotted line:
I will not poison you.

(FULL NAME, WITHOUT ABBREVIATION.)

(14)

One summer I followed my fair father & his fair cousin
to shoot Coke cans in the woods.

When it was my turn to shoot,

my father showed me safety from reload,
how to stand
so the recoil wouldn't shove me down.

I took WITHOUT QUALIFICATION
THE OATH of a medium finger
against the trigger.

I lowered the target between the sights;
inhaled;
squeezed;
& missed the can completely.

The fair men expected it of me.

For the rest of the afternoon,
I was EXEMPTED THEREFROM conducting injury
with my own paws.

Instead, I accompliced.

I loaded .22 bullets into magazines
& watched the fair men use the machine,

which breathed,
which could PERFORM NONCOMBATANT SERVICE
or unzip a medium girl's forehead into the mud.

141

(15)

Life took to dirt as it took to water.

Once, the planet was all stone & fire.

Then dirt.   Then perpetual ocean,
          which is not a question of power.

                    Then an animal staggered onto dirt
                    with uncertain limbs,
                              became Eve.

                              Then you.
                              Then dirt eye.

                                   (UNLESS EXEMPTED THEREFROM).

(16)

     The birds were VERIFYING WITNESSES of Lazarus.
     The birds were Lazarus of the meteor.

                         They took flight
                    & escaped annihilation,
          but not its SUPPLEMENTAL AFFIDAVIT.

     They watched the wind bruise the chestnut trees,
               & the chestnut trees drop their payloads.

The birds flew microfilm across enemy lines.

     Then they were turned into hats.

          Say:
                    once there was no country,
                         no treaties,

                              only mountains not yet weathered
                              by time's unrelenting melt.

                              No south.
                              No pen.
                              No metaphor.

142

There's comfort in myth.

Dirt eye is not a metaphor.

(17)

WHERETOFORE

I am dirt eye.

I SWEAR (AFFIRM)

I am dirt eye,

        SO HELP ME GOD.

OATH OF ALLEGIANCE

I HEREBY DECLARE, ON OATH,
      THAT no state can ABSOLUTELY AND ENTIRELY
           archive the ocean which delivered us;

THAT I WILL BEAR
           the archive, the railroad spike,
           the tokens of jade & brilliance of the rising sun,

                    which make manna,
                    which makes a name;

THAT I WILL PERFORM
           resurrection in the name of insurrecting joy;

THAT I WILL PERFORM
      the WORK OF the medium
           to floss our phantoms from the archive,

                    which is alchemy,
                    which is an ear;

& THAT I TAKE THIS OBLIGATION FREELY
      & in the indicative mood: our future,

                    which is *both/and*,
                    which is soil,
                    which is here.

          We are here,
                    SO HELP ME GOD.

Joseph Harrison

Air Larry

*(Larry Walters flew a lawn chair attached to helium balloons to a
height of 16,000 feet, into the jet lanes above Los Angeles; he
named his craft "Inspiration I.")*

When the idea came
It seemed, at best, a dicey thing to do:
You rig your vehicle, give it a name,
Straighten a line or two,

Then, confident you've given it your best
If not that it will carry you aloft,
You put it to the test
And it just takes off,

Lifting you over the trees
And up the sky
Easy as you please,
Till soon you are really high,

Your neighborhood, turned miniature, is gone,
And you wonder how,
Up here all alone,
To get the hell down, now

That the transcendental imagination
Has proven it can indeed
Surpass your wildest expectation,
And raise you higher than you need

Or want to go,
For now that you are "there"
All you know is how little you know,
And that here in the upper air

It is very cold,
A disenabling extremity

Your clumsy calculations should have foretold,
And, triggering all your anxiety,

You hear, then see, roaring across the sky
As dots in the distance streak into form,
The gargantuan craft come cruising by,
Perfectly uniform,

Built for speed and altitude,
So effortless in shattering sound itself
That next to them your vehicle looks crude
And fatally flawed, just like yourself,

Painfully ill-equipped to play the hero,
And actually beginning to freeze to death
At a temperature far below zero
Where the thin air burns each breath,

And you realize you must, not a moment too soon,
Jettison all original intent
And pop your own balloon
To undertake the perilous descent.

Shakespeare's Horse

He was a man knew horses, so we moved
As wills were one, and all was won at will,
In hand with such sleight handling as improved
Those parks and parcels where we're racing still,

Pounding like pairs of hooves or pairs of hearts
Through woodland scenes and lush, dramatic spaces,
With all our parts in play to play all parts
In pace with pace to put us through his paces.

Ages have passed. All channels channel what
Imagined these green plots and gave them names
Down to the smallest role, if and and but,
What flies the time (the globe gone up in flames),

What thunders back to ring the ringing course
And runs like the streaking will, like Shakespeare's horse.

Dr. Johnson Rolls Down a Hill

Even a man of voluminous gravity,
The monumental lexicographer
Who labored in inconvenience and distraction,
In sorrow, sickness, and slovenly poverty
Unaided by the learned or the great,
A man of girth and passionate appetite
Who relished with dispatch and enormous zest
Huge stacks of pancakes, bottomless pots of tea,
Along with whatever conversational thrust
Kept the mind nimble and the spirit light,
Delaying the final, agonizing hour
When he lumbered off to bed, always alone,
To self-recrimination in pitch dark,
Contains in his heart of hearts a little boy
Who played and played all day, without a thought
Of duty or expectation or penury
Or wasted years diminishing all the time.

Not to idealize childhood, least of all his:
Barely alive at birth, too weak to cry,
Infected in infancy by tubercular milk,
Rendered half blind, half deaf, with an open wound
Stitched in his little arm for his first six years
(An issue, with so much else, he learned to ignore),
Scarred by the scrofula, and further scarred
By being cut sans anesthesia,
He wasn't a pretty sight, but bore it all,
The constant pain, the perpetual awkwardness,
The fretting of parents, and the feckless taunts
Of boys who could play ball and ridicule
The rawboned, driveling prodigy in their midst,
And grew to be a man of great physical strength
Despite his pitiful incapacities.

The body had its struggles. So did the mind.
The photographic memory, the sheer
Celerity and clarity and taut
Engagement with the question, small or large,
Be it some pressing affair of state, or some
Domestic crisis pressing upon the heart
Of one he loved, encompassing his point
With honesty and syntax and good sense,
Such gifts the mind deployed with bravery

147

While poised above a vertiginous abyss
Opening wide within, a whirligig
Of deep afflictions and anxieties:
Depression, sloth, despair, paralysis,
An "inward hostility against himself"
In which his massive critical faculty
Would pulverize his puny self-regard,
And, worst of all, pure terror at the dark
Encroachments of what seemed insanity.

Now, in his middle fifties, the shadows lengthen,
"A kind of strange oblivion" overspreads him.
Beset by horrors and perplexities
The clicks and spasms and clucking of Tourette's
Markedly worsen as the great man sinks
Deeper in torpor, till guilt at time misspent
Freezes and harrows him, transfixed, become
A spectator at his own stunned debacle,
Tortured by scruples like pebbles in his shoes.
He's written nothing for years, and Shakespeare waits,
Promised and paid for but beyond him still
(What infinite riches, and what little room),
As vast resources of intelligence
Fritter away from faulty "character,"
And reason flickers, dying, all but snuffed
Out by the listless drift of hopelessness.
His friends try to distract him, to little avail,
With a club, a trip to the country, anything . . .

He visits Lincolnshire with Bennet Langton
In January 1764.
He's on his best behavior, charming both
His young friend's parents and their visitors.
One fine, dry afternoon, windless and clear,
They set out walking on the Lincolnshire wolds.
Only the groundsel's in bloom, a tentative yellow,
As they amble past tufts of grouse scrub, furze, and thorn,
But the air has a pleasing crispness, with a rich,
Effluvial hint of leaf-mold or of wood-rot.
The hills are varied by streaks of yellowish red
Which vaguely correspond to, lower down,
The low, red roofs of occasional cottages.
Everything's very still. There are just three birds:
A fluttering brace of fieldfares (or are they redwings?),
Plus a lone kestrel, hovering for a vole.

They reach the top of an impressive hill.
Admiring its steepness, suddenly Johnson declares
He has "not had a roll for a long time."
Against the objections of the company
He divests himself of pencil, keys, and purse,
Lies down at the edge, and, after a turn
Or two, is off and tumbling and picking up speed
Flattening the flora in his path
While sending up puffs of chalk dust, now he's chuckling
As his weight propels him and his heaviness
Precipitating his new view revolves
As sky and earth wheel round in blue-brown circles
And happiness is merely being alive,
As if the good life really were this easy,
As if the nightmare of his coming breakdown
Had no more substance than a child's bad dream.

To My Friends

My good friends, when you're under the illusion
That the common end of things has ended me,
Whether that end was sudden or wretchedly slow,
Peaceful or violent, untimely or, finally, wished for,

Don't spend too much time grieving, as if I were gone
To some murky underground region of swampy water
And cavernous absence, metallic and silent and cold,
Or some plush resort in the stratosphere of our dreams

Pillowed with cumuli, graced by ethereal muzak,
Or some massive confusing impersonal processing center
With lines and obscure snafus and numbers not names,
Away from the sun and the sound of the wind in the trees,

But after a short ceremony, public or private,
Listen for the wings of the birds, and ask where we're going,
Alabama or Delaware, Canada, Yucatan,
And wish me luck in the next life, who now have wings.

Mark Strand

When I came to the end of the dream, there was Mark Strand.
We were in a vast hall, where the ceiling was too high to see,
And the light slanted down from above, and a cold wind blew.
We sat on a bench in the back. A little ways off,
A teacher was teaching a class, and she asked him to speak,
But he shook his head: he was too tired. Then he turned
To me, and he said, "I don't write anymore. I don't
Even look at the moon. But I read." Then he smiled. "When you read
The books you most love for the last time, you see
The great works of imagination get better and better.
When you come to that passage where, arrayed in battalions,
With all their flashing armor and flapping banners
And bright wings fanning the starlight, the heavenly host
Throws down its spears, you wonder, although you've read it
A hundred times, 'Will it really happen again?,'
And when it does, you are surprised." There were tears
In his eyes as he said this. But were they tears of sadness,
Or tears of joy, or were they just caused by the wind,
That cold wind blowing and blowing? Then he was gone,
And the teacher was gone, with her class, and the students' voices,
And all I could hear in the hall was the sound of the wind.

Carolyn Hembree

Ghazal as Shadows Lengthen

Greet me in a dead tongue when I rise from my sunken bed—*Godana dag!*
(Gothic). Mama's here, my necromantic swamp, good evening all afternoon.

Download complete. Getaway App: charger, cash, nuts, poems, gum, curlers, slip, good
panties in case, bad panties in case, glitter, pills, morning, night, afternoon.

Carolinas spat us out. Then Queens. Quit the Catalinas when our night-
bloom soup burned at a Y2K party that last slurpable afternoon.

My aliases are *Ariadne, Ariana, Audrey*. I play
Mistress of Labyrinths. I play femmes who jump trains in *Love in the Afternoon*.

Where'd we see that Joan Crawford flick? Bette Davis. *I never wear*—was it
violets or lilacs?—*magnolias big as baby heads in the afternoon.*

Sue me. The flipped neighborhood keeps me around and out of it—another
wan revenant in house-shoes draping a groaning porch swing all afternoon.

Words over Emily's case (320). I say voices. You say German.
Friend, don't leave, we'll praise small, impartial *certain*, small *light/Winter Afternoons*—

Word of Marthe. *Of* no more *from* Marthe. Priority: Normal. Eighty-
one kilobytes. Saved. Received: 10 April, 54 minutes after noon.

East Asian Religions complete. Click to test your Abrahamic knowledge:
[click] 1. Mincha, Nones, Asr, and _____ are prayers offered every afternoon.

Approaching your destination. De-board as road bleeds into roads left. Breath-
clouds. Bye, bus. Hi, wild ducks, distant pond, low-lying lung of late afternoon.

Siri, what's it like? *Looks nice today, Carolyn. Up to 75.*
No, what about me? *Figuratively, too, welcome to your afternoon.*

---

*The eighth couplet refers to the late poet Marthe Reed (1959-2018)

A Cutter's Sestina (Prom '95)

Fuck spring. Spring's a punk in rose
leather who sings
under lacy stars,
stars the night bruised around:
My knives / are sharper / than your / knives.
Na na nana na. / Here, amid my corsage of voices—

baby's breath, filler, wired voice
I'll call Boss Fleur (my rosiest,
my loudest)—I knife
bloom upon bloom I believed. In what? Unsung,
in ribbons already, I'm around
to, what, suffer girls this Phantasmaboria stars.

Strobed grunge and stars,
you pulsing through gaps in my stall, govern these voices.
Govern these slits. Oh, we should belt a round
so we never cry, we never stop crying, should rise
on tides dyeable heels bleed, should sing
our aerial arrival, waif dynasty on a knife

edge at the dance no one dances. With knives
for mirrors, those stomped-cold stars,
we color our lips like our songs
before bright heads loll and voices
disappear down school and wild-rose
wilderness corridors. When limos round

the terraced distance with backseat cardigans, their round
necks, may every spike heel conceal a flick knife
for pinned torsos, our *oh so much* cuffed blubber, to arouse.
Feeling is a lie the crepe stars
tell the falsie hills in a voice-over
for a song

never cut. Didn't I say I loved a gothic touch, a snuff song,
a grudge fuck? Just look around.
TO THE YEAR THAT AMAZED US ALL, a voice over
the system. Have it. Where are the knives?
Where are the woods? Where are the starlets
who play my ghost and cover my creeping flesh in roses?

152

La Dictée

My mother calls to say she isn't dead
but choked on a cheap kebab. *You say you're
a writer. What's so tough it won't go down?*

What can I do? Voices from a blotted-out
planet tell her I'm not her daughter.
My mother calls to say she isn't dead

but OD'd on the shitter. I stomp, I beat,
I chew the bites I feed my daughter.
What's so tough it won't go down? She read

me French who now reads phantom doodles
on her flesh, those padded walls my author.
They call me Mother, the loving dead,

mes étoiles. I sell science my parts. Adieu.
I save love for poems. I get wet, I sing.
Écrivez-moi vite qu'elle est revenue.

Students dissect the pearly tissue
that held these bones. My cadaver rings.
My mother calls to say she isn't dead
and *Gristle!* I'm her writer. I get it down.

Note: *Écrivez-moi vite qu'elle est revenue.* ("Write to me quickly that she has come back.") From *Le Petit Prince*, by Antoine de Saint Exupéry, with the masculine pronoun replaced by the feminine.

Nocturne

My daughter molds a gun from bread.
Why do gods make us eat? Witness divine

stovetop resurrection of yesterday's sides!
I scrape my plate. August, so long, sweat

your bullets of stars over our shrinking soirée:
alluvial fluted trunks, swamp iris, lone owl

in the live oak, dropped brass of avenue magnolias,
this shotgun home's gable rookery, these leftovers.

Her flimsy Sunbeam pistol to my head:
I am not and do not like you, Mother.

Don't play with your food, Pistol. Copper skitters
on the fire. Something's done, something unfed.

I'll have my drink. What's got my get may get me too.
Play dead, each day a shallow sucking wound.

Prayer

Always with this smashing, muddy river. And my child vexed. The white sky her screams crested. The white coats rounding the kid wing. Where histories were charted, looks gauged. Under my touch. Scrolled symptoms and elevators. Chimes. A drip was hung. A bed opened, a gown. In a room with a magic mural. One wand sent forth waves of sound her tissues made bounce. Unheard echoes went. In or out of view. Bats in the mural.

Bedrails. Yet her roiling. Not to be contained. We were spoken with. I wanted any edge to punch: through. There was none. No night, no shrinking, no edifice, none. Doorframe. I went wooden too. All call buttons called. Wood still feels. Cut so. I forgot our stories.

Not I. Sang the moon in the mural. Sang the witch. Sang the fish. Until rivers rose. And a piece of water turned back into a girl chin to chest curled into herself.

Listen. The girl sings exultant songs from our house by the river that spills over walls into dreams.

Raye Hendrix

Pinson

What will it take to stop thinking
of here as home? I stay, I go, I come

again—even the shifting skyline
seems the same, new buildings owned

by old money, old trees felled
for a different kind of growth,

the streets still keepers
of slave owners' names.

The corrupt Mayor died but now there's
another reclining in his chair.

Always more, an abundance of Mayors,
a plague. The Dairy Queen torn

down and resurrected as a failing
strip mall is still *the place*

that used to be the Dairy Queen.
The husk of the grocer on Old

Springville Road still wears the ghost
of its former life, *Piggly Wiggly*

shadowed into brick by years of heat
and sun. This entire miserable town—

its dilapidated roads pothole-pocked
and going nowhere—a relic of itself

inhabited by rot, the kind that sticks
around, keeps itself alive, blooms

sickly where nothing else will—
where the people are proud

to be holdout Confederates,
each new generation baptized in red.

But there's jasmine here. There's light.
The tea is cold and smooth and sweet

and brewed by a windowed sun. Dogs
wear no collars. Cats lie fat and happy

on the warm roofs of trucks—fed full
by field mice and table scraps from

women with curlers in their hair—
unowned and belonging to us all.

The mountain breeze cools the air,
ripples the lake to diamonds, the algae

a million emeralds sunk just beyond
the shore, a jeweled city for channel

cat and bass. And the people plant
things. Put down roots. Let kudzu

stabilize disintegrating barns, hold up
the walls. Is it wrong of me to want

this to survive? To die? To leave,
come home, then leave again

and leave my ghost behind?

At Toomer's Corner, the Morning After the Iron Bowl (2019)

In memory of Pat Sullivan

An autumn sun, expected, rises;
steals darkness from between the stars

to illuminate the streets and avenues—
College and Magnolia brilliant white

with billowing paper, a southern substitute
for snow: live oaks cloaked from trunk

to acorn, ivory drifts in dewfrost catching
light like pearls on Samford Lawn.

This softness that follows the clamor
of Saturday's spectacle, the neon

sound—so quiet now the city
seems to be holding its breath,

silent streets clinging to the ghost
of last night's gathering—the true

and fearless faithful singing
Glory, Glory; Give 'em Hell

at the last game of the year. Soon,
city crews will come to clear

the tissue from the branches,
untangle celebration from the trees.

In the cool of Sunday morning
the rolls of streamer-snow will feather

into subtler pieces, flutter down
Auburn's drowsy avenues, then scatter

skyward—on the wind rise up as if
triumphant—as if dancing, joyful, free:

a white-winged flock of paper angels,
now having won, returning home.

Blood in the Milk

The calf slipped from her body
like a receding wave: breathless,

limp, landed soft and heavy
in the dew-wet grass the way

a stone might after rolling slowly
down a hill, a nine-month anti-climax—

and if cows can mourn its mother did.
Wouldn't let us close enough to milk

for days, pink udder distending,
swelling as if in place of empty womb.

She wasn't mine—belonged to the old
farmer who lived a mile around the bend,

nestled in our shared bosom of hills—
but I loved her as if she was,

and the farmer let me, gave me a key
to his barn, let my girlhood smell

of shit and seed and hay.
I walked there every day, freckles

blooming like cow-spots on my cheeks
in the early heat of April, and maybe

that's why she finally let me close:
my body not much larger than

her would-be calf's, arms and legs
twiggy, pigtails like low red ears,

my breed a mother's aggrieved
mistake for bovine. The farmer gave me

a milking stool and bucket, showed me how
to work my hands, slow as springtime,

gentle as a suckling mouth. I pulled
and when I did she looked me in the eye.

What the Water Left Behind

For the victims of Hurricane Katrina

We didn't know that it had swallowed
Biloxi whole, or that the waves
betrayed the boats in Mobile Bay.

We didn't know the French names
of the tiny coastal towns, or that the gulf
was busy burying them in brine.

We didn't know the trawling prawners
in the shallows of Bayou La Batre gave up,
cast their lines for heaven in the water's wake.

We didn't know we wouldn't eat shrimp
for nearly a year. In Alabama it was dark
for days. The water swept up power lines

and gas tanks, all the magnolias my father
planted the year before, their roots upturned,
outstretched like empty hands of need.

We scoured the house for batteries
for flashlights. Used none for the radio
and the news. When the light finally returned

the TV came back with it, drowning
out the overcast gloom. We should have,
but didn't know we'd see the bodies

on the news: face down, swollen, buoyant
in all the wrong ways, clogging the canal-streets
of New Orleans; or the new coastline, framed

by the screen—a perverted gift shop snapshot:
wrought-iron coral, rooftops islands, brown bay—
a postcard from a large and lonely God.

Thomas Alan Holmes

Belvedere

for Ron Giles

Through an adjoining wall
we hear an overamplified
new band tune up, preparing
to perform for patrons
of the coffeehouse next door
to this converted storefront,
where a corner stage, spotlit
and miked, provides a space
to share our work before
we send it out to little
magazines and editors.

Our emcee introduces us
as we have signed his list.
He chaffs the ones he knows
and welcomes first-timers.
We listen, gratified
that certain of our students
have gone beyond the wolfcry
"fuck" or metaphoric "rape"
to shorthand violation.
We take our turns and wait.

When he climbs the two steps
to the low stage, he leans
slightly left, like one hefting
a fixed flat to get a truck
on track. He stands in front
of a plum rug hung stage up,
its design a center hub
surrounded by oversized
blotched brown paisley figures
curved like fetuses, a glory
around his head. His ball cap
plugs a cancelled sitcom,

and he wears its bill low,
like a pitcher measuring
a batter at the plate,
his eyes shaded from the light
falling on his hands, the one
clasping a manuscript,
the other gesturing
as he caresses each phrase,
his voice an Alabama
accent in Southern cadence.
He speaks few true
one-syllable words—
even "home," "Nam," and "gun"
shift and settle into place
with gentle inflection
as he contemplates
a killer's hand, a careworn
shaving kit, half an alphabet.

We walk out into silver
moonlight and halogen
orange streetlight, having nursed
lukewarm beer for three hours
just to hear each other
stay hushed for two beats after
he has read his final line.

On *Homer's* Fox Hunt

At once, I'm fooled and think the view I share
is what the fox can see, the sea, a green
and jewel-like glow along the shore between
two snowy banks, but, no, I'm in the air
and near a pair of crows, aloft; from there
I see a smooth, unbroken, snowy plain,
no cover for the fox. Should I explain
my broken self I see depicted here?
I thought I am the rust-daubed fox, away
from its familiar haunts and trapped alone,
a resignation that feels languorous
and desperate. Should I, now crow, betray
some secret need to feed on what I've done?
Like crows, the snowflakes pile on, dangerous.

Road to Goodbye

The quickest route to say goodbye would be to take Exit 318 on I-65, southbound
        in my case, but I would more likely take Highway 31 North from my
        hometown, drive through the small towns where my father lived, look at
        how the roads changed, how at the intersection of Old Highway 31 the
        '70s-era roller rink still stands if only to support the local drug dealers,
        how a truck stop became an evangelical church with its own daycare, how
        Hurricane Creek Park still looks the same from the road after forty years,
        how, once I would turn left onto the other end of Old Highway 31, the
        flea market has worn down to bent wood and axel-bruising potholes, how
        the swamp right before West Lacon Road still looks as snaky as it ever did,
        and then I would turn right onto West Lacon Road,
because West Lacon Road is the only way to go to say goodbye, where I would have
        to drive by what used to be the Wilcutt place, the only money on my
        father's side of the family, being from his mother's family, and she, having
        married a poor man cheated of his inheritance by a brother who gulled
        him into signing the wrong line on a loan application, never recovered
        through the Depression and through having five children, two of them
        notorious for their adulteries in that community, one having escaped to
        the biggest city in the state after marrying a never-satisfied woman who
        considered herself better than his entire family, one having escaped to a
        smaller town, determined not to raise any children in that holler, the last
        settled there, having retired after a respectable career on the railroad and
        now eating himself to death as the only creature comfort left to him, given
        his own angry wife projects her fears about her mental health onto him,
        and my paternal grandmother's not inheriting money or land because she
        was a daughter given in marriage at fourteen,
her younger brother, instead, later inheriting the land when my great-grandfather
        died, and he selling it to purchase a big rig and drive throughout the
        country to satisfy an appetite he could not sate at home without sullying
        his reputation that was not harmed by his stories of selling goods out
        of the back of his trailer and claiming them damaged when filling out
        inventory, refusing to step foot in the family church but loitering in the
        parking lot during Decoration Sunday, and marrying a community college
        teacher who kept his house neat and her life pretty much to herself while
        he was on the road except for a scandal that perhaps escalated to false
        accusations and a trial to preserve her own reputation and who, herself,
        could not sell the house fast enough once he died,
so, I would drive past that homeplace, the house on one side of the road, the barn
        and pastures opposite, the copse of persimmon trees broken by storms in
        these years but still standing,
then continue past the other houses, the older ones in their dilapidations, the
        house where lived the widow whose attentions my great-uncles would
        come to blows over, the newer house whose owner, clearing land, found

a Civil War-era headstone and now has to accommodate gawkers who with right of ingress come up on his property, the childhood home of a serial child molester celebrated in his later career that provided more access to victims, and the patched-over structure once belonging to a recluse whose only satisfaction was his continuing to live in the oldest house in the community while controlling the single-lane gravel driveway to the community cemetery,

which is where I would go to say goodbye, as I would turn left on Simmons Lane, and I would look at that oldest house, and I would hook around it to that cemetery, and I would see all of those familiar last names,

because if I were to continue down West Lacon Road, I would pass the church which my father in his dementia wanted to buy with almost all of the money he and my working mother had saved for years, and I would come to the offshoot dogleg of Burney Mountain Road, where my paternal grandfather lost property to pay the debt his brother gulled him into, where the lushest pasture in the valley, bordered on one side by a cave-borne artesian spring, would now be mine had my father bought it for the small price an old family friend asked just to keep it among folks he knew,

a pasture my father did not buy because in purpose-driven thought he believed he would have to build on it if he owned it, never wanting to return to that community,

so I would turn on Simmons Lane instead to spare myself those last pains, and I would stand near where the great walnut of my boyhood was, now replaced by a mature cedar that I remember as a seedling, and I would feel the wind from the west as it passes over that church I will never enter again, and I would imagine that wind yet carries the a cappella hymns sung by the elderly Hardin siblings, their twangy syllables holy in their harmony.

Jennifer Horne

Morning Gift

"Still they stood . . .
As if the earth in one unlooked-for favor
Had made them certain earth returned their love."

1.
I opened the porch door quietly
so as not to wake the dogs.

By the lake, a roundish, off-white shape—
a plastic bag blown by last night's rain.

My eyes opening fully, it resolved into Bird.
Long neck, gimlet eye, fancy feathered hat.

It stood so still, watching for a fish.
I tried to stand as still, watching it.

It crept. I crept. It held. I stopped.
Two Belted Kingfishers ratcheted by,

disturbers of the peace. With raised head,
a slight jump, a shrug of the shoulders,

the heron was airborne, a flying machine
dazzling the morning.

I turned to coffee and breakfast.
It swooped off to the shallow slough.

I carried its stillness with me for a while,
the pause in the action being the action itself.

2.
I was not alone in my watching.
I called you from the bedroom

and you stood just behind me,
your breath so close, your chest to my back.

"Two look at one," you said, then
took the volume of Frost from the shelf.

You read the poem aloud,
your voice hoarsening at the final lines

(I heard, and loved you for it):
"I haven't read that poem in fifty years."

College Tour

I can see you hunched at the steering wheel,
black leather gloves holding tight,
peering ahead, willing the car to stay on the frozen road,

your good wool coat, your checked wool hat
talismans against mishap,
taking me north through the Ozarks

from Little Rock to far-away Missouri
through sudden snow on rollercoaster roads
with unseen drop-offs.

I was quiet so you could concentrate
quiet like both of us reading a book in the same room
but never did I worry you wouldn't get us through.

I knew. I'm driving now, halfway lost
somewhere north of Atlanta, picturing
your steady hands on the wheel:

black gloves, near white-out of snow,
your love expressed in getting me
where you hoped I wouldn't go.

Thanksgiving, 2020: When the New York Times *asked*

the Poet Laureates of America what their states were grateful for in this time of pandemic
I knew
what the people's answer would be: Trump & Tuberville & Faith & Family & Football

How to say in my own words that those are not my words?

I smell boiled peanuts, and I know I am once again at that old crossroads:
broken-down couch on one corner
old flag on the next
produce stand on the third
and on the fourth a lynch-tree stump with ambiguous green shoots

Somewhere a rocket

What to say, what to say?

I am grateful for everyday kindnesses

I stand still and take in the silence. Vow not to speak
until the right words arrive
breathless from the journey
and demand their own saying
tasting both of peaches and of gall

a simple sentence saying itself out saying its piece

Rachel Houghton

Wading in the Little Cahaba River

I look for words under
each beige and copper stone.
River pennies and pebble
snails cling, while crawdads bolt

before siltation clears.
Glinty rumors of gold-
line darters, Cahaba
shiners, and freckle bellies

flit while flathead catfish
lurk in cooler depths. One
boy holds his find high—Luke
Skywalker sans one arm.

I slow-creep fingertips
through mud for papershell
mussels. The Riverkeeper
says they wait and wave their

mantles, longing to catch
a fish. Glochidium
to gills is the final
impartation. My

hands come up fisted, full
of mud. Empty. The boy
cradles a flat football
he found among the
Cahaba lilies.

Burn

She eases an ear toward the fading flame
as the clash of metal on ice trespasses
up from the frozen pond. The poplar splat
follows—its hand-carved tulips drop to red

embers while she creeps oystered arms toward
the grate. Apron and splayed legs acquiesce
until only four hoary feet nestle
in the inner hearth. Two pairs of figure-

skates hang on a pecan peg by the door—
one white, one beige, the leather dry and cracked,
the matted laces intertwined. Footfalls
echo in empty space. She kneels, and with
one heel in hand, she toe-picks an oak
plank from the floor. The nails screech and the fire
crackles, while outside, ice laden limbs bow down low.

Andrew Hudgins

The Unpromised Land

Montgomery, Alabama

Despite the noon sun shimmering on Court Street,
each day I leave my desk, and window-shop,
waste time, and use my whole lunch hour to stroll
the route the marchers took. The walk is blistering—
the kind of heat that might make you recall
Nat Turner skinned and rendered into grease
if you share my cheap liberal guilt for sins
before your time. I hold it dear. I know
if I had lived in 1861
I would have fought in butternut, not blue,
and never known I'd sinned. Nat Turner skinned
for doing what I like to think I'd do
if I were him.

              Before the war
half-naked coffles were paraded to Court Square,
where Mary Chesnut gasped—"seasick"—to see
a bright mulatto on the auction block,
who bantered with the buyers, sang bawdy songs,
and flaunted her green satin dress, smart shoes.
I'm sure the poor thing knew who'd purchase her,
wrote Mrs. Chesnut, who plopped on a stool
to discipline her thoughts. Today I saw,
in that same square, three black girls pick loose tar,
flick it at one another's new white dresses,
then squeal with laughter. Three girls about the age
of those blown up in church in Birmingham.

The legendary buses rumble past the church
where Reverend King preached when he lived in town,
a town somehow more his than mine, despite
my memory of standing on Dexter Avenue
and watching, fascinated, a black man fry
six eggs on his Dodge Dart. Because I watched
he gave me one with flecks of dark blue paint

stuck on the yolk. My mother slapped my hand.
I dropped the egg. And when I tried to say
I'm sorry, Mother grabbed my wrist and marched me
back to our car.

               I can't hold to the present.
I've known these streets, their history, too long.
Two months before she died, my grandmother
remembered when I'd sassed her as a child,
and at the dinner table, in midbite,
leaned over, struck the grown man on the mouth.
And if I hadn't said *I'm sorry,* fast,
she would have gone for me again. My aunt,
from laughing, choked on a piece of lemon pie.
But I'm not sure. I'm just Christian enough
to think each sin taints every one of us,
a harsh philosophy that doesn't seem
to get me very far—just to the Capitol
each day at noon, my wet shirt clinging to my back.
Atop its pole, the stars-and-bars,
too heavy for the breeze, hangs listlessly.

Once, standing where Jeff Davis took his oath,
I saw the crippled governor wheeled into
the Capitol. He shrank into his chair,
so flaccid with paralysis he looked
like melting flesh, white as a maggot. He's fatter now.
He courts black votes, and life is calmer than
when Muslims shot whites on this street, and calmer
than when the Klan blew up Judge Johnson's house
or Martin Luther King's. My history could be worse.
I could be Birmingham. I could be Selma.
I could be Philadelphia, Mississippi.

Instead, I'm this small river town. Today,
as I worked at my desk, the boss
called to the janitor, *Jerome, I hear*
you get some lunchtime pussy every day.
Jerome, toothless and over seventy,
stuck the broom handle out between his legs:
Yessir! When the Big Hog talks
—he waggled the broomstick—*I gots to listen.*
He laughed. And from the corner of his eye,
he looked to see if we were laughing too.

New Headstones at the Shelby Springs Confederate Cemetery

Though wild, each flower has its name:
sweet william, dogtooth violet,
wild iris, wild geranium.
Some of the headstones, too, bear names:
Rucks, Murphry, Bookout. Mostly, though,
it's *Unknown Soldier CSA*.

It's late. At dusk, cool slanted light
glows opalescent on white stones,
and at the end of a long row
we stand and talk about—what else?—
mortality: unknown, a name,
unknown, me, you, and you.

          I snap
a green weed from a grave and chew it
for its sharp, sour burst of juice.
One of you—which?—breaks off a stalk
and says, "Sheep sorrel."

          It's *sorrel?* Sorrel!
She's dead and buried—and all my life
I'd heard my mother say *sheep sorrow*.
But now her teaching voice comes back
and says it slowly, properly
—*sheep sorrel*—so I will get it right.

But even she can't name these men
whose namelessness is now engraved
in marble. Adam had it easy.
He merely had to name the world's
ephemera, while we have to
remember it. Sheep sorrel, yes!
Wild iris, wood sage, chicory,
sweet william, Sarah, Norman, me,
and some red spiky thing, which blooms
at our feet as we walk back home.

Roberta was my mother's name.

Crucifixion

Montgomery, Alabama

In the hot dark they dug a hole—
quickly and with some panic dug
a small hole, tipped in the cross, braced it.
Flames surged though burlap soaked in kerosene.
A short lopsided, crude, half-burning cross.

Ah, Lord—each day, each breath, you're back
on some cross or another, nailed,
jabbed, taunted. And one eternal cross
burns through a hot night on this scorched
patch of suburban lawn. Judge Johnson's lawn.

I went to college with his son,
who, one fall day six months removed from Easter,
went to his room, shotgunned himself.

I would have said he died for us, our sins,
but I know longer know who Jesus is.
He's someone walking through his life—or hers—
until God whispers, *It's you.* And God's ignored

Two boys—one fourteen and one fifteen—
heave their homemade cross onto a truck.
God's voice grows louder as the truck
turns down Christ's street. God's shouting now.
God roars. The boys ignite the cross, run off,
run hide, and wait to see whom God has chosen.

Or does God simply choose us all?

Transistor Radio

Summer nights I huddled under
bedsheets in the hot dark
of my own breathing, ear pressed
against my father's radio.
This was forbidden: listening
to songs of cheating lovers,
lost unrecovered loves,
drink, song itself, and making
believe. I yearned and feared
to suffer that suffering
so the hurt would justify
my pure unhappiness,
at last. And now we march,
conscripts of sorrow who first
were volunteers. I hummed,
ignorant of what it meant:
walking the floor, you've got
that faraway look
in your eyes. But knowing that
I would find out, I sang
the forbidden words, ears pressed
to older worlds, in the hot
dark of my own slow breathing.

The God of Frenzies

The tall boy shook and shimmied across lunch tables,
shouting at us to shout.
"Jeez, what a jerk," I thought, but I still shouted.
I couldn't stop myself.
Strapped to his torso, pinned up and down his legs,
blue pompoms snapped and sizzled. We screamed with him,
and as we roared, he rode
our screaming, swam in it like water, soared.
We shook our pompoms at the living pompom,
and—mad, ecstatic—he
burst into flame. The boy inside the flames
froze one half-second as he changed
from flesh to fire. He raced
across the tables, and leapt toward us. I thought
it was stagecraft, part of his act.
Who would have thought that what looked true was true?
I couldn't hear his screams above our screaming.
I couldn't see him flopping on the floor.
Later we heard a story:
a match flipped at the swirling paper. A joke.
Though I know now that I was seeing terror
—a boy burning on a table—
I remember joy, the boy flung gratefully
to his full blazing length onto the air
as if he thought the air would hold him.
At that false remembered moment,
I saw terror and ecstasy,
and I would ask the god of frenzies why
with both choices before him, he chose terror,
though I know there was no reason. He simply chose.

Elizabeth Hughey

A Call to Arms

A man will keep trying
to beat the bad energy
out of his father's statue

until the man and the statue
appear to be one mark
on a timeline. Applause

comes from inside the fire
that takes down the stars
and removes the difference

between one thing and
another, between shotguns
and hands. Now we have

just one word
for everything, and we
aren't even saying it.

We are being said
though we can't quite hear
ourselves being said.

The Belongings

We have to work
with what has been
handed down to us.
We eat off of the words
our grandfathers said.
We sleep in them.
We set our drinks
down upon them.

What were we to do
with the fur stoles
but wear them
to museum balls
on the mildest
of winter nights
heat heavy
on our shoulders
like a burn from the sun
in our great-great-
grandmother's vacation.

We see our reflections
in the sterling set
that we have cleaned
of its meaning.
We could not blame
the knife
for what it divided.
We could not blame
stairs for our falls
or blame the art
for what was praised.

We could not destroy
every thing that was touched.
We still have billfolds,
swimming pools, hangovers,
wingbacks. We had to keep
birdfeeders, cake plates,
neckties and dice.
We kept all of the letters.
We kept all of the trees.

We moved into the names
that were left for us,
and we changed
the locks. Inside
we feel different now,
all sunwink, all meteorite,
but our windows
still look out
over the same city
of unearned suffering
we will not save.

Song for the Egg Filled with Nude Hose

I have called a dress white
when it was bone, gulf sand
baby teeth, dirty rice. I have

longed to be worn. I have
wanted the plum to want me
to eat it. I just want a plum

to be pleased. I wish to please
every black fly I kill. I will please
pleasure until I am loved
             by love.

A Promise for the Egg Filled with Cotton Balls

I drink down a little round white word
and wait for the unnamable ghosts
to leave my body, my body a nest
made of the finest cement.
I am asked in waiting rooms,
Is it a yellowthroat or a redwing?
It is a cowbird, I must answer,
it's a bullbird. Still, I will raise
any word I have been given with its
wide-open fig-red mouth.
There is always enough,
I lie, I can be a fraction of a mother.
I can be halved and halved again, the last
morning star floating in steamed milk,
a little bite of me will always be left
for you and you and you and you and you.

Ashley M. Jones

greens&bread

the soil remembers the names of our mothers
                                our fathers
                                    even the babies who
made their first and last milkbreath and went to heaven. greens
grow from even the dead-full soil.

greens stretch their velvet shoulders and ruffle in the south.
they bend their backs to let us wash their spines.
they remember us remembering,
remember plucking them from your father's raised bed?
remember how he taught you which ones to keep
and which ones to throw back to feed the soil anew?
remember beholding their beauty at the sink,
the way veins shined through even in the pot
gleaming with bacon fat,
even in the soup of stock and water as it pulls softness from
their mouths?

and the bread—how incomplete they are without it,
cornmeal raising up to meet buttermilk, to meet egg,
to meet the hot glaze of oil in the cast iron,
the crack of the crust a guarantee.

the pot liquor is a broth of memory. greens remember it all.
and on the plate, remember how the bread acculturates to let
its unctuous river in? softened, yes, but not weak,
crumbling, instead, toward a new identity.
and our forks and our fingers gobble it up.

hoppinjohn: *a blues*

after Tyehimba Jess

she's got some eyes—bette davis, no, black—
on our plates, she shimmies between the rice
and makes a lucky meal where there is lack—
not lima, pinto, just blackeyes suffice.

what alchemy where peas become pennies,
where even here we can be rich with pork,
this meal is tender medicine, ready
to heal what keeps us broken, to unyoke

ourselves away from helpless and enslaved.
we slice we sear we simmer and we braise
we hunt we chop we pick we stand amazed,
we serve it up and then we offer praise

the white blending around it—a whole note
supple with salt and onion and butter
this marriage on our Sunday plate, we float—
this here's a john that hops like no other.

the currency we want is born of soil,
stewed and heaped while the crops break for winter
when we need fresh warm hope, brought to the boil
so we're not chained to ruin, we splinter

and we build ourselves a future, we cook
it down until it's soft enough to eat,
we count our blessings, count the faith it took
to be here, to have vegetables and meat.

blackeyed peas and white rice on new year's day,
we pray this meal will keep the doom away—

mama, sweet as the fresh scent of new clean laundry. sweet as a curl unraveled from a pink foam roller on a fresh press. sweet like her mama taught her to be, her mama who knew what it meant to raise a child you didn't carry in your own womb. her mama who could make yams like no one else on this dull planet—who could make sugar out of laughs alone, who could cut the yams up and cook them bright and orange. could blend them up and make a pie every thanksgiving and christmas—see how the nutmeg floats its spice, see how you can slice it up when it's just a little bit warm—faint memory of the oven still lingering, see how it stays intact in your own eager hand? crust as strong as a mama. no, stronger—a black mama—strong, and it knows when to give, when to fold around the soft filling, the soft you, the soft black baby and hold—

WHAT IT REALLY IS

Coastline broke into forest into village, seas
rolled in uninterrupted waves. Somewhere,
I insisted on being born. Somewhere, countless
tribes called each other by name. Somewhere, a black panther
inches ever closer to its prey. Somewhere, the sun is a halo.
Cameroon is a whisper in my blood—the ancestry kit tells me
as it uses DNA to glue me back together. Can it catch
long strands of lineage shucked and punched to pulp? Somewhere, a clot

rubs its rigid way into my veins. It calls itself America.
And the seas were parted with my body over and over.
Centuries are cut into the skin stretched across my womb. Will
every lifted voice be silenced? When does a

theory become a threat? I return to the coastline. Village. Bright arc,
halo of sun. All this has been bloodied. Even my body, a wound, infinitely.
Earth spins on an unfair axis. Streets curdle. Again, blood.
O, come back coastline. Come back, un-shipped sea.
Remember the way my people were robbed of bone and breath?
You called it liberty.

On My Way to the Edmund Pettus Bridge, I Think of My Father

I don't know when will be the last days
of my life. Today, on the road from Montgomery
to Selma, I can't help but think of death. Can't help
but hear its familiar quiet settling down on the bright
green land. There is something in the memory
of protest called fear. Still. I feel it when I remember
the way some men beat the soft pulp
of the marchers' bodies until it was a paste.
I remember the way my skin signifies, sometimes,
chains and the necessity of force. Of death.

Any day could be my last.

I don't know who will be there when it's my time to go,
whether by nature or by force. I wonder
if my father knew it was coming when he died,
if he had a moment to see the sky before
it went black. If he smelled the sweetness
of the breeze as it passed him. I hope he thought of me,
of all of us. I hope he wished us well.
I hope his mother greeted him in heaven,
open arms made of angel wings.

I hope, when it's my time to go, I see him
in an unending garden in the sky,
tending a patch of collards ready to be plucked.
I hope he turns to me with soil on his fingers
and that thinking furrow on his brow.
Maybe, as I leave this earthly realm he'll ask me to help
him pick some greens like we did one Thanksgiving
a lifetime ago. I hope I feel the grip of their green hands.
Their veins full as my soul.

Rodney Jones

The Peasant Poem

੭

It is hard work not to be saved. Even a mediocre country evangelist is seasoned in the very rhetoric of the tear-ducts. Like a murder ballad, he plays for teenagers. Like a lawyer, he plies the nearly innocent. While his amanuensis, an elderly pianist, chums the baptistery with "Softly and Tenderly Jesus is Calling," the region high in the back of my throat, which I have identified as the soul, starts to salt and cramp. "Do you feel the presence of the Lord?" And, on this cue, a select squad of the saved and sanctified mobilizes in my direction.

੭

All human time is simultaneous. Here it is 1980. I am in a Santerismo séance in San Juan, but I came with a lawyer. Until I see the feathers and bones and the holograph of a smirking Jesus, the medium is a judge and we are in night court. Here it is 2016 in New Orleans. I live with Katy in the Faubourg Delassize opposite a brownfield that was once the Saratoga incinerator, and three retired cemeteries. At night the city over there, which, close-up, reeks of the vomit of beggars and celebrities, shines from thousands of lit windows.

੭

Maurice Merleau Ponty writes that each time we see a new image it changes our perceptions of everything that came before. The view of the city changes 1952. The first year I feel shame. I am running toward the outhouse. A neighbor woman, Modena Hardin, is bathing me in a porcelain dishpan. Shame is feeling that the place is watching.

Small houses about a quarter of a mile apart, of whitewashed or unpainted clapboard, each with a well and outhouse, a few with barns, chicken-coops, toolsheds, and smokehouses. My people are homemakers and small farmers, mainly self-sufficient. Neither much money nor light has arrived, most neighbors sign X, and, for every six automobiles, there comes a horse-drawn wagon, often trailed by a skittish and ungainly colt.

☙

The shame of provenance is not genetic. It is installed like electricity.

☙

Here I am in a cotton field north of the house. One of the pickers, a woman with red hair who just got out of the pen, is saying, "I'd rather kill a man than a dog." My mother is an unhappy field boss. My father is away, painting houses to earn money to buy more land. A boy tells me that if a rattlesnake bites me I will die, but if a rattlesnake bites him, he will live. He has the holy ghost. Now the field is empty except for my mother, my sister, and me. My mother has caught a man at the scale with rocks in his sack, and when she fires him, the other pickers decamp in solidarity.

☙

A dirt road in front of our house stretches along the side of the mountain. To the west downhill around a curve it passes the old Jones schoolhouse, which was turned into a residence when the county consolidated the schools. I am bored. There are only tattling, Christian girls to play with. When they send me out to shop, I sneak up the road and eavesdrop at the bootlegger's.

My father often tells of meeting a cousin, John Jones, who studied classics at Columbia before returning home to farm. They are standing in downtown Cullman and John says, in front of the women and the children, "Goddam, I would have been so much better off if I hadn't been born in Cullman County." When my father tells us, he spells out G-o-d-d-a-m.

❧

Wherever I go in Alabama, the story follows. The form of the story is a mystery, for it is not exactly handed down, but added to and subtracted from and totaled differently by each citizen as the sum and account, so that it can be further revised and debated. If one finds in a pasture a pistol clotted with dirt and corrosion, in the story it will be reunited with its owner: first as the toy of a dead second cousin, then as the real pistol of a man named Quattlebaum. Over that same pasture, during the Second World War, as a plane passes over, a leather satchel drops. James Hardin, cleaning his fence-line, thinks bomb and sprints for cover.

❧

I am timid like James Hardin. My sister is all outward energy. She leads. In the nineties she stands up to the Vulcan Corporation and stops a quarry. Here, she sits me in a high chair, smears bacon grease over my head, and prepares to cut my hair. In 2008 I am giving a poetry reading with Ellen Bryant Voigt at the Library of Congress. When Charles Simic, the Poet Laureate, introduces me, he mentions peasant poets. A year later in Chattanooga when I am inducted into the Fellowship of Southern Writers, Ellen introduces me as a peasant poet. On one hand, I am pleased. On the other, I prefer "postmodernist outdoorsman."

❧

1976 I am teaching the sonnet to high school juniors. One says, "We can't do this. It's too hard. We're not from New York. We're from Alabama."

Why does Fairview matter? Transformed, time-doctored, deracinated—all the houses have been wired, the road paved. Still I go back. A mastiff growls. The blind piano tuner passes with his driver. 1967 woos 1953. The life of the mind transcends the known ridges and enters the habitation of rumors. In the nearer distances live possum eaters, snake-handlers, and water-witchers. The angel of death only a few years earlier rides a white horse up this road to the house where Nancy Cooper lies dying. At the gate out front angel and horse rise into the sky, harvesting her soul. The atheist Tom Nesmith was there and he confirmed it.

❧

Because I dream I am Winston Churchill, because, in the front yard, I am never unwatched, only Sunday afternoons, in the unsurveilled hour while our parents are blindly making love, bicycle polo is played in a pine thicket on the side of the mountain. With croquet mallets and English accents. A gentlemen's sport: there are multiple injuries; hardly anyone ever scores.

❧

My grandparent's house and barn sit on the right and the Fairview Church of God to the left. Their house is a neat square two-bedroom house with green shutters. It stands a little in front of the concrete porch of their previous house, which burned. The church, too, is tied to disaster, as it was moved from the southwest corner of the valley after a tornado blew away the previous church. A few old men still blame the tornado on women who wear jewelry and mascara.

❧

The church is nondenominational. Like gravity, it holds things together. We go there three times a week to keep things from flying apart. To my mother, who was reared Methodist, the church needs finesse and a more dignified service, free of foot-washings and hollering. My mother is a philosopher. She studies and allows some gospel but does not condone Paul, whose pronouncements on marriage strike her as fanatical. She suggests to my sister and me that we should not be indoctrinated. Nevertheless, salvation, like hard work, is expected.

Jung explains my resistance to salvation: introverts are not joiners. I take comfort in the thief on the cross, who converts a moment before his death. Also, in my mother's brother, Bill, who had been dozing in his pew when the minister made a call for new church members to come forward. When the man next to him rose and walked to the front, Uncle Bill went along, joining the church half asleep.

My father is disappointed when I decide I am an existentialist. He is a good Christian, I know, but am I not a good existentialist? I neither regret nor see the point of it.

One Wednesday night, in a discussion of the eleventh chapter of Corinthians, our pastor mentions that not all Christians are saved in churches. He describes one woman's second birth in a corncrib. A few Wednesdays later, he declares that tonight each member of the congregation is to testify how long and under what conditions they have been saved, then drop one penny in the offering plate for each year that they have been a Christian. One by one, the members stand, speak, and go to sit beside him in the choir. Alone in the pews, considering the strategies of Mark Twain, I rise and walk to the altar. "I was saved in the woods behind the house a year ago," I witness (as I dig for the missing penny).

In 1965, I renounce public prayer. Briefly, I identify as a Druid: I pray to trees.

꙳

Thank you electricity: convivial brightnesses, hot and cold running water, ovens, heaters, well-pumps, refrigerators. Where once they played Rook with neighbors, now my parents sit up late, listening to radio dramas and country music. My father wires our barn. My mother watches "As the World Turns." In New York, John Cage writes "Indeterminacy;" in a village in Nigeria, Georgia Yorama discovers, above her husband's grandmother's bed, a signed photograph of Dolly Parton. In El Salvador at the New Year's party, the fishermen dance to Herbie Hancock's "Headhunters." The titles fade from books. Our toothbrushes come from China. The very chickens we eat are strangers.

꙳

The common idea of Alabama shames me, but it is only an idea. The port of vision is one room, one field. Here it is 1959. Junior Flowers channels Fats Domino and Picasso. When he is not beating on a guitar, he is painting enormous, unwieldy abstractions. One day when I give him a stick of gum, he says, "I will remember you when I am famous."

꙳

In one year, my sister and I select two caskets. The Hardins sing at both funerals. My sister picks the songs. Rain on a night in 1958 beating on a tin door. The seven of us huddled in the storm pit listening, praying, as if we might patch the leak in infinity. And the cyclone passes.

꙳

We make five trips back to Fairview to clean house. Careful at first, we winnow the receipts, box the intimate apparel, tape names on furniture, and give hammers and gadgets to cousins, but the archive is vast. On the last trip my sister rents a dumpster. Finally, everything rolls away, but everything has been touched, and the idea follows me back to the Faubourg Delassize. Some of the packages we throw away have not been opened.

J. M. Jordan

Three Miles Below Lake Eufala

The drifting gunwales cleave the water lilies
    as night collects its tricks and passes down
in grey tides to the bay. The amber glow
    of rusty lanterns swinging in the prow,
like morning stars at dusk, begins to fade,
    and darkness drops behind the stately palms.

And so begins the day. The river banks
    now bloom in bright green fields of maidencane
where just before was shadow. Argent flames
    across the water, framed in swamp and sky.
Then, throttle-down, the miles stretch out in spray
    toward the swamps and unmapped cypress groves.

The outboard rumbles and goes quiet. Now
    the day is on us: hard and bright and hot,
the river-world around all motionless
    but for the quiet paths of dragonflies
and the long low drift of a snow-white egret
    that dips its wings and slips into the pines.

The trolling motor hums us towards the bank,
    and there, the tale, the rumour that we sought
half-hidden in a canopy of oak limbs:
    a rounded wide inscrutable expanse
of darkness in the whiskey-colored shallows;
    a cipher, a deep black patch, a hole indeed.

A quiet pulse of knots and tackle, then
    the lines go out in soft sibilant whirs
and arches catching light before they drop
    like threads of spiderwebs across the water.
We reel in slowly, slowly, tighten up,
    sit back and set our caps against the sun.

And now we wait. A chorus of cicadas
    upwells in the hot bright day like a prayer

that this last patch of night will offer up
  what turns in silence there beneath the surface.
We have our lures, our luck, our lore, our secrets
  to summon up the wish from the unknown

but sometimes darkness deigns to keep its own.

The Old Logging Road

I lived all alone on the outskirts of town,
a field-hand in a small field-hand's hut.
Odd as a barn owl, wistful as a wheatfield,
I showed up for work and kept my mouth shut.

But trouble still found me the way that it does,
walking home one night from the Dixieland Bar.
It rose from the darkness of the back road around me
like the last long note of a lap steel guitar.

They missed me at work in a week or so.
They got no answer when they knocked at my door.
I got three column inches in the local weekly
and a MISSING flyer on the post office floor.

Now a flicker of thrushes sings my thoughts for me.
My fingerbones scatter like stones in a creek bed.
Wildflowers poke through the slats of my ribs,
and honeysuckle crowns what once was my head.

So hiker and hunter and lover, pass by.
The searches all failed. I'm alone once again.
Go whistling by freely but stay away from
the old logging road when the night closes in.

Rearview 1973

Our ragged-out rag-top rumbled down Main,
its engine keeping slap-bass ryhthm as
I watched my pop's long skinny fingers
drumroll the dash with a rockabilly flare.
He grinned that broken whiskey grin of his
then turned the wheel in a slow easy circle,
the Charger's front-end nosing craftily
through lazy lines of Friday night cruisers
like a gator sliding through ranks of swamp grass.
His dark eyes watched the crowded sidewalks,
the storefronts and the doorways flicking past:
Dixie Liquors, Merle's, the Starlight Inn.

And there they are, he said, *as I suspected*,
then flicked a still-lit cigarette out the window
and took another quick pull from his bottle.
He reached a hand into the glove box and
I saw that faded tattoo on his forearm
illumined in a sudden patch of street-light:
memento from the war, a washed-out dagger
encircled by a banner with the script
Homeward Be My Prayer, O Lord. And then
I saw that shiny silver Colt revolver
floating in the darkness there before me,
like a magic object in some ancient tale.
But after that I cannot separate
the flash of the cigarette in the rear-view
with the sudden muzzle-flashes in the darkness,
the hemi rumble from the POP POP POP
and the smell of burnt powder as Jerry Lee
banged out *Boogie Woogie Country Man*
and a woman screamed somewhere in the background.
I only know that next we were outside
of town, beyond the stretch of streetlights,
roaring down the highway toward the mountains.

Back home up in the woods, he went inside,
kicked off his ostrich boots into a corner
then passed out on the couch. So now I sit
and watch the moonlight on the gravel road
that winds up through the pine-stands to the house.
Wherein lies duty in this broken world?
What is honor, justice, faith? Perhaps I should

just kiss his head and leave him to his nightmares
then slip out back, into the mountain darkness.

In the hills you are free, he'd always said.
At fifteen I could make it on my own.
But now I see a line of cars below
assembling on the highway through the trees.
They shut their headlights down, and, one by one,
turn off onto the road that leads up to
our place, the only home I've ever known.
I hear the crunch of tires on the gravel.
I see the brakelights flash the trees with red
as if a sudden devilish conflagration
was roaring through the woods around our cabin.
My pulse is in my ears, my breath is tight,
my father's pistol heavy in my hand.

Amelie Langland

Boxcars

And in 98 or 99
my grandfather sketched
the slant required

on the eye of a wheel
of the train car coming
to a bend so it might

better ride up
the lip of the iron
before rounding out

the bend, and
even then
as young as I was,

living some other life,
I knew, for certain,
the reason he knew

what he knew
was his father
scratched out a living

as a train conductor
in some turn of the century
caboose on some

lonely and gas lit
Michigan rail line,
and these tales

and explanations
and feats could spur
treatises from him

on ball bearings
through on
to battleships

and trains and dolls
and dead apple trees
and sailboat keels,

but mostly—
like overheard
thunder gods,

or ghosts left behind
in a machine
half-remembered,

the slow wrestle
of wristed metal
on hammered rail.

6 AM

The hack and clash
of three day old ice
hewn off stone steps
as the sun wakes up.

The clack and rush
of a coal train on track
as car then car rolls down
to some far off hub.

The buck and wince
of wind on bare limbs.
Dead leaves picked and stuffed
in a gray squirrel's mouth,

their nest just a few hops
on more limbs, to a wire,
a rail, a post, through
a hole in a roof

back to their home
full of small kin,
as they too
must wince

and hug to keep warm.
Mom still on her way
with a mouth full
of not yet spoiled

things. And me—
my puff and curl
of smoke all hush
in waves of hair.

I'm Not Even a Boy Anymore but I Still Love Them

in my sleep
in my deck chair
on my futon
in every corner
of the yard

against the fence
while watering tomatoes
waiting on their rounding
out from green

&
in the fern section
of Home Depot
imagining triceratops
sniffing at fronds
snorting at stems
chewing the best
to mush

&
up and down the aisles
of Walmart and Target
parsing scrunchies
in off odd grays

&
among the 2 buck bottles
chaotically displayed
on an endcap
in Whole foods

&
in the What-a-Burger
drive thru at 4:26
in the morning

&
cruising past cypress knees
twisted in heat
bending back
to bog water

&
picking up
an americano
before work
without milk or cream
just like some boy
probably told me
was cool one time
in passing

&
his dimples deepening
the way crawdads
might streak
shoremud

&
his black hair
falling around
his skinny ear

&
these days
a wound blossoms
like a poem or a peony
becoming red
like hurt

Growing Up Diptych

[i]

Al.com, an ex-newspaper based in Birmingham, talks
of a squirrel sneaking into a Methodist balcony,

and the article bestows a spiritual skill
to squirrel catching, to joining in on the hunt

amongst the choir, the congregation hungry
as the preacher for a dove in that one Lyle Lovett song, and

I don't know the metaphor here. I don't know why God
would choose such a bird over the other except

there aren't squirrels in Sinai.

[ii]

Well aware of my ability
to pass—

to blend in
to code switch:

jeans to sundress, mustache to
bald lip,

growing up in Bama, there was
always shame:

too easy to disappear,
suck dick in the dark.

Matthew Layne

The Comoving Distance of the Peach in Cosmological Equations

Circling down in a tightening gyre,
the crow charts its course
to the silver orchard,
pencil trees
in perfect parallels
until the horizon, where,
anarchy! Lines meet, centers fold,
Euclid rolls gravely and wads
the chaos of glooming arithmetic
into a confused ball. Look
to the farmer. Her twilight fingers plot
 a new geometry as they trace
across the paperbark.
Here, soil is x and fruit is y,
and we solve for no endpoint but infinity.
Beneath each callus lies the spiral formula of creation.
Beneath the bark, spiritus mundi pumps sap heavenward
to where peach blossoms unfurl luscious truths,
and there, my firm friend, past the pluck,
past the fuzz, flesh, nectar, and pleasure,
turning and turning, beyond the world's
widening eye, is the grooved pit of it all,
intricate as your brilliant brain.
The stony core of its center
holds the key. Press
it to your ear
and hear it
lover-whisper,
be sweet.
Be sweet.

In Eve's Defense

Surely the apple
in the sun,
warmed and ripened
to sweetest perfection,
sugars crystallizing a knowledge
unable to contain itself,
surely that fruit above all fruits,
longed to be picked,
longed for the shadow
of the first hand to fall across it.
This singular orb deserved a fate
greater than worm castings.

How it must have shuddered
as fingertips first grazed
its smooth flesh, and then,
joy!
Wrapped firmly round its body.
The pure pleasure of the squeeze,
the pull,
and finally,
Oh! The pluck!

Surely the apple
desired to be consumed.
It must have rained joyful tears
as lips brushed its skin
in that first forbidden bruising kiss,

the teeth,
the tooth,
the crunch,
the juice,
the tongue.

"Oh! To be tasted.
To know and be known,"
the apple surely whispered.
"The blessing.
The calamity."

What We Leave Behind

108 red stitches lined the baseball
my brother flung at the wooden hive.
The whack.
The whirling buzz.
The bees swarmed forth.

I stood in the field, not far away,
four years old and oblivious.
The heat rose from the soil.
A breeze broke.
It felt so good
I closed my eyes.

My brothers flew away,
so the bees found me.
Each golden-gave itself completely
before falling like forsythia blossoms
by my Buster Browns.

My mother tweezed each stinger out,
lined them upon a mirrored tray.
As she counted, every number,
an exclamation. Every hurt,
a little prayer.

Still, when I found bees in the cattle trough,
desperate yellow bodies bombinating that dark water,
I scooped them out by hand, tilted their soft fuzz
onto a board. The rare bee clung to bury
the lancet of its stinger
in the plump of my palm.

Imagine if our kisses were finite.
Would you covet each one as the magnolia
clings to its withered blossoms,
or give them recklessly as the honeybee
until nothing remains but the memory of sugar
and the soft sting of goodbye?

Kindling

Tell me your story, and I will tell you mine.

A rag of colts splinter across the Arizona desert,
white dust rises behind them like smoke,
like dreams half-remembered, like a living prayer.

The gray tortoise watches from beside the black road.
Her back is the weight of the world.
There is no chance of rain.

You have heard that horse hooves sound like thunder;
this is not true. They are the sound of goodbye.
They are the sound of a station wagon door shutting

and shutting again. They are the sound of our father's voice
calling out that last list of things for us to forget.
Then there is no voice, no hooves, no rooms, only the vast

open plain of your heart beneath this purpling bruise of sky. Look,
there are the galaxies that were wrought the moment you opened
your eyes and reached for them, and here you are: infinitesimal.

Come sit by the fire, and I will tell you how wild horses spirited
our father away as he lay dreaming of a tortoise and her clutch.
In the morning, we can share all he remembered to leave behind.

Southern Fried Hymn

Stewed tomatoes and okra and blackeyed peas.
Boiled down turnip greens and macaroni cheese.
Green beans, butter beans, red beans and rice,
field peas, crowder peas, sweet potato pie.
Fat back, heart attack, Southern till I die.
Cook 'em down in boiling water or throw 'em in deep fry.
Collard greens, kidney beans, gravied mash potatoes,
ham hocks, pork chops, fried green tomatoes,
fried chicken, fried catfish, country fried steak,
fried corn, fried okra, apple cobbler bake.
Buttermilk, smooth as silk, slide into my belly.
Corn pones or rolls or biscuits with Bama jelly.
Southern food, Southern soul, raised up Southern hard.
I ain't gonna touch it if it ain't been cooked with lard.

Quinn Lewis

Quarantine

for my mother

Allowed the air.
Allowed the surrounding pasture
as we pleased. I followed you there,
keeping a distance between us
in the woods, so as not to step
on the heel of your boot, wrenching
it off. You always hated that.
It made you whip around and snap,
a wolf at her cub that has not
waited in the tree line for her mother
like a good mirage. But I did love
that warm apartment. We lit the fire
and the lamps until we glowed. The mice
burrowed in beds we left for them—
empty cigarette boxes with the foil
torn out and folded into stars we taped
to the ceiling. We ate yogurt and wild
strawberries, let our hair grow long
and slept with it wet against silk
pillowcases, taunting fever or infection.
You allowed the soft, brown rabbit her loping
over our cream duvet, leaving
a trail of blameless droppings. It was like
a field of snow under which we lay,
over which every creature for a time
freely roamed.

The Carnival Queen's First Understudy

Another play within
a dream. Another dream
in which I'm not
the actress, not even
the understudy,
but a maker of signs.
I paint down the board
in a vertical line
the letters A, B, C.
I scrawl them ugly,
meaningless as they are.
Even my cat has a role
as the panther who attacks
Prince Hamlet. Waking,
she stages scenes, cuts off
the heads of field mice
with her teeth. In the dead
town, a carnival rises
for "Hometown Days,"
the sign strung across
the newspaper office
that's never open.
The depot's come alive—
a surprise—from nothing.
No fast food, no
coffee shop. The hardware
store's bald stock
is a few pale shelves
of dust and mousetraps.
Cash only. Dollar General—
the county seat. The people
at least have something
I want. They've flooded
hand in hand, links
in a chain, from their houses
on the hill today for alcoholic
slushies, blue snow cones,
four seats on the tilt-
a-whirl, and I alone, turn
my car around, take
my thirteen-gallon trash
to Art's junkyard, where dogs
comprise the corps de ballet,

and Bev—wary wife—waits
for her turn, behind the curtain.
Thinks, *The hell's she doing
here?* Another sign
hangs before me across
steel dumpster doors.
In letters wild it reads,
Do not open. If you can't
throw it over,
take it back home.

The River Ex

They rush to drink
the black water.
So they might speak.

Push of my heel
keeps them
drowned. What news

could they bring
of a future, being only
past. Their faces

bob like apples.
They cast
their tongues

from beneath my foot
like fishing lines
and suck

what they can
from my hair.
Long as it's grown,

the ends dip in the river.
I let them
go at it. I've done

as I'm told and arrived

with a question.
Who in darkness

would take my hand?
Each at a time
tells his story.

I've listened.

Calypso Contemplates a Cowbird Mating Pair

Think of Penelope, eating alone
in her room. Tired
of her mind's grief's appetite,

she goes downstairs one night
to join her unwanted guests.
It's true a horde

of cowbird males might court
one female in the breeding
season, might throw

a smaller fledgling
from its nest to make space
for the new brood. Where

is her son, Telemachus?
Let's say just one
of her voracious suitors

isn't arrogant like all the rest,
keeps to himself. That she likes
that, which surprises her.

Maybe this night Penelope and he
get to talking. Turns out he's
a herder, too. In some ways

seemingly dull,
the cowbird male has nothing
striking, nothing that flashes

like lightning, except
contrast. The division of colors
between head—brown

as the trunks of wet trees—
and glossy body—black-green
like the storm on the sea.

This pair shares a branch
on which to perch, pecking
at olives doused with oil.

Maybe after all these years
she prefers ham and fig
and a glass of wine by the fire,

a book in each lap, and needs
no show of ire, no revenge,
but the way he loves to watch her

drive the cattle in, the ones
the other suitors haven't
slaughtered. All day

it is evening. Everywhere wings
seek shelter from the downpour.
They leave their muddy boots

in the boot room, laugh
under the loom at the bleating
of goats in the middle of it.

And what of Odysseus?
How they've both
come in from the rain. She

in her foyer, and he
in this cave. What if she wrote
to him, thought long and hard

at what to say. What if
she wrote to him,
and told him, *Stay.*

Meanwhile, Flies

You must go out to the paddock
where it's never warm.

The ox must be slaughtered
for his shoulder blade.

The ox you loved, even. The one
who watched you turn away,

going back into the house.
Attend the body

in the field for days
letting beetles devour the meat,

washing the oracle bones
with wine. Meanwhile,

flies will give birth
in the ox's eye, be drawn

to the barn cat as she dies, zeroing
around her. Soon you'll ask

the necessary question.
What is a season?

A thing of beauty to be loved
in this life.

McLeod Logue

Oh Honey, Bless Your Heart

There's nothin' like Nana's kitchen
with the wide tiled ceilings and the sound
of everybody bein' ugly.
                              It smells like biscuits
year round, even when we got the heat runnin'.
Salt clings to the air and ain't nobody goes hungry

unless they choose to. It's the kind of place
where the same people who brush your hair
will smack you into next Tuesday.
                              There's love
and then there's Southern love. They never did
have trouble sayin' I love you here. They say it

like the world's gonna end, like they watched
their parents lay hands on their brothers. They say it
like they're doin' you a favor,
                              flickin' your wrists
for gettin' seconds. I swear things would be different
if we all just knew how to act. I'm always doin' this.

Swearin' at the wrong time, sayin' the wrong thing.
I damn near broke my Nana's heart sayin' I won't
eat her chicken pot pie no more.
                              She calls me *soft*,
but she's wrong. I'm bone thin, my lips rusted shut
since the day I learned what was good for me.

I do as I'm told, bend waist down to pull the dish out
the oven. The heat knocks me back like a corkscrew.
Laughin', she says if it were a snake
                              it would've bit me,
would've swallowed my left hand, would've slowed
my heart to ready rhythm, would've filled my veins

with butter. Everybody's waitin' at the big table,
their mouths waterin' more than they can swallow.

I wipe that ugly thing off my face.

                                  It's too late now
to cause a scene, my hand still red from impact.
When we sit down to say grace, I wait

for Nana's voice, count her perfect syllables,
close my eyes, squeeze my hands so tight they go
numb. I pray to God

                    someone remembers
to bless this meal, to save our earthly bodies. I know,
sure as hell, it won't be me. My tongue knows better.

Currency

In the beginning, God said, *Eat
and be merry*, and surely, someone did.
He said it is good to love something

enough to consume, and it was. He always spoke
about the things we held in our mouths.
Chew, he said.

[   ]

She stood at the window shucking corn. Peeling
plastic film from green exterior. Two layers
littered the kitchen floor like light.

Her fingers revealed kernels underneath. She bent
down to eye level. *Look*, she said. And we did,
our mouths watering in harmony.

She hummed a hero's song, her black curls barely
grazing her neck, a balancing act. We bit our nails
to give back the sound of teeth against body.

She pulled our fingers from our mouths, that foul
look on her face. We loved to tear—skin
from nail, nail from flesh, close enough to feel the hurt

vibrating through our arms. We were
soft and there was so much to pull from.
This is what we knew to be true.

[   ]

The corn was naked now, fleshed to the stalk
like a ladder. We wanted to climb each
yellow round in our hands, in our mouths.

We wanted to watch our mother rip them
from the thing that helped them grow,
throw them into boiling water, smother them in butter.

Everything she touched was soft and full of life.
We ate from the big ceramic bowl and prayed.
Chew, she said, our mouths clenched for eternity.

[   ]

Life ran out like a blister. It was so gentle,
to leave the inside out. We wanted to know
how small something could taste.

Fight Club

We're street fighting in the middle school parking lot, bloody
noses and hair curled between knuckles. Time moves a wobbly
table leg and we've got nothing to do but see how far
it'll bend. There's blood on my face that isn't mine. I'm scared,
but I won't say it. The big girls swing and don't miss.
Kaia's got a mean hook, sure, but she's all talk, waiting
for Carmen to knock her back. Over and over and over. I am
so close I can smell the copper release of open wounds. Their noses
crooked and red. I don't remember why we fought, only
that we did. We wanted to see just how much we had to lose.

After dark, me and Mary hopped the fence and stood in open
waves of that warm night. Blood still caking the white lines
of the parking lot. We laid down on the earth and traced chalk
around our bodies. I was hungry for a taste of that hurt.
So when Mary sat up and swung her skinny arm across her
chest, I grabbed and twisted so her body went soaring. Out there
in the heatstroke center, so far from forever, it was a cry we had
to make. The grownups never showed, but if they had, I knew

they'd be sheet white and horrified. It felt good to be misjudged.
Sure, we were nice girls in our jean skirts and camisoles
but if we didn't like the way somebody looked at us, we'd make it
known in the flesh. Our Christian names sliced into skin.

The Governor's Woman

From the banks of the wooden wraparound porch,
I could see her through the window, the governor's
woman. She was naked, changing I assumed, how stupid
of me, and she admired herself in the mirror. I watched
her, distorted through the glass as she cupped her chest
and arched back, ribs lining her shape. She was glossy,
or maybe it was the window. She twirled, examining
the ways her body was smooth, pearly, enough
of her to be grasped in handfuls, the way my mother
held peaches at the market. She was a woman,
not a wife, my father made the distinction, a secret
no one planned to keep.

Later, she packed her bags and sat in the convertible
out front, picked her nails and thought about nothing,
her face a stretched canvas. Later still, I stripped down
to pink and stood alone in the mirror. My skin licked with salt,
I pinched my hips and pressed my palms into flesh. I did my best
to build sandcastles on my chest, forcing my skin to slide
inward. I traced lines around my lips with one finger, covered
my nipples with flat palms to see the half moon shadow below,
waxing and waning, not yet knowing what it was to be full.

Maurice Manning

Reading a Book in the Woods

The spindly trunks of two trees
have twisted twice around each other.
This is what I see when I look up
from reading. I've read the page on the right
then turned to the left-hand page and read.
I've read the book all out of order,
beginning in the middle. Now,
by looking up, I know the book
is reading me. And there I am
in a middle chapter, whistling,
and knocking the back of my hand against
the motionless fruits of a hawthorn tree,
an action that has no consequence
unless the lifted hand and the branch
left swaying after are symbolic.
I could see it that way, but also see
how simple it is, how very little
is happening—no memory
is leaking out, no evident
signs of despair. There's sort of a dot,
dot, dot at this point in the book,
and I don't think the ending offers
much more. Maybe the sun goes down
and someone whistles in the dark,
or maybe it ends with pale light
still visible above the trees
and one has been changed, and walks farther
into the woods and farther than that.

A Crooked Star in Pencil on a Page

For some reason, I misremembered
a star someone made in the margin,
but there wasn't a star when I went back
to the page of the haunted, Gothic poem
that hangs in my mind like a coat on a hook.
Only a few words in ink,
here and there, to explain a passage.
One little fragment I like is this,
"pessimistic about life." On the page
before, "gun" is underlined,
and later, a darker line is drawn
below "imagination." It's strange,
but you can skim these notes, almost
illegible, and get the feel
of the larger poem and what the poet,
the younger one, was apprehending.
She—for I think it was a she—
puts it well in a difficult sentence:
"Time is man's enemy
can't stop time." Being
a later reader of the book,
I put a star beside the sentence
an unknown reader made between
the stanzas of a poem I love
and drag behind me like a shadow.
As for me, I have no enemies—
I guess I disagree with thinking
I have an enemy—but I like
the difficult sentence, as sticky as tar
to say. That's why I made the star.

Licks

We each were given three licks
for throwing snowballs against the side
of the school and making them stick. It snowed
so rarely we didn't know what snow
could do. Lessons were over but we
were lingering outside before
we walked the alleyway and the field
where our tracks in the snow would jumble together
and then untangle on our way home.
I had the farthest way to go,
but not so far, and a paper route
and other chores before the dark.
Homework was nowhere in my mind.
I was trying to make a face on the wall,
but it just looked like a bunch of blotches.
That was all right with me, though, I liked
the blotchy white against the brick.
It looked like several moons were stranded
in the cold universe of the wall.
The principal said we'd broken a rule,
but we didn't know the rule existed.
Our protest sailed over his head.
The principal said we were lying now
and he was going to light us up.
So, that's what he did, three licks each.
A horse in a painting over his desk,
where we had to bend and place our hands,
was supposed to wink with every lick.
Whipping a boy with a wooden paddle
doesn't always change his mind
about the universe or snow.
It wasn't exactly the plank of reason,
that paddle on which we signed our names—
a record the principal liked to keep—
and there's not much principal behind it
and it didn't even hurt that much.

White Oak Shadow Half a Mile Away
for Charles Wright

One thing I hadn't noticed before
is a tree that's standing on a hill
nearby, and I had to climb a hill
that's nearer in order to see it. Declining
November light, a solitary
tree, and its shadow darkening
the hill behind it like a smudge
of India ink. And I saw the shadow
before I determined the tree was there,
a dreamy little paradox.
To determine means you reach the end
of something, but I don't think I've reached
the end of the tree. It's entered my mind
and I'll keep looking at it there—
a thought or two will come from it,
I suppose. The tree will leave a mark.
I'm fine with that. It's good to have
a tree alive on a hill in your mind,
and then to study the actual tree
to see if it has other aspects.
The tree must be an oak because
the leaves are still attending it
like a bunch of people who haven't been
let out of church. That ought to evoke
a Scripture or bring to mind a hymn,
but I can only summon the story
of Zacchaeus, who climbed a sycamore,
and I don't think that really applies.
But that's alright. It's nice to have
something to think about and not
know where you're going. You'll come back
to it some day and then you'll know.
You have to believe that things come back,
though when they do they may have changed.
I don't know why I said the shadow
looked like a smudge of India ink—
it's not like I have a special thing
for India ink. It's just an expression,
it's just something that came into my mind
and it seemed like the right thing to say,
because the shadow looked like a smudge
of something that from a distance was dark,
that was made, ironically, by the light.

I've Got Those Mean Old No. 10 Washtub Blues

Everything is a metaphor,
even the bent over heads
of grass that's gone to seed and the sway
they make, and the rhythm of the swaying,
devoted little emblems of green.
Sometimes I turn the washtub
over when I think a rain
is coming in, to let the rain
thump the bottom of the tub,
a nice, low sleepy sound, depending
on the rain. I enjoy that kind of truth,
the daydream wanders into the light.
More often, however, the washtub
only hangs by its handle from
a nail in the barn and the tub is mute
except when it catches from the distance
the old man farther down the way
calling his cows home for the night
with a high-pitched whoo and whoop
and the open tub cradles his voice
and lolls it lightly back, as if
a hymn is being sounded out.
It isn't despair I hear in his voice,
but I like to hear the lonely in it
and how the washtub makes it ring.
An old man's voice and a washtub,
a daydream making its way to the light—
very particular instruments.
We might as well add a spicebush
to the scene and work it in to the low
refrain, the thumping, low refrain,
depending on the ringing rain.

Kwoya Fagin Maples

What Yields

The following sonnet corona relates to the eleven or more enslaved women who were subjected to medical experimentation by Dr. James Marion Sims. Between 1845 and 1849, these experiments occurred in Mount Meigs, Alabama. Each woman suffered from fistula, a condition created by traumatic childbirth. Sims performed a series of surgeries without the use of anesthesia. To keep the women subdued, he addicted them to opium, which he would only administer after the surgeries, for pain. In addition to pain relief, opium contributes to memory loss and confusion. By 1850, Sims declared he had successfully healed fistula and published his findings. At the time, he was considered a pioneer in the field of gynecology. Today, gynecologists still use tools he developed, namely Sims' Speculum.

I.

The day we were born, we belonged to you.
These clay-sculpted women—yours. There is no
respite to offer—such exquisite wrongs
remain. Our vulvas: the future you wrote

against the back of your hand. Born to be
seen by you, we are the bodies you
strive against. The triangle axis gleams.
It is June, your glinting silver blade new—

you—slick as butter. So yours, we wonder
if the saliva in our mouths is still
ours. We're denied water to protect sutures.
My parched tongue circles for wisps

of spit. You could leave me this one thing. Thief,
all night you drink water from my body.

II.

All night you drink water from my body.
You sneak from your bed, taking the worn way
toward the wood shack over the chickweed
and white clover. We call it shack. You say,

hospital. You stop bedside, and full of
need you straddle me, squat down, your haunches
hovering low, graze my throbbing vulva.
You claw the back of my neck so my head

falls aside like a pansy, then you call
for the water in my body to rise.
Come up, you sing. Dizzied and stunned I watch
it rising like so many beads of wine.

In the mornings I am bare. I am shut.
I am dead where I lie, already plucked.

III.

I am dead where I lie, already plucked.
Yet all afternoon, sir, I have risen
up out of this whiteness—out of its touch
I come and though my mind is dim

I will say no, split your trembling lip by
my refusal. I've been longing to see
the rush of blood to your mouth, your pink lie
distended, the flush of blood to your cheeks.

I've been reaching for the surface to show
what my fists can do. My eyes reach for you
out of reach. I am too much to feel, too
impossible to be known. All afternoon

you slept in down, snug against your wife's dove back.
Bodies above virtue are never black.

IV.

Bodies above virtue are never black:
sprawling dewberries grow along your fence;
since most days we are hungry, we take
them—fill hemp sacks we hide against our hips.

When each bite unravels in our mouths
we imagine a sweeter history
and more hope than you could ever allow.

Desperate, we gorge on dewberries—

the heady berries and our molars' slow
grinding drown out the distant cries of
thief. Crushed berry over berry over
berry, this joy—the closest thing to love.

Sated, we hide the blue-stained sacks again.
Our eyes blink back the river to be lost in.

V.

Your eyes blink back the river to be lost in.
You clutch your elbows, pacing the sickroom
walled with basswood, eleven beds sinking
like monuments into a red clay floor.

Our bodies taut in their sheets, locked in place,
calculating your restraint. We keep our
breath, waiting. Then you begin your complaint:
we aren't trying to heal. Unchecked urine

in our wet beds instead of the waste pail.
Piss compromises the stitches and we
know it. And how many times must you tell
us to lie still? You leave us. There will be

no dosage today. The held cries lift.
First, you'd have to consider us women.

VI.

First, you'd have to consider us women,
realize our hearts beat under the bush.
You'd have to think my heart longed like yours
and that my mind wasn't mindless, awash

with nothing. I am a hot quaking body—
prime material subject. To you,
I am only worth what can be gleaned.
And you would have to know I meet the pain

how your wife would: imagine her blushed pink

frame, gap-legged like a birth-slick colt, quaking.
But you cannot hold both of us in mind
at once. My ability to bear is

immeasurable. Pain discriminates.
Material subject—I am rabbit.

VII.

Material subject. I am rabbit.
I skitter the path to crooked river,
scratch up the perfect stones and carry them
to my litter and when they clamor to nurse—

their soft seeking nostrils nudging my teats—
I beat their bodies, stoned against the rocks
I trample, crush red skulls, dash. Panting
blood into the grass, their buff fur bodies

set in an array of poses, the weeds
bowed down, draining blood that will not cry out.
My babies sink into the ground, drowning.
I am only fit to be without.

I swallow the last stones. Your shadow looms.
Now, the whole earth has turned to look at you.

VIII.

Now, the whole earth has turned to look at you.
And we see the gray hairs curling out of
your nose. We nod off like pine trees as you
stitch. Always sighing, you hover

over us. Fool, we know you will never
be done, though you promise promise promise
it will work this time. We've grown wiser
to your kindness. We watch you thread our missed

days and nights. Your needle unmends our seams.
Silk? Catgut? You should have known the catgut
would fester. How careless can you be?
Did your dumb mama drop you dumb? You smug

reckless thief. The whole earth can hear you breathe.
Even the clouds agree: we're dead where we sleep.

IX.

Even the clouds agree: we're dead where we sleep.
Between sleep and waking my gaze follows
yours as you scan the room of destiny.
Picking through the moss of your mind so

carefully, you decide who you will heal
today. Your hair has grown gray right above
the ears, you could be a wren standing near,
shifting foot to foot in the door, nervous.

You pull out the notes from your leather bag,
reading and murmuring through surgeries—
failures, the almosts bore against our backs.
Every note marked becomes the symphony

you compose, and yes, we will render it.
We are rotting fruit, yet our bodies yield.

X.

We are rotting fruit, yet our bodies yield.
How easily we yield to you, for you.
We slide into our poses, blossoming.
You examine our stalks for blight, mildew

and rust. One morning your eyes examine
the field and we are ripe. Through sixteen
seasons you have tended us, kept us tilled
and well-drained. You've cultivated after each

rain and sewed crimson clover in the rows
between us. Not one boll weevil has stained
our leaves. With care, you have nourished the soil.
And now, the time has come for you to claim

the crop that you've sewn. Your harvest will be.
We must yield, even if you lie to reap.

XI.

We must yield, even if you lie to reap.
Untuck the lie from the roof of your mouth
and set it free. If you write it, it will be.
It will set right the frown on your wife's

lips, make it worth it. Is it worth it?
Her unspoken question, she doesn't see
what wealth can be gained from digging into
an empty woman. She never believed

it was mending when she heard wails sound
their way up to the house, sounds like rabbits
dying she'd said, but never fixed her mouth
to help us. Write history, it will be.

Try out the words in your mouth. We're healed.
The day we were born we belonged to you.

Jason McCall

Why I'll Never Ask About My Birth Certificate Saying My Momma Was Born in Illinois

Because I know
the journey to a promised land can bring more
horror than milk and honey. Because I don't want to

see her and my grandmother carrying their gods
in pockets stuffed with gods and hope and cold chicken.
I'm talking about dead white gods because that's easy

compared to talking about a live black woman
who moved against the tide of the Great Migration.
I don't know the altar

she left behind or if she ever found god
waiting for her in the damp of our Montgomery
air that traps so much more than heat. Maybe

there's someone in a Chicago suburb moaning
over a piece of pound cake born from my grandmother's recipe.
My mother's face might be the best

part of someone's fading memory of their Midwestern childhood.
Maybe she spent a few days blurring in and out of sleep
until the big shoulders of Chicago transformed

into the baby steps of Appalachia.
Maybe it was days of nonstop lookout
for the danger they left behind

until they made it back to the danger my grandmother knew well
enough for all of us. But I won't
ever ask because I'm afraid

there's at least one tear between
the house she left behind and the house she made for me,
and she can keep the story if it means she gets to keep the tear.

John Henry Makes a Special Guest Appearance on Shark Tank

I'm going to stop you right there.
Somebody has to

call you out for what you did
when you said the algorithm would be the answer

to your shipping issues.
Now, I was never actually here

to invest in a program, anything soft-
ware related. If I believe in anything,

I believe in people being the best
investment you can make.

I'm here to buy a piece of you
and your dreams. There's the truest part

of an opportunity like this. In the end, I just want more
from you than excuses

about automation and China. Look it up.
I know how to deal

with automation and China. I'm worth more than any
machine or overseas contract. But are you

ready for this moment? I can make you
a household name. Do you know how

many millionaires I've made since I laid down
my hammer and turned to business? Now, I'm always losing

count of them, but I'm sure there's more
room on my shoulders for you.

Feel free to counter. But you won't be
able to find a better partner. The train is

leaving the station. Come on, you have to
make a decision. What's it going to be?

The Right Tool for the Right Job

You want to think about Thor, the myths
of who the world wants to see
as worthy. Just the right hands
will reach for the hammers
that build our walls and monuments.
There's honor in work,
pride born from splitting
a log to keep the fireplace burning,
from splitting a skull to keep
the altars of your gods burning. Let's pretend
the weapons are only waiting to be
transformed into tools. Swords praying

to be plowshares. Fat Man and Little Boy aiming
for a future without fossil fuels. My father keeps
a bag of tools in the laundry room.
I know there's something in there
that can cut me because he told me
to be careful the first time he sent me searching
for a Phillips-head and the sense
it took to not come back to him
with bloody hands. And isn't that when you know
you've mastered your craft? When you can blame
the blood on the tools and have the world believe you.

Rose McLarney

American Persimmon

I have tried to carry a persimmon home,
to share one fruit. I passed the tree running,

a pursuit which allows no pockets, no bags.
Needs no equipment. No team.

I was many miles away,
and could not clench my fist.

I told myself to hold my hands like good men
every time they choose not

to use their strength.
But a good persimmon

is already halfway to ruin.
A ripe fruit falls,

wrinkled and dark.
Too fragile to bear reaching the ground,

it bursts. Too fragile to bear touch,
the skin of the fruit I gathered

skidded off. Pulp pushed past
my knuckles' best intentions.

Men can be considered good
for what they don't do. How small

of a taken action could be a saving
grace then? I tried again, another day,

dropping a persimmon in the emptiness
between my breasts.

Home, undressed,
there was only a sweaty smear

no man could find sensuous.
Some things are best

enjoyed alone. Some things can only be
enjoyed alone.

And so, this morning, I eat right
on the roadside, picking grit from fruit's soft insides.

Across town, a man I love sleeps.
Around the world, the hungry and sleepless.

Here, my fingers so sugared
I can't suck them clean.

Motionless

In the photos of Sherman's March—no action.
Cameras could not yet capture
subjects in motion. No battles, just battlefields,
landscapes after. Trees, bark blasted off,
burned bridges and barriers overcome.
Broad strokes of blackened fields, sweeping
the eye from the small interjections of fallen fence
and fireplace, standing alone, to disappearing points,
detail broken down in the indiscriminate texture
of rubble and wreck.

For film to register faces, people had to keep still
so long they wore iron neck braces,
not to tremble and blur the picture. Bodies
gun-shot didn't pose such a problem,
and must have piled themselves before the photographer.

But how hopeless the honesty of showing the dead,
when, in a composition, trees can function as a frame,
form a place where tensions are only between background
and fore. And the shattered buildings, the splintered beams—
they thrust up into the shape of branches, growing back.

*(after the photographs of George N. Barnard,
photographer for General Sherman)*

On the Move

Crape myrtle's confetti of flowers.
Magnolia polished to mirror shine.
Live oaks that never will drop

their leaves, some standing since
the Civil War. And shacks,
empty of sharecroppers fled North.

Scenery of the South. Of survival.
For which trees still try. Seedling by seedling,
tree species can seek higher ground.

Can move, migrate where it's cooler
as the weather, one kind of climate, changes.
Many believe every *how it has always been*

will stay. While even rooted symbols,
to endure, edge away.

Seasonal

Neighbors have erected an inflatable pumpkin
out of which arises an inflatable dog. Then
it descends, then rises again. I had imagined
a life set in another landscape, long stretches

of rivers and fields. Now I know it is autumn
from the lawn decorations, the lawn mowers
trimming the football field. Men measure
and spool out string, lay straight lines

of paint on the canvas they've been given,
the kind that keeps growing grass through
their accomplishments. Showing great care.
As I suppose they do padding and helmeting

five-year-old sons sent so soon to practice
struggle. Why not such a field as subject for study,
rather than a farm's, which was never pastoral
for many, not in the land of cotton, not for those

who hoed and picked it? And though the rivers here
are few, there is rain. When that water falls,
equally and indiscriminately soaking everyone's shoes,
it weights the inflatable dog. Now, nothing comes

from the pumpkin, and my love and I admit,
over our early supper, we are made earnestly sad.
We've got none of our young loftiness left,
nor laughter for others' losses, no matter their bad taste.

When the dog did work, its unfurling was slow,
one eye unfolding, a limb lengthening. It had done
this since September. A limb sagged out of sight,
an eye was sucked back, how many times already?

Yet we want all the measures, so much extension,
even of these days. Because the children on the field
rush forward. As bidden. Coaches screaming
that they can't cry. When they aren't. Five and already

they don't cry. They try for strong faces. People put up
what they'd like to look at. It doesn't stop them,
that the elements will take all ornament down.

James Mersmann

Mel Kneels Down in the Confessional Beside Bill and Carl

> hog in sloth, fox in stealth, wolf in greediness,
> dog in madness, lion in prey.
> —Wm. Shakespeare

> There is a wolf in me . . . fangs pointed for tearing
> gashes . . . a red tongue for raw meat . . . and
> the hot lapping of blood—I keep the wolf because
> the wilderness will not let it go . . .
> I got a menagerie inside my ribs, under my bony head,
> under my red valve heart . . .
> —Carl Sandburg

Well, boys, it's a zoo here too!
There's a mess of owls and skunks
in my timber, and noises

that'll keep a camper awake!
I'm an ark full of grunting and baying.

Noah never heard such a din.
We didn't come just from wilderness,
but from something older and blacker.
We rooted deep in a cornucopia
that still hasn't stopped spilling its stars.

The snake and I
were among the first stuff spit
like a cork from the astral bung.
We rode here on the tail of a bronco
comet waving our hats.

Every summer the snake and I writhe
and chafe our way out of last year's skin.
Folks swear it's a fine fit, but if
I can't slough it, I'll die.

I have a crow in me who thinks he's a lark.
He can't hit a note, but longs to sing
at heaven's gate. Worse than any magpie,

he loves his squawk. Words are seeds
for his beak to crack. Nothing is too black
for him to contemplate with his piss-yellow eye.
The crow and I came from a long-ago
sneeze of the stars. It was we
who made the black hole black.

I have a fox in me
that can smell a female
miles away; my nose can track her
down the center of a creek; double cross
or loop her trail as she will, she can't
shake me—it is I who circle ahead
and spread my allure, and behind a log
watch her puzzle and sniff
my scatter of flattery
and praise, every best word
about loveliness and the shine
of her hair, until at last
she will have to come to me
and admit I have the most
elegant tail in the woods.

I have a pig in me who farts his way
through slops of macaroni and cheese,
and a moose with a hard on like a misplaced antler.
The moose and the pig and I came from sputum
hawked from the throat of a star.

There's a weasel in me, albino
and cowardly blind, weaving and ducking
along ditches, ready to hide
behind every stump of an excuse,
avoiding my friends like enemies, wanting
only a narrow hole full of my own smell
to worm into, where I can sleep behind
a fake snarl, my butt against the back wall,
my teeth bared toward the door.

After the first cosmic blaze snuffled out,
I and the weasel wriggled up anemic
out of the pale ashpile.

I have a hound in me who howled all night
the day my friend died, howled with such

a wavering howl that leaves fell from the trees
and neighbors nightmared in their sleep.
The hound and I were the last broken-tailed stuff
scraped from the cooling caves of fire.

But all of these things are not as strange
as the other things I need to confess.

In a world perforated with gunfire
and darkened with lies, I still feel
stirrings of other stuff got from the stars.

Though I wade knee-deep in toxins
through landfills of stress

many days there is a porpoise in me, effortlessly arcing
out of the sea. And some mornings a butterfly
leaps up in the light and hangs between geranium
and hollyhock unable to decide. There are days
when a mockingbird inside rarely pauses
in his blissful recitals, and a hawk
climbs on spirals of wind, high up, until he can see
everything, every hunched mouse, its one
exposed whisker, all of it, with a perfect eye.

Watching My Mother's Breath

for Regina Mersmann (Oct. 15, 1899–Aug. 28, 1990)

For hours after the stroke
you were like a house being closed;
one after one the blinds came down.

Now on this high bed, your face
says death, but your heart clings
to an old habit; you
have not been here for days.

You sleep and sleep, as if to sleep
for all those nights waking
with children in the cold house.

I put drops in your eyes, swab
your dry, gaping mouth with a sponge,
say to you the few things we would not
have known how to listen to together.

Beyond washboard and breadboard now,
your thin body is pulled
into the sheets by an immense
and eloquent fatigue. Will you
have to sleep for years
before you can go on ahead?

In unmistakable stages your breathing
alters; sometimes stumbles, and stops—
then, comes again, weaker
from a deepening cave.

90 years of sand hurries from the hour-
glass back toward its first ocean.

In you now the breath backs slowly away,
bowing, toward the wings; the flame
wavers smaller and smaller,
re-entering the ember.

All those years of gardens
arrange themselves in the palm
of your hand.

In the root cellar, potatoes
settle shoulder to shoulder;
the rock weighing down
the plate on the kraut jar falls
more deeply asleep.

Time moves away down the walk, waving goodbye.

In your ears, violin cases wrap themselves
shut over the gleaming wood;
chairs are being stacked
and leaned against the wall.

In your mouth the table is cleared
for the last time, the floors
swept and shining.

Your sleep slides deeper,
your breath rocking you lower
and lower into your self, back

through the rings within rings
to the hut in the woods where
the master takes your head in his hands
smiling at your perfection;
and leads you to the hearth
where you crawl into the fire,
and the sky opens its hand,
full of stars, and the wren's eye
looks out bright from the hole
of her small house.

Breaking New Ground

Everywhere, as if a cable from my elbow tows her,
my nine-year-old follows me like a small boat,
bobbing, spilling questions on all sides, shining.
Together we will begin the garden somewhere
in this new state, this strange yard
where I probe hardpan chert and clay
for a vulnerable spot, and one more try
in my transient's life for growing space.
She hears my spade bite like gritted teeth,
watches it bounce away empty. Already I am
counting the years I will need
to rebuild and restore life here.

"Is the soul any good, Dad?"
(Even before we came South, her tongue,
sometimes twisted, was never tied.)
"It's soil," I say. She tries
to taste the difference; turns it
on her tongue like a sweet mint.
"Soyerl," she says a dozen times
and can't shove the sound beyond
halfway. "That's okay, Sue," I say,
"at least I think you've found
the middle ground." She sees my smile

and knows there's something there
she hasn't got, but has her own
things to grow, and wanders off
tilling her syllables like rich loam.

"Soyerl, soryul," I hear her go—
and I know I, too,
have had some trouble
keeping the two
apart.

"For Counting Your Blessings," She Said

Again this April morning, she knocks at my door,
this time prim in a pinafore of sunshine,
wearing only a light perfume of New Dawn roses.

Oh, today she's proper enough, seems almost virginal.
We could go anywhere, to the lake or a fashion mall.
But sometimes she comes to me so outlandishly

we can't leave the place—in her excessive gown
of wisteria, her red mouth swollen
crazy with a lipstick of geraniums,

jasmine way too heavy on her shoulders.
But outrageous or prim, lady or unlady,
she's always eager to kiss and roll with me

until we smell like bruised petunias.
Last fall she came to me with hair
full of goldenrod and hayseed, and brought

me for love-gift a skypocket calculator,
a musical Vee of migrating geese honking
high up and glittering like a live abacus

"for counting your blessings," she said.

Morning, Easter

This morning the sun laves light on new leaves
and red barn, takes over and claims for its own
every thing willing to give even half of itself away.

Everywhere light is boss, on the pond cane,
on wet rock at the well lip, on fresh pentangles
of sweet gum and serrated edges of young oak leaves.

(No matter that the rail fence keeps its backside
black, or hoards a lattice of shadow on the ground,
or that any tree's west side hangs on to a darker life.)

The single light sliced and barred by vertical pines,
horizontal fence, and bright diagonals of forsythia;
light parceled and multiplied into geometrics

of difference, italic gold scripture of particulars
my body reads as well as my eyes. A king's
treasure scattered over the prodigal grass. Even

the water is wet with the overflow and splash of it.
Even the porcupine scuttling across the garden
half-awake is needled with it. And there, see the bit

that shines in the open mouth of the stallion
where he frolics, head-high, over new pasture,
carrying the riding light

on his quick and gleaming back.

Daniel Edward Moore

God of Repeat

Imagine being rearranged by repetition
taking the form of you in me,
as Elton calls us *Tiny Dancers*,
molecular ballerinas in leather.

Imagine learning to twirl on the scratch,
that two-inch grave in 70's vinyl,
beginning on the dark edge of me and
ending in the radiant center of you.

Imagine being wronged into song
hearing our voices join a dog
starving to death outside a store
where a neon sky blinks *Safeway*.

Imagine being heaven, an egg
with a shell waiting for sperm
to storm the coop and give
beautiful feathers permission to fly.

Well, there you have it,
the god of repeat, that
brutally, bashful, elegiac old chap
who never knows when to stop.

Dear Neurodivergent

souls like me thrashing in the turbulent sea of transition
worn down, like rocking chair arms
home to an elbow's support of confusion

graciously holding the chin like a child
as ankles and calves rode evening's waves
like a sunburned saint on a Malibu board

headed for the mouth of a great white god
hungry for varieties of innocent flesh
found at the spectrum buffet

                                        praise the wild unruly grey matter
                                        few have the courage to touch

                                        praise the way words spin like a top
                                        on the pre-school floor of your tongue

                                        praise the misunderstanding look
                                        others dress you in daily

then rest and relax Adirondack style
far enough away so the waves can't bite
but close enough to prove you were there.

Dear Body

Let's talk about a preacher's daughter's belly:
                              the bastard beginnings of me.
In Selma, in a trailer, where nightly she grew
                      a soldier's seed into an Amorite's rose.

There in my private greenhouse of glory
                      I learned to prune beauty so strangers
would pay to harvest the womb with adoption's turbine.

The mind does what it can to borrow & steal
                      when it can't deal with holes that remain,
can't change them, ignore them or fill them with time

when judgment's dark ink blackens the sky
                      & the Red Sea of her & the Moses in me
find nothing delivered or free.

Jim Murphy

Junk Travel Through West Memphis

Woman with a starshell light behind her eyes
turns slowly on the sugar of a ride cymbal,
and moves her hands to the Pleiades

she imagines strung across the dancehall floor.
Other hands are soft on her white taffeta,
and the fingers everywhere in her things

only add their brushes to the torsion.
What a love this is, at the core of quiet music
where rings and wallet can be gladly given over.

Shoes, too, and a bracelet with eight red stars
swinging from the band are offered to those most
interested in need. Her frayed hem sweeps up,

and the bassist at his hat rack lifts an arm
to the backward-rushing bride. She unfolds
the packet of her tin foil heart, invites each one

to touch it. She wants them all at her cotillion.
What matters is the glow around her mansion,
though the eaves are overrun with creepers

and the portico is strewn with broken glass.
The alloy in her brain's blood shimmers—
she slips and taps inside its iridescent wave.

River Minstrels, No Date Given

Invisible from the angle of this image,
         a low rumble of vast Indiana tree line
must swell before their open eyes
         along the heavy envelope of the Ohio.

The boat's prow cuts a seam, dividing
          neutral air and water, while the great
wheel churns depth to surface and back
          down. Four stiff figures, posed

in a brittle pantomime of friendship—
          hands clenched at hips and chins,
with banjo, fiddle, drum and cane fife
          splayed at their feet like captured flags,

flat on beaten boards. Strange bearing on
          each face—no showmen's grins, almost
bitter, lined and freighted with stark
          knowledge of the world, its drifting

tastes, peculiar wishes. Barrels of salt pork,
          rye and brandy, ristras of chiles,
bamboo crates of chickens, strings of long,
          skinned hares—provisions furnished

above decks or below, beyond the lens, yet
          lending texture to the whole. Who will
pay for these indulgences? Who will pocket
          the change or play? Who will step

forward from the camera's deadly-still
          embrace to claim a partner, then set
to dance, and break down in the paneled cabins?
          These four players—Black men without

burnt cork, each a solitary traveler in communal
          exile, trained in subtle warcraft, plying
trades along the rivers—stand disguised quite as
          themselves, bent to survive the times.

In the photograph, a mere suggestion
          of the unrecorded music, custom,
thoughtful variation, a semblance dignified,
          demeaned, drastic and denied—

no solid land or portage tracks in sight.

Brian Oliu

Alabama Basketball Fans Drown Their Sorrows In Arby's If They
      Lose, But Minnesota Timberwolves Fans Get a Free Arby's French
Dip Sandwich if They Hit 12 Three-Pointers

Because there are two sides to every sandwich and I grew up knowing something about loving losers—last second shots clanging off the back iron if we even let the game get that close. Most days it was a quick dap up while the clock was still running, the refs allowing for an extra shuffle of feet because it was time to go home and the game has been out of hand for a minute.

There is pride in seeing the end of things—not needing to beat the traffic because you're going to get stuck in it anyway; that there's always a train stopped on the tracks, or worse—one that crawls along just slow enough to let you know that it is moving at a pace you can do nothing about. Me, I've stepped up and over the crushed ballast while I checked the box scores to see just how off our off night was; to check in on the west coast road trip with its late tip and its potential for a parlay.

A confession: I've never drowned my sorrows in a five-point loss that was never that close, and I've never celebrated a hot night from beyond the arc in the same way that I've never wanted to fly that close to the sun—that there is some duality in this world; light from night, here and then not here that scares me to dare put my finger on it. I am scared to know about winning because I must know about loss—the duality of doorways, of how souls and bodies are separate, that we can lose loudness but gain quietness the same way we lose a person but gain a legend, and how I'd trade a thousand myths to get back the voice telling them.

Today, I learned that another word for the track on a railroad is "the permanent way," and the word for railroad ties is "sleepers," and these are things I wish I did not know because they make me not want to go home, ticket folded in quarters after another close one—that in another world I live somewhere else. Instead, I am here, shuffling home in the dark. But soon, the bridge behind the floor that will always bear your name will be built. I am here, caught in the middle before whatever satellite or angel lights up my pocket. I see the Wolves are only down three and we've got the ball. The order is ready. The Tide is still dancing even with the loss and you are still dancing. We are so empty, yet we dance for the nights you kept us full.

After Growing Up In A World With No Sonics, There Are Now Sonics

Instead, we rely on rumors: of girls in roller skates traversing through cracked parking lots to your open car window, of a combination of drinks so infinite that we forget about counting stars against the farmland sky. Ordering your height in hot dogs on a dare. Mythic proportions.

A decade passes, and there are neon awnings in the West End, spaces to pull the car I drove as a teenager into adulthood—the window not yet unable to roll down on its own, a long grease-stained receipt stuck to the outside of a paper bag of not yets. The menu, a glowing beacon of childhood possibility, of every constellation and asterism, of decadence overwhelming.

On my television, the seats are always filled; friends cracking jokes about French toast sticks and peanut butter bits, a small child leaning over the arm rest to steal the tater tot that has fallen to the bottom of the bag. Me, I am alone in a town that I do not yet know the side streets of, and I am not that hungry but I need to eat something because I am alone.

Even now, I fill myself with the hypothetical—of driving up the hill where I'd get four bars on my flip phone, texting friends who are slipping away in between tots, ketchups on the zero key. Another decade passes and I do not know what I sent or even who I was talking to, but I remember the act of it; how it felt to be less empty despite not being less empty, of the joy in the ritual, of how I learned what items were too messy to eat with a steering wheel in the way.

And yet it was never quiet—sounds travel in waves, whether they come from a crackled speaker or the sound of chewing inside of a mouth inside of a person inside of a car inside a city where nothing was known except the void that was attempting to be filled—a reward for making it through another day, another dance floor, another time where it felt like everything stood still even though it all rattled at the slightest humid breeze.

An engine hum. A key press. An order repeated back to you. A thing that gets you through is the thing that gets you through.

Em Palughi

Pastoral for My Trans Friends Living in Alabama

You get trouble for being
                liminal: grafted
         fruit tree with starling nests in the branches,
not in the orchard
                but at the thin edge
         of a mother's backyard.
Sit, sit, eat
                a honeyed biscuit
         nestled in the roots,
peel the strange
                sweet of the fruit. Nearby,
         a river: brackish
and alive, the catfish
                braiding each other's barbels
         like girlfriends.
You are estuary—salt and fresh
                swamp, ocean, wetland,
         too many things at once,
as alien to man as briefly-eyed comets.
                Don't mind the mudlarks combing
         your hair for
the sellable—they'll go home empty-
                bucketed. Instead, watch the slip
         of an alligator ride
on her mother's back,
                not concerned with naming
         the place that keeps her fed.

Gay Epithalamium

The whole swamp
> will sing tonight!
>> Blue Catfish will shine

like fine silverware
> in moonlight,
>> crickets will sing like birds

and birds will dance
> like we do,
>> without skill.

Think of the way
> fresh water meets salt,
>> or how doves flirt

by flying in wide arcs—
> This is an estuarial
>> melding.

Make a home
> in the canebrakes,
>> decorate with Spanish moss

and mermaid purses, listen
> to the life outside,
>> to the tittering love.

Hunting season for the White-Winged Dove
> begins a half-hour before sunrise,
>> but you have been hunted before.

A wide spray, open chokes,
> aimed lead rain from below,
>> gray feathers in red mud,

everything was once unimaginable—
> survival, most of all.
>> Nest however you can.

Alluvium

Before the delta was swarmed with condos,
my father would take me fishing
unlicensed. Gray mornings over
brackish horizons
                    live oak treeline behind
our backs, cheap sunscreen smell mixing
with the earthy cup of nightcrawlers.

He always had me bait the hooks, made sure
the point went through each piece twice.
Once I pushed it through the body
of the worm and into the meat of
my hand, where thumb joins palm.

A river is formed by erosion, carved away,
but deltas are built
                    sediment carried
by currents made into beds where
alligator gar hunt turtles and bluegill,
and miles of sweetflag hide heron nests.

My father pushed the hook
further into my hand, until the barbed tip
pierced my thin skin again, and reached
for the wire cutters. For a moment,
he was tethered
                    to his creation again,
                    holding onto the fishing line,
in control of my flesh
like I was again an infant in his arms.

Charlotte Pence

Stingray Valentine

Two teenagers, shiny as polished agate,
wander the beach, whirling a neon-yellow frisbee,
color of tease and hormones.

They soon return frisbee-less, swinging arms, holding—
not each other's hands, but a three-foot stingray,
dying between them, each knuckle-deep in eye socket.

Wings splayed out, the ray resembles a grey,
heart-shaped valentine
while inside a real heart pulses to stay alive.

The new couple shriek, complain of its heaviness,
its thrashing, command one another to hold tight,
avoid the barbed tail. I'm alone, watching,

while other wave-hazed beach goers point
their phones. Sunlight diffuses. Shadows slow.
The ray breaks, flops to the ground,

attempts to swim on sand. Someone suggests water,
but we are only surrounded by it. Someone suggests
shovel, but we only have plastic. Someone suggests

risk, but no one takes it, including me, rationalizing
like a war correspondent. The new couple sidle off
in search for the frisbee or their next toy.

One wing flaps. The other is slow to follow.
Meanwhile, a woman kneels with her camera, closes
in and shoots, as if there is no god to punish us.

Alabama Backyard Haikus

I.

Two orange cats sleeping
on the shed's roof. One awakes,
arches: a sunrise.

II.

Swinging her legs from
the park bench, the girl asks when
she'll no longer swing.

III.

The chicken struts by
the Cadillac in the drive.
Even the dog snores.

IV.

One shrimp pot, two men,
four folded arms. Nothing boils
except their tempers.

V.

August, the white rose
fattens, while in the shade,
the grey cat flattens.

Rusty Rushton

Humor Tends to Cowboy

Humor tends to cowboy on an earnest—
now leaning left to ogle himself in a polished spur,

now standing suddenly up in the stirrups
with a shocking codpiece.

Humor, deep inside, would mimic earnest earnestly
but can't sit still, his shiny fanny slides.

Never a completed turn about the ring
but at some grave caesura he will pick,

for all to see, his whatnot—
the riffraff hurling kerchiefs from the stands,

earnest stalled as if tethered to a stud.
Humor does this half on purpose, making love and fun.

On certain days the hue upon his clowning darkens
and laughter melts into the scars of his face.

Others, he'll toss his rowdy vim then watch it sail
embarrassed down, like toilet paper from a tree.

Deep in the craw of a subsequent mood,
humor recalls his quips of old: perfect cows

in the headlights of his inner eye, an ardor burbling
through his veins like Listerine.

Midnight Ride

Rolling home in the old Saab
from the Wildwood Ten,

kick ass mind fuck flick
still urgent as a comet's tail,

Bartok's fourth string quartet on the changer
waging war on grace,

sky roof yanked back for the stars
and the whirling wind,

now the highway
now the wooded streets

forgetting what they can of the day's heat
and hushing down,

my forty-fifth year dawning on me
like a reprimand,

deep inside desire
a rain cloud over thirsty turf

and the promise of a tree
on which to hang

these votive syllables,
this preface of a life.

To a Waitress at Dreamland Barbecue

Sweet spontaneity,
whose goodness I don't know the half of,
sent to my table from above
(unless it was from below),
your cropped wilderness of hair
arranged without a care
yet perfectly...

with priority
half blurred,
I give you my word,
which you may take for the kiss
(and every other bliss)
that cannot be,
while I return to life away from you
to picture you
in all your sly straightforwardness—

your pitch of consciousness,
your rhythm of hip and footfall,
the something not quite even in your smile
(is it a chipped tooth?
some way you lay your tongue?),
your ancient, mischievous truth
wrung
from the very garden
itself, a thing that will never harden,
however much invoked by rascals,
into tune—

in short, the way you swing it through the room,
my feisty sauce of dreamland
hugged in the palm of a flowing hand.

The Bard's Glare

Our holy fodder, whose art of heaven's
   hollow as a name,
   our kingdom's done
   (or will have done)
        for mirth as it has for madness:
given us dismay for daily bread
and enlivened us to trust asses
   (or agree to serve those
        who thrust asses against us)
to lead us into slim nations
   like a river of upheaval,
for swine and for Ding-Dong,
   on the power of a story—
   a fruitless endeavor, our men.

The Enunciation

He read his poems over and over
till the ears of the people he dreamed
fell away, and the beloved fever
of his voice appeared as a honeycombed

arc on the dove-white page, and the floors
of his mind gave way, and the syllables rolled
in their quiet aisles, and the careful doors
of their joining kept out the cold.

The sun discharged an ominous grin
into his immaculate attic of signs,
but to him the window's troubling shapes

had died, anesthetized by the slow spin
of his seamless circle of lines,
dumb tautology of his waltzing lips.

Athena, My Daughter

Athena, my daughter within me,
whom I randomly paint as it pleases me,
who speaks, when she speaks, in Pinocchio's
dream, whose rarefied war with dust unrolls
in scrolls of colored ink—
wear something respectable and new
as your beat-up streams unfreeze,
if one day you should chance to meet,
Athena, my daughter without me,
made up in inscrutable decrees
and dancing some green bedevilment:
"whose woods are these?"
let her ask, and bring her this moon
polished bauble for comfort,
among your other tasks that day,
when her one bloom constant and eternal now
spreads fretfully or gaily in two
at her first startled sighting of it
and bears her her own companion, perhaps,
supple, translucent, removed,
for you to know and to know you.

John Saad

Microburst on the Madison River

for Alyson

Somewhere the summer fires still burn
and so the mountains I promised you sleep
behind a gauze of smoke.

You learned long ago to write down
my promises about this place, and how things
I learned here as a boy are lost

beyond the timberline. And you've learned fast
how to mend a fly-line and make good use of wind.
We earn a rainbow each

before the downburst makes its claim.
The guide paddles into the calm
behind a bench the river cut

ages ago. We pull the willows
in tight and let the brief rain heal
the valley of smoke.

Fan Mountain rises. Then the Sphinx,
its brother the Helmet, and the range in full.
But beneath the river's skin we trace

a silent trout holding its sway
against the current, back and forth
over the riverbed, with a shining thread

of wake unraveling behind its tail.
This easy stroke will be the stone
we take back home with us,

so place it on the windowsill
above the sink with our other travel grails.
Someday we'll need it for ourselves.

Longleaf

The duff,
the fernspine

underfoot,
where light

coils
the crooks,

leaves
needledrift

on holes
and shells,

the shagged
blowdowns,

and scales
darting,

lithe,
crimping

early red—
say

a crowning
syllable

without
waste,

come March,
burning

candlegrass
into

a tendered
clearing.

100 Miles Out

Dad and Mr. Rod swear
this oil rig is a jackpot
of grouper and amberjack,

and they tell us boys that men
live up in all that cable and steel—
but not one is seen,

not one man. We don't even
hear bootsteps echoing off
the catwalks. No, the rig

looks abandoned and jagged,
like a cicada's leftover skin,
and is quiet except for the steady hum

of the wellhead. We chum
the waves around us and send
our jigs down deep. Then,

after hours of no signs
of life and bobbing,
always bobbing,

up comes my breakfast into
the gulf's four-foot chop.
I hear my father

over the wellhead's throb.
It's ok, son. Just focus on the horizon.
But I can't turn away

from my floating retch,
billowing like boiled milk
in the dazzling ultramarine of sea.

Dark fish rise.
Something in my throat constricts.
I swear they must taste to see.

Austin Segrest

Yellowhammer

state bird of Alabama

Not yellow much or much of a hammer.
His brain, the mass of two paperclips,
spared what hammering there is,
the force diffusing through his bones like grace.
Between wingbeats, a lull, a loping measure
like the mind repulsed at the edge of sleep
or dropping to the next line or stanza.
Doesn't raise hairs or the dead with his rebel yell,
nor maketh he much of a pretty singing.
No more a coward than the rest of his kingdom,
glorious bright striking light of redemption
he is not. Yellibama, hallelujah, yellowhammer—
another name by violence yoked together.

Door to Remain

Whidbey Island, WA

A shipment of mist is coming in from Japan,
rain ground to grist, blotting out the mountains,
lightning pushing pins into a pincushion.
An outlet to open ocean has warped the windward firs,
wind barreling unobstructed down the strait,
blindsiding the island as if the Sound's
Eustachian tube were stuck open, as in the ear
of an anorexic tortured by the white noise between worlds,
inner and outer. This door to remain unlocked
during business hours, signs on the mainland read.
God's tenseless infinitive, wielded as imperative.

Barrel Roll

I knew enough about love to know that when
my uncle flipped his open-cockpit twin
during his mail route, which he'd let me
co-pilot on special occasions, I knew when he
turned and asked, calmly but somehow
loud enough to breach the airshaft's window,
"want me to turn it back?"—I knew with a steel
swallow I could only nod. The pistol
he handed back, the color of pond-ice, seemed
heavy enough to pull me out. When he said,
"put it in your mouth and I'll turn it back,"
and I started seeing red spots and shook
my head that I didn't understand, and he said,
"like this," and lipped the barrel like a sky-god,
I knew enough about love to know this pact
was my uncle's way of asking me to defect
and verge on that jagged yellow rim inside
his eyes where it was like his other side
was always leaning over the abyss and catching
itself at the last instant, leaning and catching,
the way he used to toss me to the rafters in his den
while Mom threw a fit—I knew enough then
about love to know I had done all I could,
and my upside-down eyes, marbled with blood,
rolled away, and when I woke up he'd caught me
under the arms and was lifting me, putty,
from the plane. Not long after, he let go
for good. And when I heard, I saw him through
the sky's scope, riding the horizon like a bullet,
frozen, one perfect steel. Though I tell it
like it's over and done with, who can stop
reliving the past? Any minute we'll scrape
the wiregrass racing under us, my uncle's grin
twisting, waiting as long as it takes me to turn
the gun on myself. My god, what might I have
unlocked? The barrel's bead singeing the roof
of my mouth, the long barrel balanced on the edge
of my teeth, and lips closed, the warm surge
and roar of engines as he rolled us out with love.

Across the Street

I ran across the street, I didn't know any better.
Ran out in the street, I didn't know no better.
I just knew a woman was there, though I'd never met her.

She sat me in her parlor, distracted me with trinkets,
milky glass birds and fish, distracting trinkets.
She said my mother would be fine, but did she think it?

The world was a blur of crystal wings and fins.
My tears were casked in crystal, wings and fins.
She was the first of many lady-friends.

The tree shadows shortened, she brought me a drink of water.
Morning matured, she brought me a glass of water.
I drank it so fast, she went and brought another.

I kept looking out the window, she didn't ask me what for.
I watched out that window, she didn't ask what for.
The seconds broke off and lay there on the floor.

I imagined my mother's route, as far as I could.
Her long morning walk, followed as far as I could.
Nothing I could do would do any good.

Suffer the little children, and forbid them not.
Christ said suffer the little children, and forbid them not.
Said love thy neighbor, sometimes she's all you got.

The End of Analysis

At the end of analysis you should face your analyst.
It's recommended that you enjoy a lengthy goodbye.
You've spent a long time together.
After years pinned to that couch, staring at that painting,
the old man of the sea will yield his true form.
For example: a slender gay man in his late thirties,
clean-smelling and bald, his anonymous sky-blue tie
and fitted slacks, like a holidaying uncle
in a French Impressionist painting, except
instead of the Rhine it's the Ohio.
The spell is broken. You can see him now—
around town, maybe, or driving home behind you
in his Honda Civic, which he's always done,
but which you've never noticed.
Imagine you've entered the painting.
It's midnight, you've got him pinned. His colony of seals
sleep piled like slipper shells. You can ask him anything.
He's no longer slippery. *Who am I? Can I love? Am I real?*
The hero's question is always what's holding me back.
It implies something went wrong and can be made right.
That the past continues to operate, that there is disorder.
And that there is disorder is predicated upon a prior state
of greater order. Once he commented on your slovenly appearance.
Once you went back for something. A question maybe.
You knocked. A no-no. He wasn't all yours.
Having seen your old man in you, having seen you weren't all hers,
your mother asked and asked, what happened to the old you?
I don't know, you'd say, squirming away. Or, nothing.
What happened to your mother? the physician on call after hours
working on her asked wearily, befuddled from behind his glasses.
Knowledge and propitiation are demanded of the hero.
Where are you getting this? Your Latin teacher?
What about you? your analyst asked. Maybe you're in love with me.
Suppose you were supposed to say no. What happened
to the old you? She didn't mean you, maybe, so much as herself.
The one she wanted back. The one you never knew.
Is that what you went back for? Because nobody ever told you?
Your mother's very sick, the physician on call had said.
Meaning dead. You gave it till the end of the week.

Jordan Shoop

In a Bedroom in Dogtown, Alabama

a J.D. combs an electric razor and crafts a mohawk,
staring in a mirror, wearing a ripped
tuxedo shirt and fishnets. CHARLIE CHAPLIN WAS GAY

is scripted on a poster on the wall, next to two butches
in floral tops rimming mouths. He believes he's his
parents' little devil, while they mock

                                        rather he imagines the screaming
symphony of "Gimme, Gimme" sung by a dude in drag
while a man in a striped Polo is chained by a leather scaffold

crawling on all fours. The J.D. sharpies a pink triangle
on the side of his head, staring at a poster of a nude
man with an erection spilling FAG POWER, and he smiles

not silenced in a deviant revolution
                              a readying reclaimed RIOT

Tough

His heavy body eroded
with tattoos of his ex-lovers,
names carved in curvy letters,
some in a bold type font, some
just lonely initials. He
sat with his legs outstretched,
as I sat next to him at the bar.
He exclaimed, "I am wild
guy, very masculine, rough."
He bit his lips as he forced
his finger to his flexed
bicep. "But I cry when I accidentally
drive over a squirrel or when
my mama calls me from Anniston
or during that part of the child
talking about an angel
getting its wings in that nice
Christmas movie." Harsh
eyes of fireball whiskey reflected
myself nodding, picturing
him later a little spoon in my
tiny frame as he cried after he
orgasmed. Grabbing
my arm, he led me to a corner
of the bar where he pressed his
lips against mine
while choking me, his rough
finger tips felt my heart
every time it beat as I felt his
tongue swirl and taste my slippery
spit. I stared down at his bicep
and placed my fingers over
my initials scarring though.

Like a Crushed Coke Can

Picture this: A Hockney painting but with plummeting
clouds angled low, dim   yet smooth, heavy yet
cotton yet formidable. We were both thirteen, and you
were running your parents' Shell gas station while
they vacationed on a Wednesday afternoon. You sat
faded   in a folded lawn chair in the hazy heat.
The only outside noise came from a   re-run
of a baseball game on the static radio and slow
cars on the highway in Tuscaloosa. You rimmed
a gallon jug of Milo's sweet tea while I tapped and
tapped my toes. "I spy something   yellow," you said
as you slapped sweat from your fair forehead
and rolled up your shirt sleeves.   I pointed
to the tiny amber weed in front of a gas pump that had
crippled through the cracked concrete. "Stop
guessing it."   Your coveted eyes felt like a crushed
coke can ran over by a tire   your same eyes
that would become so blank after being found
on your parents' bathroom tilted tile floor years later
after finding your father's assault rifle with a note
saying you didn't want a mess.   But then, you were
innocent and I had dug my own innocence away as I craved
your biceps exposed under your rolled up sleeves.
"Do you think you'll ever leave this town?" I asked. Your
head fell down like a slow start   of a drop of rain
in the steady summer and you hunched your shoulders.
Your mouth steadied open for a few then stopped
and your hand held my skinny inner thigh   "You ain't
gonna mix a John Wayne and a pussy." Your eyes lit fire.
"Or at least that's what my papa says." I stared back
at the amber weed.   Other summers, you ended up
banging your head as you worked the drive-thru window
at McDonalds. Every Sunday, I would order a fudge sundae
just to watch   you smile for only a second.

Lauren Slaughter

Alice the Corpse Flower Blooms at the Chicago Botanic Garden

In September, 2015, thousands gathered to see Alice the Amporophallus, one of the Chicago Botanic Garden's "corpse flowers," named for their rancid stench, when she unexpectedly bloomed.

And what woman

hasn't been thus
gathered round,

a mob of cell phones
raised like torches

poised to snag the spectacle

that is her efflorescence—
pompons peeping out

(glimpse of thigh
or thong)

ovules swollen
with her fertile redolence?

Because smell is indifferent
to video or maybe more

the dare you take
to taste the sour milk

a queue of tourists forms
to step right up to Alice's enormous

sex and nozzle in—
whole heads will disappear

in a cunnilingual pantomime
the wincing faces say

reeks of rotting flesh,
or fish, or death.

~

We use real words
at our house, not prim

approximations, not
the *birdie* of my childhood,

or *girly bits*, or *vee-vee*,
or *hoo-hoo*, or *kitten*,

yet despite my professorial directives
my young daughter

refers only to her *private*—
that is private

in the singular, like signage
on her bedroom door

years from now, and as if
understanding, somehow,

she must enlist
a part of herself always

to serve as her own soldier,
her very own private,

her protector,
and I won't correct her.

The Neutral Ones

My daughter's fed up with getting called boy.
She wants to trade in her brother's short hair

and hand-me-down athletic shorts
and polo shirt with the collar popped

for picture day. She wants to replace her handsome
smile for never explaining herself again.

How many girlfriends you got? I imagine the photographer
will tease as my daughter scans the room

for that teacher on a field trip who scolded her
for using the wrong restroom. She prefers

the neutral ones with half-skirted
stick figure signs

where everyone belongs and can be hers
as the sky is hers. Eleanor. My daughter

reveals she is about to cry when red stains streak
across her cheeks and I swear I could

slit that teacher's throat with the teeth
of a tiny black comb. With my teeth.

I have learned to murder anyone, mother
that I am—a fool at Target with a Starbucks

and hangover scanning The Girls Section
for a get-up my kid could stomach—

something ribbon-free and sans *Princess*—
bulletproof, perhaps, in a pretty shade

of math, refusing to conform, and always
speaking up. My own bowl-cut childhood

was roly-poly bugs and jacks, jeans
with the knees ripped out going for the ball

and still the fluorescent glare in here
is brutal boomeranging between mirrors

and the blank-faced mannequins—my face—
my mascara—my strong legs—my desires

that strange morning years ago I woke up
out of time into a middle space

between dreaming and perception
and for a flash was no one, just me

267

without a body, a Lauren-y existence
before corporality snapped me back

to shape and brain, this sale rack place
of dumb graphic t-shirts. *Roarsome!*

says the T-Rex. *Hang in there!*
jokes the cartoon sloth. *They/them/theirs*

demand my gorgeous students, fierce
in polyester, violet fades, and fedoras,

fluid as the ocean and complex as the night
out of range of any manufactured light.

Sometimes You Just Have to Grow Up

My OB says when I ask
about another little one to tend

this want bloom heart
stuck in a jar perfuming

the room with its flesh
stink until the whole family's sick,

all four of us. (Bounty already:
one girl, one boy

as prescribed.) I learn petals
fall off. Off and off onto

the counter tacky with spilled Os
milk and finger jam. The mad cat

meme says, *Go embrace life
somewhere else* which I quote

here as it pleases me
to do so. Seasons of one's life.

Season of indulgence. I indulge
my therapist with my accomplishments,

help myself to a tissue for each
until the box gapes back

in sudden emptiness. And yet,
Dr. Viv says, you're not happy.

Let's explore this. My mother
likes to tell a story called

All the Punishment You Needed
of the Cinderella birthday

I attended as a girl,
how I licked every last child's

cupcake clean of its beautiful
pink icing until nothing

was left and hid in the closet,
ill, filled with the sunrise

pinks, sunset pinks,
pinks of the inside of things,

the body inside
the beating body breathing

breathing
because because

R. T. Smith

Deer in the Sedum

All summer the ruminants
let the loosestrife thrive
but nipped the wild lilies,
low-growing roses
of Sharon, gold iris
that cost us considerable,
any ivy, exotic hostas.
The French sunflowers
once yellow as finch
feathers have withered,
and cool weather has
us deadheading a plot
of perennials we want
back. Soon Orion will
be striding across cold
sky, his outline implied
by silver seeds, but this
morning, rising to meet
my body's needs, I stare
into the garden until my
old eyes find four does
browsing on the season's
last petals, sedum, also
called *stonecrop*, which
we love because they linger
into September when
the remnant cicadas
wind down their chivaree
and because succulent
clusters of magenta stars
harbor pollen to bedazzle
both us and the bees.
I used to throw stones
and shout at the foragers,
who'd take a step or two,
then resume their feast.
So now I pause to gaze

before a casual hand clap
and *scram, scram* as
they perk ears, twist,
quickly and leap easily
over our shoddy wall,
flashing their own flowers,
the moon-white scuts
which must not be confused
with admissions of mischief
or flags of surrender.

Mourning Dove

This morning my wife found the dove
huddled against our back door
for shelter. We thought the dog,
in her eagerness for play, had killed it
last evening. Rabbit, deer, chipmunk
and squirrel—on her flex line
she seldom catches anything but loves
the chase, her own voice across
the dark. The bird was shivering
in tremors, one wing clearly broken.
The first half of my life I hunted,
knocked them from the sky,
finished any wounded ones swiftly
and stashed them in my game bag
with little sympathy or attention.
It's best to guard your heart and turn
a blind eye, but this one I had to lift
from the grass fluttered off thirty
yards to settle under the dry birches.
I could still feel its heat in my palm, see
the rich coral of his feet. Retrieved,
he was done for, near eye eclipsing,
the left wing barely twitching,
so I fell back on my old ways, twisted
the neck till the head detached.
The bubble of blood that pumped
from his body was finer than any ruby.
It wasn't easy, but I flung him beyond
the shrub cedars and into the understory

where sentiment plays no role at all.
So this is what it's like to be an angel
of mercy. I washed and rinsed my hands,
scrubbed them again, but the blush color
of his breast stays with me, the feel
of a small life suffering, struggling
for one more breath, another moment,
a final performance of soothing song.
Did I rescue him from his misery?
That's the story I was told so long ago.
For penance I went in and embraced
the puzzled dog, glad she'll never
need to understand, relieved that I had
no son to whom I could not explain.

Snake Church

2016

I'm Reverend Cody Coots
from over in Bliss, Kentucky.
Don't you think this pink
suit looks snappy but holy?
Come by on Sunday,
we'll be high in the faith,
braving rat poison
and torch flames, eight
snakes I count so far,
one young copperhead,
likely last Easter's hatch.
Listen here: I've been
bit six times when my
heart was off harmony
with Jesus, but I prevailed
over Old Scratch and sport
crippled fingers that can't
half work a guitar or
button my own shirt,
but the Lord will provide.
His eye is on the sparrow.
It's foolish to be afraid.
You might not guess,

but fangs feel at first
like the touch of a feather.
Angels sing in color.
You think you can fly.
By the way, have you tasted
Sister's biscuits? Light
as breath. We'll have
four plug-in guitars,
a drum kit and tambourine
with some new glory
music. We'll all wallow
in His grace and make
the rafters rattle like
looms at the towel mill.
Joyella will be there, too,
to witness with me, as
we expect our assembly
to increase, guessing
from the feedback we're
getting on Facebook.
But God's a healer. Don't
never forget. We're all
Heaven-bound. Drive up
early and we'll break
bread, then step over
to meet the snakes.
You got to look them
in the face, creature
to creature, to be saved.
You know, as you breathe
and behold, even among
cursed serpents, the eyes are
the windows to the soul.

Torpor

Hummingbirds do not sleep
but go deeper, nightly,
into a dream where hearts
that beat a thousand a minute
under the sun slow to a hundred.
They feed on nectar, savor
foxglove, hollyhock, rose
of sharon or snip mayflies
in mid-air. How tiny
the wishbone, swift the wings.
The brain, relative to body
weight, is the largest
of all birds but not so heavy
as its eyes. They survive longer
than anyone would think.

Starthroat, rufous, berylline,
calliope, lucifer—all billed
with needles, all migratory—
they gather, experts say,
not in *flocks* but *charms*
to make their long journeys.

Memory: the hummingbird
flies backward. One summer day
in the Sangre de Cristo Range
I stripped to union suit, boots
and visor, pausing for water
on a ridgeline, then heard
the burr of a host of wings,
saw the blur of their swarm,
that charm, their javelins
so close I feared they'd mistake
my scarlet outfit for a flower.
I covered my eyes, afraid
to be struck blind,
even in the midst of a marvel.

Don't tell me noon's desert
is dead, all that hunger
and divine pattern. Morning
glory, day lily, hibiscus,
sweet pea, lupine, ditch iris—

all invite this ravenous precision.
I've read that each specimen
remembers every flower
it's ever courted and sipped.

Torpor it's called, this
nocturnal suspension practiced,
also, to conserve energy when
sustenance is scarce. Like
prayer. Their wings do not flap
but rotate in an oval pattern.
They can hover in sorcery
bird science barely fathoms.
As they rise from stasis
they rocket off at full velocity.
Their calls and cries are diverse,
enigmatic—for mating,
greeting, angry songs
to warn trespassers—
zeek, and *chip* and *chirr*.

Now I lie wordless,
still as a hummingbird
in starlight under a limestone
overhang and waiting for rain.
I have no azure wing feathers
to thrill nor splendid auriculars,
but my stillness is not sloth,
this silence not quite stupor.
I am learning how quiet
a riddle is. Wingbeats,
heartbeats, syllables or breaths—
how can we measure a life
and know when to say *Surrender,
it's all over?* But I pray
my idleness this time is only
some human torpor—poised
on the threshold of wilding awake,
recalling every single flower
by taste, tint and smell until
I am once again kindled or,
in a chorus of amaryllis, slaked.

Anastasia Sorochinsky

April

And then it was a matter of scale. The broken
car, the trees coming into themselves, the terrible
growth. The killing thing and the thing inside
and the thing itself. The itself inside myself. The
body of proof in the brilliant light of day. So
we sat in the shadow of the oak trees. So we sat
directly underneath the branches and the sun
still bled through where the knots had not burst
into leaves. Where yet was yet. And not was
still to come. I hate how the thing assumes itself
even in language. Even before it exists. The
possibility. The cruel architect of negation. Myself.
Spread thin as a widening gulley. Even as it is
not so wide. Even as it is still quite narrow. So we sat
dividing in that day and I thought about how
a car needs a starter to start. How the body can be
a mechanical thing. So it breaks. So you must
open it. So you open it many times and find a pump
at the heart of it. And then it won't be the heart.
It will be something else. The lungs. Its liver or
its spleen. The car hood laying the whole thing
bare. The elbow bent awkwardly beneath the weight
of the skull. The downward leer of the unmoved
sun. Waiting. Again we are waiting. A beat of sweat
breaks free of the skin on your thigh and finds its
place in the earth. Falls onto the red clay and lingers
there a moment. And all the while. Then all at once.

Elegy

Moon-white
snow on your crown.
Road-like, time settles in grooves
on your brow and pauses
before you pick up

speaking, on there or
then. Wishing to
say: what is this—?
The wood and its table.
Work of our being here.

Spring Cleaning

The dogs are chasing the finches chasing the dogs around
the yard. The earth is increasing its tilt relative to the sun.
We bring the chess board out to the patio and you choose
the side shaded by the awning. You play white. Your mother
watches the pieces move from her cigarette. I think she thinks
it is indulgent but I think she understands. The way she is
watching. The way she is already not watching. The way she is
searching the pines on the horizon. When she leaves she tells
us there's no longer an excuse for avoiding the yard work. So
one thing tilts into another. So one thing tilts away. You look
so small when you kneel in the dirt by your brother. I imagine
you younger. Starting fires in the woods with your father.
Learning. Starting fires alone. Lately, we've been talking
about starting a garden. I think it'd be nice to grow something
together. Strawberries first. A plot in the right hand corner of
the yard. You tried to do it yourself but the soil didn't take.
Last year. I wasn't here yet. Somehow the yard work always
was. The tilting keeps tilting. The dogs nip at your muddied
heels when you walk back. You light a cigarette. In the sun
your skin gleams with sweat like it's the first time.

Soil Horizons

We got caught in a wormhole
documentary the other night. The general principle is

that anything is possible. Theoretically. In physics. For anything that is
there is also something that isn't. Think
inertia. Equal and opposite
forces. And so: space,
time, wormholes, etc.

Turns out the universe itself rotates!

That was a Facebook headline I saw. I guess
the algorithm knows I've been thinking about
unthinkable things. How lovely, though
to think we're spinning in a big way.

Even if it isn't true. There was a debate
in the comments about the veracity of this and the
authenticity of that and whether you could or should trust anyone or anything.
(This is in line with the general principle I think).

The bees are back.
When I come home in the afternoon I sprint across the porch
and the neighbors laugh. I took a walk through the woods and that shade
of green was everywhere. And buzzing. And I got
a piece of the gravel by the creek stuck
in my shoe and had to stop and take it off and
so many small things live in that silt.

Or clay or mud or sand. Every stone
a confluence of time. When I pressed on the shale
it came apart in thin flat sheets that didn't skip
on the water. That dropped like the last year.
Heavy and low. I watched

the fall. The gravity of entry
and the flood of reverberation:
the water climbing the air in defiance
along the edges. When Salvador Dali, late
in his career, changed his signature to a crown,
it was because he'd seen a stroboscopic

photo of a drop of milk. The splash
like a coronet. The coronet like him.
I thought I saw a hawk with your face
when the sky was breaking
into evening.

With your likeness, I mean. The silhouette like
your movement along
something glowing like sunset
fading away. Relational, in motion
like a signature, like ink

sinking in the page. I keep
the postcard you painted by my bedside.
The crabapple tree from Maine
in watercolor. The general principle is
here and there and then and
now. I meant to send you a history

of sedimentary rock and lichen. The white
imprint of gravel in the flesh
of the foot. A note on the nature
of force of art of truth of the woods
between us. The earthworms curling in the loam.

Rain Song

In the coherence

                                                  in the luminous
                 drift of heavenly bodies

          we are naming rain
                       as rain

again. The rain
               as rain
                     is pooling
                            is running is
                                      washing the dust
                  from our feet

and the long bones of our shins
                     and their long calcified
                            clemency. The rain is

        falling lenient

                    and I am waking
            in the valley.

                        Where I am born.
      Where I attach
            my arms and legs
                   to my mind
and call it
                           like it is
        the rain and the bone. How
                        is it already

History?   Isn't it?

       Reprise of silt.

     Water-heavy

         hum.

Kimberly Ann Southwick

The Perception of Need

I.

Take me to the green park first, then you dash in for groceries:
dog food, grapefruit juice, dish soap, seltzer, bananas,
—massive BPA-laden receipt revealing an etcetera.

We don't need a new container for dish soap.
We don't need the sink's pipes replaced at least yet,
they are fine. You say we need to redo the entire kitchen
for a garbage disposal so I'll wait.
We don't need a new roof or white painted trim or
gray painted trim, we don't need a duvet of parachute down.

Four friendly neighborhood gunshots & then someone else's dogs in our yard,
again. Say something about neighbors & fences one more time. I'll consent:

the fencing we need. The broken dishwasher sitting helpless,
haying the grass it tops, we need that
to work. I am tired of using my brief free time to hand-wash the dishes, tired
of buying dish soap, of having an argument on whether the dish soap
should have its own container it's too early for this we are too broke please rewire
the one in the yard, & when you leave to buy such & such a tool
that you need to rewire it aside from that come home empty handed

for once. This time five friendly neighborhood gunshots.
The birds in the trees unperturbed, the flowers
unruffled, the baby asleep in the other room.
Someone drives by with music blasting entirely too loud.

II.

The dogs were asleep on the porch. If I had to make an inventory
of everything rusting in my yard, I would fail. /// Heavy open parenthesis
topped with a wheel. Orange chain attached to pulley attached
to gallows. Giant springs stuck in place, seeming to grow
out of the ground like the purpling flowers they're beside.
I can't tell the difference between the lawnmowers except:
push, push, riding, riding. /// I'm not even mad though. I'm not
even mad about any of that.

Sometimes when the baby cries, I want to cry, too.
Sometimes I force myself to cry so we'll stop or to get out
of being blamed for something I'm being blamed for—is that
every woman's not-so-secret card except some of them
don't ever have to use it & sometimes I can't tell if I'm really crying
or forcing myself to cry. /// I guess some of it I do know: Funnel
for something to do with gasoline. Broken dishwasher
Broken oven. Working though rusting washer & dryer.
Some sort of mechanical saw. /// How can I be mad, though,
when there are sometimes those soft cookies with colorful frosting
& sprinkles in the refrigerator, when he saves the last one for me.

How can I be mad when there are all these flowers.
He pruned the bushes with (redacted) & now
there are so many more, so many that the baby & I
pluck an azalea here & there & no one can tell any are missing.

Sometimes, we try to put them back, touch beheaded pink bloom
to breathing pinked bush, & it falls to the neatly mown grass.
We gather our failed recouplings & practice raining petals
over the dogs as they bake in the spring sun.

In Alabama, They Renamed the Praying Mantis the Boxing Mantis

The most common wildflower
In Alabama is no longer
The dandelion

Kids blew their tops
Seed explosion
Huff, puff, poof

I send my daughter to the foot of our property
With a bell jar à la *Beauty & the Beast*
To preserve what's left of ours

They reflect yellow in the light
Green claws close like a fist at night
Everyone likes butter

Red buckeye, Cardamine,
Wild Ginger—these grow like weeds
Light a match & burn the lawn down

To lop the head off a dandelion
Is a crime in Calhoun County
Punishable by up to a $300 fine

Precious now like the Praying Mantis once was
Before they renamed him the Preying Mantis
Before they renamed him the Boxing Mantis

Fists balled
By his face
Ready for a fight

Cheyenne Taylor

Harvard researcher says dreams indicative of virus fears

The people are dreaming
of buffalos going long,
sacking lean pines
in their own endzones,

of buffalos in prairies
surging from cattails.
Lightning girds the herd
like a championship ring.

The people are dreaming
of empty porches,
wasps building organs
in disused offices.

A lanky quiet pops
its knuckles all the way
to Ocala, carried on birdsong
spat like chewed seeds.

The people are dreaming
of pregnant elephants,
carrying in them smaller selves
made of vegetable salt

and something unobserved—
a groaning baleen
clarinet, or milk-fed
churchyard root.

The people, tired
of themselves
are dreaming
of just about anything.

Anniversary in an Election Year

with phrases from The Iliad, *translated by Caroline Alexander*

The hours release their horses. Full on marsh parsley
and clover, they rush toward us. I've loved

this shivering world to my white bones, been fucked
on dirty feet, am ashamed to refuse but afraid

to accept the call to always be a child of peace.
Drunk as men, I've put my faith in sparrows

and braided the strings of my limbs. I've hung my head
like a garden poppy, let my name down

to brush the senseless earth. I was never a star
washed clean by oceans, just a back bristling with spears.

But we either grow or die: time is a swift consolation
of fire pressing us into the tide. Over the whole

unbroken chine of you, my hands turn years, all gold,
grip, and body. And at night when dread nods terribly

over me, you send missives past the rampart
of your teeth—wild rock, holy salt, crowned oak.

With the taste of each other's mettle in our mouths
we couple with the dust of our country.

Humble // Tremble // Triangle

We talk of children with terrible, naive joy.
The body tends toward nectarines, bulbous
lamps, pinnately compound leaves.

In the kitchen, we nourish each other
fervently, hands soft and scalding, dying
to take the other's shape. Why invite

the world into this equation? A child
is a doorway to the disastrous light

of other people, a leak in the membrane,

a fearsome structure pulled from some
chromatic pool into a stair of bismuth.
And we want it like water. Like a greasy

bone to lick at the refrigerator door.
At night we are astronomy, morpheme,
in, come, -ing. In daylight, flesh,

concentric objects on an axis
of loblolly pine. Why invite a child
into this world? For witness.

To give our greedy beauty form.
That she may do a good deed.
That he may love nectarines.

Where the Congregation's Gone

Come Sunday, blue skinks abandon their tails for higher mercies.
But we must have faith in our reflections—says the house finch,

stained fleetingly in glass. Nothing's ever really filthy, says the sweat bee,
thorax throbbing on a soothing leaf. Even in the sweat-wrecked night,

we have pistachios and milk, says the raccoon flexing its starburst paws
at apartment balconies. So we drink from the cupped hands of satellites,

keeping watch like callow bucks coursing the woods in threes.
Yes, we will go forth and multiply, we will try to forgive ourselves

for being unable to forgive. We know an empty bed when we see one,
make love above hundred-year-strong heart pine floors. Say the neighbors

and the stray cats eating dry shoots in our crawlspace. We enter each other
to make the weather come. Says the brief flood of sugar between trees. Says me.

Does the tough mountain love? Some nights I walk into bars and say
"I am a person who doesn't believe in anything." No one cares.

In this holiest glory, I am overwhelmed, heart a knot of deer mice.
Says the fire ant tasting my ankle. Says the rabbit I cannot see.

Walker County Rites

One average night you catch yourself
combing summer's stour through your hair,

slicing the moon like fruit with a pocketknife.
The night undoes the hooks behind her back

for you, white freckles tossed across her skin.
Before the massless hoots of barred owls hail

you back to camp—your wet, unbaptized body
bruised from testing instinct—you're convinced

that something's watching. Fatwood fatigues.
You loom up to the fire, trusting heat. You say

I sort-of-think, and *I would* like *to pray*,
and marvel at the coal barge hauling

light between banks. When someone thanks
the Lord for camp potatoes, aluminum foil,

rootstalks spread for tortoises, a mammal howls,
and you want all the earthly knowledges.

You steel yourself with whiskey for the river.
You plant yourself ashore and suck the mud.

Jeanie Thompson

The Little Boy Next Door

After a black and white photograph of Helen with an unidentified child

I knew first from a distance his ramble across the yard
        toward the porch to sit with me on the rock wall:
his smell of infant sweat and something else, a milk
        musk mixed with his mother's talc
and the dark rich dirt from the backyard arbor.
        He played there late. When I moved
in my garden, touching the rose trees to shake their
        fragrance at close of day, he ran
quickly to nestle against my skirt, his small dumb
        hand patting my thigh to signal, *I am here.*

One day a visitor thought to photograph us
        and so we posed as I imagine a mother
and child do for a memory book. His warm, damp
        body next to me, he pressed his head against
my breast with a quiet knowledge, let me finger
        his toes to feel dust powered there and learn
where he had played.
        I was younger then,
        and felt the quickening of a mother's desire for his
small body on hers.
        Later, when you did not arrive
        to take me from Alabama, I mourned the child lost
to me. There would be no difference to lose him—one I would
        never have—or that child, pressed from my body,
the dark smell rising to tell me at last who I am.

Memory of Ivy Green

Tuscumbia, Alabama

The first time I entered a wave
          my feet swept up under me
                    by a force stronger than wind
or Mother's arms—
          nothing held me—

          The salt water touched me
                    like an earlier time, featureless air,
a bland surging engulfed me,
          just a babe—who could know
                    anything of loneliness or death?
I was alone, tumbling
          in the deep element of myself.

When my little feet found no bottom,
          no sand scratched my toes—
                    I was
cut loose—returned to an elemental pulse—
          with no thought of exit,
                    or birth.

          * * * * * *

Flickering leaves
          played across the bathroom floor—
                    I toddled forward, arms outstretched—
Then this—
          the receding sound of Mother's

breath at the phantom's ear—
These she cannot claim,
          they are not hers,
                    language has not taken her—
little soul cast off into the deep
          ocean of herself,
                    no mooring, no anchor.

Imaginary Farewell from Russell Cone to Helen Keller

The Golden Gate, traveling to the Far East, April 1, 1937

Ma'am, you see it was good work
because it was safe work—hard hats,
no drinking allowed. One stunt
at any height
and they were off the job.
But the best we gave them
was the net. Suspended
under the bridge, like under a circus tent,
designed to
catch a man, a can of paint,
a ton of scaffolding.

On that morning eleven men
worked the platform, prepared steel
for the orange vermillion
to paint her right into
the California landscape.
On the north tower
two men already in the net
scraping away debris.

Like a big sigh, five tons
of scaffolding
gave way and hung crazily,
tilting the men to the water below—
then all fell to the net

like babes into a mother's
outstretched apron.
The relief we felt you can imagine,
a moment's joy.
The tearing we heard next
was like a machine gun's crack
or the rip of a picket fence splintering.
All down—men, wood, net
220 feet into water
you now cross.

Twelve fell, two lived.
One man knocked unconscious
by a piece of lumber then

shocked back to life
in the icy channel.
Strong swimmer, tangled
underwater, he made it, broken,
lived to tell so I can tell you, Miss Keller,
the worker is never
truly safe. One man builds
so another can cross.

March 26-31, Helen and Polly Thomson traveled overland by train from New York by way of Chicago to Kansas City to San Francisco where they boarded the Asama Maru on April 1 to sail for Japan and Korea. Moving under the newly opened Golden Gate Bridge, Helen remembered workers killed during its construction. Much of the imagery comes from an historical account of constructing the Golden Gate by the project manager, Russell Cone.

The Myth of W-a-t-e-r

It was not a single word and there was no utterance.
You may have your play, your frozen moment in time
if these please you. But understand, Teacher lead me
to the well house to distinguish between *water* and what
holds it for drinking. I held the cup under the pump and she
wrenched the handle. I could smell her sweat, though
I didn't know its name—only that it mixed with the garden
and told me she was near. The liquid hit my fingers
where I gripped the cup's handle—in my other upturned palm
she spelled the letters over and over, like fire.
There was a moment when everything came,
that my mind accepted thought like a body
crossing a threshold through the opened door.
It was illumination and joy, then more words until *Teacher,*
Helen, world, go. Go into your life!

Allen Tullos

Great Unreported Events

One morning Highway 80 fronting the downstairs
we rented from Miss Marybelle delivers my load of shy:
curb-jumping eighteen-wheeler crushing
the three-wheeler beneath unscratched me.
(According to those familiar with the situation.)

"What thumbsucker won't eat a parched peanut!"
Consigned to sit outside myself and sing for a piper's
disappearing into seamless stone. All for peanuts.

Foil-folded twice-chewed Juicy Fruit token
passed cousin to cousin under the table.
Kiss on my cheek, no one looking.
Saying pass the syrup repetitiously,
no grownup hearing, jawing,
preferring a mutterless child.
Biscuit of buttermilk lightness,
cold for its anointing.

Kinskein pondswimming cumulus tufts.
Fishing bird's return.
Catchy title, catchy tune, if you can.

Seasons, one and another.
"Hear somebody come to the door, what boy runs hide.
Nose smelling of book."

"Away you go," laughing.
"You'll remember this years from now."
"I remember it already."

Elements of Composition

Tuskaloosa, the sixties.
Near the banks of the Black Warrior,
Marcel Smith of Smithtown, first generation college,
teaches us Romantics: "More is not enough. All is enough."

Blake or Marcel?

"You're almost entirely" he blackboards:
O, C, H, Ca, N
"But doorknob dead without the smidgen of
iodine, iron, selenium, copper, zinc, chromium,
fluorine, manganese, molybdenum."

"You never know what is enough
unless you know what is more than enough."

From mail-order plans, Marcel and brother Perry
(who'd published a praisesong for the grasshopper
in *Evergreen Review*) measured, sawed, and nailed together
the first geodesic home anyone'd seen.

"Orgo, bio, physics, math, econ, poly sci,
more than enough. But not all."

"He was a serial zealot," the obit quotes Elizabeth,
knowing more than she lets on, if not all.

Between Rivers, Years Between

Small towns have gone by the wayside. But this one's going to come back.
—North Mississippi Herald

Across the loblolly desert, death and the interstate call.

"Where you at now? Where?"
Skittish Angus huddle the locust grove at a pasture's edge.
Carmelized thunderheads and "Blue Bayou" roil the exitburger.

Circling the courthouse square, west on Mesopotamia Street.

Pecan limbs clack what's coming from the Gulf.
Dirt devils chase a mascot practicing bagpipes.
Papersack luminarias spit along the elementary curb.
Memory picks on something its own size:
late summer's arm, my first teacher's grip, "Are you white?"

Park on the county road shoulder, ghost cousins drive by in rain:

Leonard, gunning his go-kart across Tombigbee bridge
jambed under a pulpwood rig;
camoed Kip in a burned-out Euphrates Humvee.
And children of the living, windows down, tongues stinging.

Beneath a Brown-Service canopy on folding chairs from church,
aunts light citronella, rehearse the missing, sick, and shut-in.
Out of earshot, spider-veined uncles add a box of Piggly Wiggly salt
to the goobers boiling in a steel pot, noodle washtub ice
for cans of Bud Lite, pledge new lost causes.

Sidling wet broomsedge and cedar I trace the path near the bluff,
follow sweating flagstones inside melting iron fencing.
Lichen claims unknowing names, possums night's persimmons.

Adam Vines

Squatter

In a squatter's heap of trash, I looked for grubs
to fish for bream on beds. Vienna cans
and ripple bottles tossed aside, I dug
through compost only offal and coffee grounds
could make. That sweet death twang pricked up,
the kind of stink you find unspooled across
the logging roads when bucks in rut, thick necks
erect, their senses dulled from estrus in the wind,
would turn their heads and freeze in the headlights' eyes.
I found a nightcrawler, then deeper down,
an open mouth of a minnow trap. I pulled
it free, the belly crushed, a rat snake coiled
inside. Licking the air in frantic swaths,
its tongue, a Bible's ribbon, tasted me.
The snake had shed a skin, the brittle length
half-curled like a mate, a pallid dream.
A couple mouse skulls rattled when I shook
the trap, and tiny vertebrae fell through.
The mice had made the same mistake before
the snake, the opening a vortex. What lured
them to that place, the hole becoming smaller
and smaller until the chicken wire raked across
their backs and they slipped through? And what
would cause the squatter to ditch the minnow trap
(he could have pulled it round again), and what
became of him, the man who squatted on
this square of land when seams of coal went thin?

I want to lie and tell you that I clipped
the wire and let that critter out and watched
it wind away—Rainbow, Rainbow, Rainbow. . . .
But at the time I was a boy with fish
and nothing else much on my mind.
I tossed the trap off to the side without
a care for that rat snake. I found some grubs
and caught some fish.
                    I know now what it's like

to crawl into a hole and hope it will
open to something new but never does
and narrows, scraping up your back. I've seen
the belly crushed. I've curled up in a ball,
while staring at what someone shed for me,
a pallid dream of you who loved me once, the me
who wouldn't cut the wire, the you I left inside.

This Little Piggy

–for Mary

Like a cat lured by its tail,
my daughter doesn't yet know
her feet are hers. She chews
and slobbers on these strange orphans,
slaps them together
as a punished student would
chalkboard erasers.

In her crib, hands clasp feet
in a spire of unstable flesh,
then she plops to one side,
looks at me then doesn't
through the bars as I kneel,
and I see clearly that the red
in my beard is the red in her curls

but also that *my* daughter
is not *mine*, that love is not possession
or a mere pronoun or an apostrophe
in the sympathetic system of language,
that one day she will realize that her feet
conform to *her* will, *her* heart,
and she will walk away from me.

Question from a Bowl of Beans

–for Mary

A bite of beans, a long milk draw, and then
a side glance: "What's it like to be a boy?"
she asked. Tiresias first came to mind,
the mating snakes he struck, the female dead,
his seven years in women's flesh that followed.
Didacticism at its worst, I thought,
especially how to explain his lie
to Hera, pleasures of the wee and woo,
and homosocial bonds, the kind
of myth an eight-year-old like mine would dig
then dig at me until I broke, explaining different parts
and dumbass boys, the birds and bees. My wife
was teaching dance that night and would have struck
me blind if I had gone that way. Instead,
I merely said, "it ain't that bad," a lie
of course, then took another bite of beans.
"The penis seems to be a lot of trouble,"
she said while looking down into her bowl.
And, once again, I thought, *deflect*. I could
bring Nana into play and how at eight
I told my class about my front-tail, unzipped
my pants to show them when they said I lied,
Miss Walker's scream, the long walk down the hall,
how Nana let me think I had a tail for years,
until that day when I walked home and Daddy
told me about the penis, the stiff-tailed ways.
I knew "it ain't that bad" would hardly do for this.
I said, "you're right—it is a lot of trouble. Stay away."

Maintenance for the Heartbroken

Consider the houses we put together,
the maintenance we do and don't do,
the rotten eaves replaced, the shutters
that a friend half-scraped three years ago
before the night took him back
to needling that vein he thought he'd closed.
Consider the toilets we spray with blue
then flush down, the ball of our love's hair
we snake up from the shower drain
and lift in a pinch of nape
as if it were a mouse. Consider what we see now
at 2:00 a.m. in the kitchen, the grout
we might or might not finally clean; the bond
that holds this floor together will remain,
soiled or not, we know. Consider the neighbor's generator
still chugging after they have long gone to bed,
though the power to our houses is back on.
Consider the meat and milk that didn't go bad.
We will hear the engine sputter and cease before dawn.
Consider the storm that dumped nine inches
of snow in Lubbock, Texas today, yes, Texas.
Consider the woman in Montana tonight
curled into the hollow spoon of her husband
after telling him of her affair.
Consider her lover as merely a context
for another repair. Consider finding ourselves
not as agency but as a slow cracking of our shells
from the weather of our lives.
Consider a sand dune that takes its shape
when the clouds drift, allowing the moon
to untuck its light. Consider how the clouds
seem to occupy the same space
as that moon, despite their distance,
how we distinguish liquids, solids, gases
by their properties, their distances apart,
the way they veil and unveil themselves to us,
though, at times, like tonight, we find
in our chests that they must be compliant
to their elemental change
but at their core are just the same.

My Father's Rod: Fishing the Skinny Moon

—in memory of Vann Allen Vines

While waiting on the Opelousa bite,
or channel cats would do, our fingertips
plucking our fishing lines below the first
eyes, twitching livers we had hooked and cast
into the river's craw, my father would
relax, the only time I witnessed this.
He'd stretch his legs and dig his heels
and match a Lucky Strike to life. He'd drag
and exhale that the night had pocketed
the moon; the cats would bite. We'd be all right.
I'd dig in deep like him and hum a hymn
I still don't know the name of—nor did he,
I don't believe—but in that dark, that settling
loam and that Alabama clay, that hymn
was ours, and God was there, or not. It didn't matter.
The bills were paid. He held his rod. He'd be all right.

Jason Gordy Walker

Elegy for a Friend

Unlaced and stale, his boots lounge
on the ruffled mat, their toes a rusty orange
like the light that slinks
around the corner where a door closes,
a mirror slants. Tonight, on the lake
behind the house,
the wind is not the wind.

Half-moon. A plane billows the blue.
B minor clouds the horizon.

You are alone, paddling an old boat
whose owner doesn't paint anymore.
He doesn't daub the calm in your face
as you palm the rain,
nor contort your posture.

Only, now and then, a whistle stretching
like a contrail.

He said the wind would wrinkle the water,
but the wind is not the wind.

For the Woman Whose Name I Forget

In Bombay, millions
of people breathe. An old man
inhales the remains
of a blemished sky while a pregnant
girl mutters goodbye. But in my small
Alabama town, at midnight, nothing moves
except my fingers across the keyboard. Last month,
a woman—whose name I forgot—was shot
six times in the abdomen.

Her son might have done it.
Come Sunday, I'll pray
just like the preacher
tells me to. For now, leaves crackle
under my feet
as a train rushes through the night
toward a damp city. Maybe her name is
on a wall somewhere,
sprayed in hollow letters.

Villanelle in Blue

I always hear the color blue at night
(our waltzing feet, my drowsy hands upon you)
before I down my pills and flip the light.

Obscured with moss, the trees encircled a dike,
like early years of sleep. I hate—like you—
to always hear the color blue at night:

the foaming waterfalls or waves that strike.
I almost touched a planet or star (or you?)
before I downed my pills and flipped the light.

The smartest man I've ever known, unlike
the wisest man you knew, will never know you
had always heard the color blue at night.

I laugh at a void that lingers within sight;
my life returns to dust (and where are you?)
before I down my pills and flip the light.

An aura—white and overarching—a weight
prevents my dance from reaching God or you,
and still I hear the color blue at night
before I down my pills and flip the light.

Ode to a Dog Park

On a Sunday at the dog park when no dogs sniffed rumps and the ditzy squirrels
cracked nuts, I sat on a metal bench listening to the conspiracy of the birds

as people came and went—a pair of power-walking grandmothers, a giggling
yuppie couple, a bronzed woman in jalapeño hot-shorts, a texting, weed-sticky student—

while a sedan coughed its way up the hill in front of me, and I thought of Peace,
that blur of white noise people kill for, that space with no boundaries, no figures,

not even trees, until a limb snapped, fell into a pile of red-orange leaves, and I saw
the trees around me, some oak, some whose names I didn't know and still don't,

their bark grooving, their roots rippling above the ground, and now some limbs
slumped their dark green leaves down in what looked like surrender. I, too, surrendered

to their tilting in the sweet breeze, which brought with it the scent of sawdust
and chopped grass blades that I passed earlier on my stroll here. Then

the crickets sang enormous hymns to themselves, the music sneaking
into my skull, doing away with thought, doing away with the anxiety of thinking

about thought. I had been rattling my gears for weeks, cranking away
just to crank away, but this, this sitting on a bench at the start of September as the 5pm

sunlight warmed the upper fullness of the leaves, this quiet, this cooling air was enough
to help me forget the onslaught of mosquitoes to come, the losing of blood, the thirst.

Richard Weaver

Blessing and release

Blood was the first priest,
the body's primal paint,
and fire its besotted bishop.
The fleshless amber of miracles.

Water became carpenter
of rock and wood, an anodyne
of age. Wedge and fist.
Archangel of unspeakable mercy.

Air emptied the world
into a bucket of parables
with fountains of singing fish
accompanied by the atonal
cries of anorexic angels.

Wind and its significant other,
its partner, rain, came around
asking for indulgences but were denied
by the sun's absolute whiteness.
Had they dreamed at dawn
the trees might have bled tears.
But, instead, they grew silent,
hardened to resin.

Slowly the earth yields
its hieroglyphs of shadows
and spreads wide
the comfort of its grief,
resigned to desire
and the shuddering
the lost body the loveless
anxiety of obliquity.

This dark Heaven

What trees have survived
the daily shelling now bow
in respect this bleak September.
My friend, August Macke has died.
Dead in Champagne.
Dead in senseless war.
August dead in September.
Only two months of war,
and the body count
includes my brother painter.
Conscripted. Too young.
Too foolish. Inspired like me
by the temptations of language
and rhetorical paroxysms.
His last painting, oil on cardboard:
Farewell. A cloudy morning.
Faceless women and children,
and a pet dog sniffing
the way a dog does best.
And at the right edge
the backs of men turned away,
not spineless, not afraid.
Simply wearied by light.

Afternoon of enigmas

The blackened forest is white with ash.
A red-winged blackbird burns dark blue
in protest against the sun's yellowing claim
to life. Its future claims to death.

The search for the painter who found you,
who was stolen and then lost
but unlike you was destroyed;
the false light of day cannot be extinguished.

I see one thing and paint another.
My eyes, my hands, the finite.
Paints do what they can. The last window
of morning ignites the walls beyond.

Whatever I find is destroyed
destroys itself each time I paint or write.

The lingering color of the bee
deafens whatever song light may buzz.

Afternoon light changes its mind
and refocuses on red sun's hammering,
ignoring for now the new century's
enigmatic pulse. Pride's false hope.
Ambition's gypsy wife.

Show me a color that raises a man
and raises my friend, August
from the unseeable light.
Show me that color
my hand's invisible dream
in the tidal dawn of September's stars.
Show me that color and I will cover
the twisted earth with every tone
every shade every variation to undo his death.
Light as deaf as wind swells the dark red river Meuse.
Without the flight of birds nothing reflects.
Nothing hovers in no man's land, struck down
in the amber of dawn.

Stranger's Lament

A blue shadow mimics
its bruised cloud cousin.

No Moses looking for a mountain.
No mountain monk seeking shelter

in the darkened valley below.
Because yellow can never see red,

and red will always envy blue;
and green, don't even ask about green;

because the marriage of pure colors
can never be, and the marriage

of true hues obscures the eye,
there are dreams leaving the body

untethered   to dance naked in trees
whose leaves laugh when the wind stumbles.

Because never is the ultimate curse
offered as the last prayers of the damned,

the black mirror's lies go unquestioned:
the length of light across the earth,

and the hunted dead of Verdun,
one falling body becoming another,

swimming in death as never in life,
your husband breathless beneath a green sun.

Reconnaissance

When the call comes this morning, I ride
as I have ridden these past months
along the river Meuse, new coordinates
buzzing around my head like hot orange hornets
beguiled by a relentless Spring.
I answer as I have these past two years.

Beneath hardened layers there remains
another skin spotted with darkness. A deaf monk
kneels in an intaglio of leaden prayers, whispering.
Holy deep blue timelessness Holy Hell on earth.
This broken mutilated earth.

Where trees once greened upright and shadows fell,
we slip past the tenuous light. We trust the compass's
true North but find no hope in the cloudless sky,
no joy in the steady, ritual march.

The next letter home I write erases my hand.
A fire melts painlessly in the window.
Your smile explodes in delight and shadow,
the hungry focus of color fills my eyes as the wind
echoes budding branches. I squint into my field glasses,
narrowing the field of light, my brown eyes
unaccustomed to such filtering.

Nothing in the distance is tethered
to the ongoing mystery my eyes insist
blooms in the valley below:
an undiminished rushing in the heedless rain.

Patti White

Weeks Bay

Down in the pitcher plant bog where slash pines.
Down in the estuary where shrimp and oysters.

A heron seen from beneath the waterline. Wings
like clouds passing over the sun as we look up
through seagrass, ask everyone for directions,
how to find the surface or how to read the light.

Out in the gulf the drowned forest smothered
in anemones like a memory of frost. The world
colder once and cypress clinging to mudbanks
miles from the barrier dunes. Then came water.

We are water all the way through I know and
we rise with the moon or fall into sea caves of
loss, suffer the tides inside our skulls, seek
shelter from the braided currents of confusion.

We are water and wear the ocean on our skin,
our thoughts swimming in salted blood, traces
of minerals floating like continents in our eyes.

Deep in the cypress forest beneath the salt
and silt, beneath the precious bark, behind
the nest the octopus has built, our dead
souls gather like crabs and pick each other
down to the bleached bones of time.

Deep in the pitcher plant bog the ants
crawling on the rim of cupped petals.

The estuary riffled by wind over reeds.

Red shrimp breeding. The oysters, as always,
silent. Keeping watch over pearls.

Sestina: Kentucky 1970

Do you remember a hint of musk
from a roadside skunk, the maples
turning silver before the rain, my eyes
hard and green like Amazon granite?
A shot of Wild Turkey vintage glass
and the way my thighs took hold

of yours as we leaned into the hold
a motorcycle cuts into curves, musk
rising from our own sweat. The glass
of our skin a mirror for the maples,
the road a limestone and granite
geology of time. You said my eyes

were like grass. I thought my eyes
made fieldstone fences to hold
race horses, creeks with granite
water, my uncle's trotlines for musk-
rats, the black and white maple
trees looming. I had a glass

full of images like your sunglasses
fell into the septic tank, like eye-
witnesses to pancakes with maple
syrup and Keeneland tickets to hold,
two dollar win place or show, Musk
Dancer or a horse named Granite.

Where the river cut, a granite
bridge. Bourbon in a short glass
and you said it tasted of musk
of oak of tobacco like your eyes
just that brown and I could hold
that memory until every maple

makes spinners in spring. Maple
fudge ice cream after the granite
of Steppenwolf, remember? Hold
the lilac vase and the cut-glass
perfume bottle, smoke-filled eyes,
and slice what my dad called musk-

melon. The silver maple and the glass
of bourbon, granite river stones, the eyes
of old horses. Hold that like skunk musk.

Corn Maze

You are not here, says the sign, and she believes it. Such a long time since she has
been anywhere, and what could be more natural than this affirmation in a state so
completely flat and polite? from a field late in the season, its stalks dry and rustling?
A blue sky drones overhead as she makes a left turn and then another. She sees dust
rise from the far reaches, imagines a family lost and panicked, thin blond children,
empty bottles of plastic water. She walks along a curve that spirals back. There is no
shade or there is only shade. The corn occupies a dead spot in the GPS grid or forms
a pattern that can be seen from space. She knows the secrets, has heard the corn
in high summer, a knife-bladed whisper beside the highway, uncanny words green
and serious. She turns left again and still is not there. The sky darkens or shows a
dawning. Another sign offers an arrow that spins. She thinks she might reach the
center in time, or it might be years of cornrows and zombies and kernels dropping
onto the earth like coins.

A Cairn for the Princess

Let she who is without diamonds come forward.

Let her walk naked of light. Rich slate beneath her feet,
the globes in the lobby dimmed, slick ebony crowns inlaid
in the doorway. Her lashes edged in charcoal. She has no
diamonds, let her walk naked in darkness.

Let she who walks naked in darkness come forward, her head
uncovered, her wrists open to the paleness of the dim lobby,
her ankles uncertain on the slate, let her lashes sweep her cheek
like the ashes of stars falling from deep space, let her walk.

Let her walk as if entering a bath, naked in darkness, a towel
slipping from her hip, entering the lobby as if stepping into water,
let her move through charcoal shadows, her lashes sweeping.

Let her walk into the night. Let her sweep through the lobby,
her lashes flirting with her cheeks, let her move in shadow, as if
without diamonds. Let her walk. Let her come forward, let our

diamonds fall upon her like a galaxy splashing into a bath. Let her
walk through the door as if into darkness, into a rain of diamonds,
walk into diamonds as if into rain, as if from darkness, as if stars,

let her walk no more without diamonds, here are our diamonds,
let her come toward us and we will give her diamonds. Let her
walk out of darkness into the light of our diamonds. Let she who
was without diamonds come forward. Let her walk. Let us wait.

Let we who are full with diamonds be generous, let our light
rain down upon her as if droplets of bathwater, lashes falling
startled upon her cheek, let her come toward us in shadow,

let her leave us covered in diamonds, covered in diamonds,
oh let her be buried in diamonds, she who was without, let
her walk out of darkness into the fullness of light.

Thicketty, SC

Folks in Thicketty speak with slow tongues,
move like molasses, grow heavy as bees.
Spider-web accents leave syllables strung

like tendrils of smothering moss. Flat feet
pound in slash-pine pollen, raising dust
that hovers like corn-meal flour; and leaf-

hopper eyes count government surplus
for burley-base boys and soil-bank farmers.
Words in Thicketty come wrapped in burlap,

cotton-mill towels, great bales of grammar;
sentences crawl through summer swelter,
drawling, sprawling, baffled by commas.

Time lingers longer there; vine-draped shelters
house redbone hounds and passenger pigeons;
afternoons stretch like love-languid daughters,

like weed-choked creeks of smoky bourbon,
as poignant as peanuts boiled in the shell.
Oh, thick Thicketty's bulk-balky southern

talk, like sweet pecan pralines that melt
on the tongue, the slow syntax strung
cat-by-catfish on lines, is a hot spell

salt-swallow, a sullen storm, a mush-
mouth, chokecherry, snaggletooth hush.

Jake Adam York

From A Field Guide to Etowah County

Alabama

Bluets, larkspur, common violets in the jimson
and queen-anne's-lace, tangles of boxwood
and honeysuckle and smilax in hydrangea and pine,
thick from which Spring Azures drift,
among the first to emerge, then Swallowtails'
gunmetal iridescence, obsidian-with-stars
wings turning like pages in hands of wind.
Thrashers tear in the leaves for earthworms,
salamanders, some morsel, their stipple
of sunlight-in-leaves blending then reappearing
in a crash of meal. If a snake uncurls,
the bird will leaf it in bibles of territory, protection,
and someone's aunt of grandmother, passing,
will slow to note that summer is on us early.
But this one merely stands, its wing in a ray,
feathers a concrete mottle of grain and pebble
like a roadside table turned into brush long ago.
Here, there is no cankered plum or split persimmon,
sap or juice to bead, mimeograph bright,
on the grass's nibs, and the grass does not whorl
in cursives of moonlight and dark each night,
but this is where they found that postman
from Baltimore, walking his integration letter
to Ross Barnett, three hundred miles to go,
shot in his head and neck, copies of the protest
scattered and streaking in the April dew.
It was September, honeysuckle in full perfume,
the woods a riot of grackles and jays,
when the grand jury broke and let the suspect go.
The facts are simple, my grandfather said,
the D. A. said we couldn't make a case,
so the words they never wrote coiled
in field reports and requisitions, and three days later
a church-bomb in Birmingham
blew the stained-glass face of Christ

313

like a dandelion head in the roadside weeds.
Snakeroot, aster, and blazing star, some
toxic to cows, should not be eaten, though many take
the greens and fruit of poke, more abundant
in Spring, as correctives, small poisons
to set things right. Goldenrod blazes the highway's
shoulders, all the way to Birmingham
or Chattanooga, and starlings gather
like glass, like grackles in the trees, such
sociability an advance of colder weather.
The Swallowtails and Azures have disappeared,
but you may spot the Great Purple Hairstreak
bumbling, slow and easy to observe,
even in the clouds of goldenrod that dust
when they land. The cones are brilliant
but delicate as their gossamer wings. Touch,
and the color's written in your skin.

At Cornwall Furnace

Cherokee County, Alabama

Blown out just after The War.
The stack's granite gapes. Each year
saplings try, as gravity has
longer, a reclamation masonry won't allow.
Lichens and moss do more.

Promises of love and forevers
mural its inside
above constellations of beer cans and glass,
ashes. The lid of sky's diameter
remains the same.

In water only yards away,
confluence of the Coosa and Little Rivers,
mud ebbs from a bed of scoria,
slag I can find in channels
miles south. Algae homes in its pocks.

The friend who has brought me here
stands waist deep in the rivers,
taking pictures
near a deadwood stump
when her feet find something odd.

Together we struggle from the water
a mass of pig-iron the size of a liver.
It's why Noble's men built it.
Probably a product of the last blast.
Too late. We can imagine

the boys who mined and cut the rock,
brought the hematite, ore, and limestone,
the slaves
sweating in their tunnel under the hill,
but do not. We know what fire

will burn here tonight, what
fumes will rise.
Flawless architecture of a monument.
Silent,
we heft the pig and give it back.

Letter to Be Wrapped Around a Bottle of Whiskey

for Bob Morgan

Water so thick
light just stumbles through
the cordials you've poured,
making a welcome table
of the cedar chest
the glasses lens
in some compound eye
to observe the story
of a rug or a plank
or a glass of whiskey.
Body and plant, body
and land. Conversations
are naturalists
or rivers, knowing
the schist and the batholith,
ginseng and Genesis,
gathering as they go.
Rise into the balds,
following streams
to their first ideas,
and the fork of the voice
will tremble, strike rock,
and draw the flood.
As corn, once wheat-thin,
will rise from any ground.
As it holds its sugars,
days it's concentrated
to such brightness
we distill, thought
to form, in the hollows
where we remembered
how to cut cadence
from a limb, a ballad
from a family
tree. As the maker of fire
brings the guitar
and the country song
from a turtle's shell
and the stomach of a lamb.
As what begins anywhere
started already somewhere

else. Here, in the ridge
and valley of voice
where you draw the well of song,
the spring that's warming now
in your talk, maybe
it is snowing now,
and a string band threads
the bruise of night
where windows are
crocuses offering their saffrons
to the cold and the snake-handler's
arms in the one-room church
antennas raised
to the broadcast Christ
the zircon in his pocket
shaking the mustard seed
from the mockingbird,
gospel from the air,
the peavine of melody curling
on his tongue an air
the wanderers know,
having passed mouth
to mouth, over the sea,
guitar to glossolalia
in tangled lines.
As from the stalk
the pone and the potable,
from the blue-hole
the bluegrass and the blues,
you keep pouring,
so conversations are naturalists
and rivers, each step,
each stumble an address
to the ground or the stars,
until we are chests,
until we are rooms,
until we are radios
playing all stations,
a ballad on every one.

THE POETS

PALAVI AHUJA (she/her) is a poet and filmmaker from Birmingham, Alabama. She earned her BA in English w/ a concentration in Literature and a minor in Media Studies from the University of Alabama in Birmingham. She is currently working on her MFA in Poetry from Columbia University School of the Arts in New York City. Palavi's experiences as an Indian woman in America strongly impacts her work, leading to impactful stories of her cultural identity and family history. Her poetry is featured in University of Central Missouri's literary journal of new writing and reviews, *Pleiades*.

DANIEL ANDERSON'S work has appeared in *Harper's*, *The New Republic*, *The Kenyon Review*, *New England Review*, *The Yale Review*, *Poetry*, *The Southern Review*, *The Sewanee Review*, *The Best American Poetry* and *Southwest Review* among other places. His three books of poetry include *The Night Guard at the Wilberforce Hotel*, *Drunk in Sunlight*, and *January Rain*. He teaches in the Creative Writing Program at the University of Oregon.

LANA K. W. AUSTIN is the author of the novel *Like Light, Like Music* (West Virginia University Press). Austin's writing has been in *Mid-American Review*, *Columbia Journal*, *Sou'wester*, etc. Winner of the 2019 Alabama State Poetry Society Book of the Year Award, a 2019 Hackney Poetry Award, the 2018 Words & Music Poetry Award & the *Still: The Journal*'s Judge's Choice Story Award, Austin has been a finalist & semi-finalist in many other competitions. Her MFA is from GMU. Austin's poetry collection, *Blood Harmony*, is from Iris Press. A Pushcart nominee, Austin teaches creative writing at the University of Alabama in Huntsville and is in the Peauxdunque Writers Alliance.

Born and raised in Birmingham, Alabama, NICK BARNETTE currently lives in Las Vegas, Nevada where he received an MFA in Creative Writing at the University of Nevada, Las Vegas. His work has appeared in *Cold Mountain Review*, *Desert Companion*, and *Nevada Humanities*. He has upcoming work appearing in *Grist* and *Southland Alibi*.

CAROLINE PARKMAN BARR is a graduate of the MFA Writing Program at the University of North Carolina at Greensboro, where she served as Poetry Editor of *The Greensboro Review*. Her poetry was awarded an Honorable Mention in the 2022 *Spoon River Poetry Review* Editor's Prize, and appears in *Best New Poets*, *Four Way Review*, *The Pinch*, *RHINO*, *South Carolina Review*, *NELLE*, and elsewhere. She lives in Birmingham, Alabama.

GABRIELLE BATES is the author of *Judas Goat* (Tin House 2023). Originally from Birmingham, Alabama, she currently lives in Seattle, where she works for Open Books: A Poem Emporium and co-hosts the podcast The Poet Salon. Her poems have appeared in the *New Yorker*, *Ploughshares*, *Poetry*, *APR*, *BAX: Best American Experimental Writing*, *Catapult*, and elsewhere. She teaches occasionally through Hugo House and the University of Washington Rome Center.

JOHN BENSKO'S four books of poems include *Green Soldiers* (Yale UP, 1980, winner of the Yale series of Younger Poets Prize), *The Waterman's Children* (U of Massachusetts P, 1994), *The Iron City* (U of Illinois P, 2000), and *Visitations* (U of Tampa P, 2014, winner of the Anota Claire Scharf Award. He is Professor Emeritus at the U of Memphis and lives in Rapidan, VA with his wife, the fiction writer Cary Holladay.

RANDY BLYTHE lives on the family farm in Etowah County, Alabama. His first full-length collection, *The Human Part*, was published in 2014 by FutureCycle Press, and his second, *The Wish Furnace*, was released in April of 2023. His poems have appeared in a number of publications, among them *Tar River Poetry*, *Chicago Quarterly Review*, *Aji*, *Pleiades*, and *Northwest Review*.

EMMA BOLDEN is the author of a memoir, *The Tiger and the Cage: A Memoir of a Body in Crisis* (Soft Skull Press, 2022) and the poetry collections *House Is An Enigma* (Southeast Missouri State University Press, 2018), *medi(t)ations* (Noctuary Press, 2016) and *Maleficae* (GenPop Books, 2013). The recipient of a Creative Writing Fellowship from the NEA, her work has appeared in *The Norton Introduction to Literature*, *The Best American Poetry*, *The Best Small Fictions*, *Poetry Daily*, and *Verse Daily*.

TABITHA CARLSON BOZEMAN lives in the foothills of the Appalachians on Lookout Mountain in Gadsden, AL with her husband, children, and 93-year-old grandmother. Her poetry explores the intersections of her life as domestic violence survivor, mother, educator, and mental health advocate. An English Instructor at Gadsden State Community College, Ms. Bozeman is also editor of the *Cardinal Arts Journal*. She received her BA in English from Jacksonville State University, and her MA in English from the University of Alabama at Birmingham. She is currently completing an EdD from Sam Houston State University. She previously co-founded the Riverside Writers Group, and has been published in the *Birmingham Arts Journal*, *Southern Women's Review*, *Mud Season Review*, and *HERE Poetry Journal*, among others.

SHANNON BRADT is a person who lives in Alabama and writes poetry. Nothing else is known about her.

TINA MOZELLE BRAZIEL won the Philip Levine Prize for Poetry for *Known by Salt* (Anhinga Press). She has also been awarded an Alabama State Council on the Arts Literary Fellowship, the first Magic City Poetry Festival eco-poetry fellowship, and an artist residency at Hot Springs National Park. She earned her MFA at the University of Oregon. She directs the Ada Long Creative Writing Workshop for high school students at the University of Alabama at Birmingham. She and her husband, novelist James Braziel, live and write in a glass cabin that they are building by hand on Hydrangea Ridge.

Poet and critic JOEL BROUWER is the author of the collections *Exactly What Happened*, *Centuries*, *And So*, and *Off Message*. He teaches literature and writing at the University of Alabama.

Dr. TAYLOR BYAS, Ph.D. (she/her) is a Black Chicago native currently living in Cincinnati, Ohio, where she is an Acquisitions Editor for *Variant Literature* and an Assistant Features Editor for *The Rumpus*. She is the 1st place winner of the 2020 Poetry Super Highway, 2020 Frontier Poetry Award for New Poets Contests, and the 2021 Adrienne Rich Poetry Prize, and a 2023-24 National Book Critics Circle Emerging Fellow. She is the author of the chapbooks *Bloodwarm* and *Shutter*, and the debut full-length *I Done Clicked My Heels Three Times* from Soft Skull Press. She is represented by Rena Rossner of the Deborah Harris Agency.

DAVID CASE was born in Birmingham and received his B.A. from the University of Alabama in 1982. He later earned a Ph.D. in English from UCLA, and he died of a heart attack in Gainesville, Florida, in 2011, at the age of 49. He is the author of *The Tarnation of Faust* (Gunpowder Press, 2014).

SHELLY STEWART CATO'S writing has recently appeared or is forthcoming in *Rattle*, *Poet Lore*, *Washington Square Review*, *Harpur Palate*, and *New Ohio Review*. She lived in the Mississippi Delta for twenty-five years and now lives and writes near the Warrior River in Walker County, Alabama. She is passionate about genre bending and short forms, blurring lines between truth and imagination. She is passionate about loving humans in this space in this now.

ALYX CHANDLER (she/her) is a writer from the South who received her MFA in poetry at the University of Montana, where she taught composition and creative writing. She lives in Chicago and works as a poet-in-residence for the Chicago Poetry Center, as well as a remote workshop facilitator for Free Verse Writing Project, which hosts workshops for Montana children who are incarcerated or reside in psychiatric in-patient centers. She is a reader for *Electric Literature* and *Poetry Northwest*, and a former poetry editor for *CutBank*. Her poetry can be found in *Cordella Magazine*, *Greensboro Review*, *SWWIM*, *Anatolios Magazine*, *Sweet Tree Review*, and elsewhere.

Originally from Birmingham, Alabama, CARRIE CHAPPELL is the author of *Loving Tallulah Bankhead* (Paris Heretics, 2022) and *Quarantine Daybook* (Bottlecap Press, 2021). Currently, she teaches at Conservatoire national des arts et métiers (CNAM) and serves as editor-in-chief of *Verse of April*, the digital anthology of homage to the poets. Some of her recent individual poems have appeared in *Iron Horse Literary Review*, *Juke Joint*, *Nashville Review*, *Redivider*, and *SWIMM*. Her lyric and book essays have been published in *DIAGRAM*, *Fanzine*, *New Delta Review*, *The Iowa Review*, *The Rumpus*, *The Rupture*, and *Xavier Review*. She lives in Paris, France.

ROBERT COLLINS has published poems in various literary magazines, including *Ascent*, *Cimarron Review*, *Louisville Review*, *Connecticut Review*, *Southern Humanities Review*, *Prairie Schooner*, *Shenandoah*, *Southern Poetry Review*, and *Tar River*. He has received two Individual Artists Fellowships from the Alabama State Council on the Arts, been nominated for a Pushcart Prize several times, received the Ascent Award for Poetry, and won the Tennessee Chapbook Prize. He taught American literature and creative writing at the University of Alabama in Birmingham for thirty years where he founded and then edited *Birmingham*

Poetry Review for twenty years and directed the creative writing program for a decade. He is the author of seven books of poetry, including *Naming the Dead* (FutureCycle Press 2012) and, most recently, *Drinking with the Second Shift* (Word Tech 2017).

H. M. COTTON is the managing editor of *Birmingham Poetry Review*, contributing editor for *NELLE*, and production manager for both journals. Her writing appears in places such as *Greensboro Review*, *Poetry South*, and *SmokeLong Quarterly*. She is the founding director of the SPARK Writing Festival and teaches at the University of Alabama at Birmingham.

Raised in the Appalachian South and now living in Southern California with another writer and two feline boys, CHELLA COURINGTON is a writer/teacher whose poetry and fiction appear in numerous anthologies and journals including *DMQ Review*, *The Los Angeles Review*, and *New World Writing*. Her recent collections of poetry are *Good Trouble* (Origami Poems Project) and *Hell Hath* (Maverick Duck Press). *Lynette's War*, a micro-chapbook, was issued by Ghost City Press.

T. CRUNK, winner of the 1994 Yale Series of Younger Poets Prize and former writer-in-residence at the Alabama Writers' Forum "Writing our Stories" project, is the author of *Living in the Resurrection*, *New Covenant Bound*, *Biblia Paupernum*, and *Parables and Revelations*. He lives in St Louis, Missouri.

LAURA DAVENPORT is the author of *Dear Vulcan* (LSU Press) and the chapbook *Little Hates* (Dancing Girl Press). She received an MFA in poetry from Virginia Commonwealth University and has taught creative writing and composition in various places. Her poems have appeared in *Boulevard Magazine*, *Best New Poets 2009*, *Crab Orchard Review*, *Tinderbox Poetry Journal*, and *Connotation Press: An Online Artifact*, among others. She is the recipient of a Hackney Literary Award, James River Writers/*Richmond Magazine* Best Poem award, and a *Meridian* Editors' Choice award. She serves on the board of Seersucker Live, Inc., a nonprofit promoting literary events and community in Savannah.

DANIEL DEVAUGHN is a writer and teacher from Birmingham, Alabama. His poems appear or are forthcoming in *The Adroit Journal*, *Southern Humanities Review*, *The Nashville Review*, and *Poets.org*. He has received fellowships from the University of Oregon and the Vermont Studio Center, scholarships from the Sewanee Writers' Conference and Norman Mailer Writers Colony, and an Academy of American Poets Prize. He is currently a Voertman-Ardoin Teaching Fellow at the University of North Texas, where he is pursuing a PhD in creative writing.

WILL JUSTICE DRAKE lives in north Alabama, where he teaches English literature and coaches soccer. His poems and articles have appeared or are forthcoming in *Mid/South*, *the Dead Mule School of Southern Literature*, *Flyway*, *Trinity House Review*, *Poetry South*, *Raleigh Review*, and others. He received his MFA from North Carolina State University.

ANSEL ELKINS was born in Anniston, Alabama, of a mother who is half Puerto Rican and a father who was the son of sharecroppers. She spent most of her childhood in Talladega County. She earned her BA from Sarah Lawrence College and MFA from the University of North Carolina at Greensboro. Her first collection, *Blue Yodel* (2015), won the Yale Younger Poets Prize, selected by Carl Phillips. Her poems have appeared in magazines and journals such as *The American Scholar*, *The Believer*, *Oxford American*, *Virginia Quarterly Review*, *Guernica*, *Best New Poets*, *Gulf Coast*, and *Southern Review*, among others. Elkins is the recipient of a "Discovery"/*Boston Review* Poetry Prize, and has received fellowships from the American Antiquarian Society, the North Carolina Arts Council, the National Endowment for the Arts, Bread Loaf Writers' Conference, and Lighthouse Works. She lives in Lexington, Kentucky, where she is currently Visiting Assistant Professor of Creative Writing at Berea College.

KRISTIN ENTLER was diagnosed with cystic fibrosis at 6 months old, and first came out as LGBT+ several years after her diabetes diagnosis at 12 years old. She currently serves as Poetry Editor for *NELLE*, as Access Coordinator for Open Mouth Literary Center, and lives with her service-dog, Azzie, whose name is short for the Greek God of Medicine. Entler can be found in publications such as *The Bitter Southerner*, *Gulf Stream Literary Magazine*, *Porter House Review*, and *BOOTH* among others, as well as on twitter @findmycure.

WILLIAM FARGASON is the author of *Velvet* (Northwestern University Press, 2024) and *Love Song to the Demon-Possessed Pigs of Gadara* (University of Iowa Press, 2020). His poetry has appeared in *Ploughshares*, *The Threepenny Review*, *Prairie Schooner*, *New England Review*, *The Cincinnati Review*, *Narrative*, and elsewhere. He has an MFA in poetry from the University of Maryland and a PhD in poetry from Florida State

University. He lives with himself in College Park, Maryland.

KATE GASKIN is the author of *Forever War* (YesYes Books 2020), winner of the Pamet River Prize. Her poems have appeared or are forthcoming in *The American Poetry Review, The Southern Review, Guernica*, and *Ploughshares* among others, and her work has been anthologized in the *2019 Best American Nonrequired Reading*. She has received support from the Sewanee Writers' Conference and the Vermont Studio Center and is a poetry editor for *The Adroit Journal*. Currently, she is a PhD student in poetry at the University of Nebraska-Lincoln where she is also a writing instructor.

JULIANA GRAY is the author of three poetry collections, including *Honeymoon Palsy* (Measure Press 2017). Her poems have appeared in *Best American Poetry, The Cincinnati Review, The Hopkins Review*, and elsewhere; her humor writing appears irregularly in *McSweeney's Internet Tendency*. An Alabama native, she lives in western New York and teaches at Alfred University.

REGAN GREEN recently received her MFA from the Writing Seminars at Johns Hopkins University. She is now a junior lecturer there and the Assistant Editor of the *Birmingham Poetry Review*.

A native of Miami, Florida with ancestral roots in Alabama, Georgia, Mississippi and the Bahamas, SHARONY GREEN uses interdisciplinary approaches to teach History at the University of Alabama. Her recent honors include the 2020 PEN America Jean Stein Grant for Literary Oral History. She has written four books including *Cuttin the Rug Under the Moonlit Sky: Stories and Drawings About a Bunch of Women Named Mae* (Anchor, 1997), which included poetry. Her next book *The Chase and Ruins: Zora Neale Hurston in Honduras* will be published by Johns Hopkins University Press. A documentarian, Green also co-directed and co-produced a documentary about Grant Green, the late jazz guitarist and her former father-in-law.

THEODORE HADDIN, former director of the UAB Haddin Forum for the Arts and Sciences, is a poet, editor, musician, and Emeritus Professor from the University of Alabama at Birmingham. His publications include a chapbook, *The River and the Road*, and a book, *By a Doorway, in the Garden*. A second book, *The Pendulum Moves Off*, will appear soon. His poems and reviews have appeared widely in the South, Midwest, and West as well as in three anthologies.

AUDREY HALL is a poet, literature scholar, and marine science enthusiast from Mississippi. Her poems appear in *Okay Donkey, Hunger Mountain, Atlanta Review, Cola Literary Review, Alaska Quarterly Review*, and others. In 2022, her poetry was nominated for a Best of the Net Award. She has received her BA in English from the University of Mississippi, her MFA in Creative Writing from the University of Florida, and her MA in English from the University of Alabama.

KATHRYN HARGETT-HSU 徐凯蒂 is the 2023-24 Senior Poetry Fellow at Washington University in St. Louis. Most recently, she received the Academy of American Poets Prize and the Lynda Hull Memorial Poetry Prize. Find her in *Best New Poets, Pleiades, swamp pink, The Margins, Hayden's Ferry Review, Arts & Letters, Muzzle Magazine, TaiwaneseAmerican.org, Cherry Tree*, and elsewhere.

JOSEPH HARRISON was born in Richmond, Virginia, grew up in Virginia and Alabama, and took degrees at Yale and Johns Hopkins. He is the author of five previous books of poetry, including *Someone Else's Name* (2003), *Identity Theft* (2008), and *Shakespeare's Horse* (2015). *Someone Else's Name* was named one of five poetry books of the year by *The Washington Post* and was a finalist for the Poets' Prize; *Shakespeare's Horse* was also a finalist for the Poets' Prize. He has received a Guggenheim fellowship in poetry and an Academy Award in Literature from the American Academy of Arts and Letters, among other honors. Mr. Harrison has directed the Anthony Hecht Poetry Prize since its inception in 2006. He edited *The Hecht Prize Anthology* (2010) and, with Damiano Abeni, *Un mondo che non può essere migliore* (2008), a selection from the poetry of John Ashbery that won a Special Prize from the Premio Napoli. He lives in Baltimore, where he teaches privately and works as an editor.

CAROLYN HEMBREE grew up in Bristol, Tennessee, and Birmingham, Alabama. Her third poetry collection, *For Today*, is forthcoming from LSU Press in Ava Leavell Haymon's Barataria Series. Her poems appear in *Beloit Poetry Journal, New American Writing, The Southern Review, West Branch*, and elsewhere. An associate professor at the University of New Orleans, Carolyn serves as poetry editor of *Bayou Magazine*.

RAYE HENDRIX is a writer from Pinson, Alabama. She is the author of the poetry collection *What Good Is Heaven* (Texas Review Press, 2024) and two poetry chapbooks. Raye is the winner of the Keene Prize for Literature (2019) and *Southern Indiana Review*'s Patricia Aakhus Award (2018), and has been awarded fellowships from Bread Loaf and the Oregon Humanities Center. Their poetry appears in *American Poetry Review*, *Poetry Northwest*, *32 Poems*, and elsewhere. Raye is an editor at *Press Pause Press* and *Dis/Connect: A Disability Literature Column*, and is a PhD candidate at the University of Oregon. rayehendrix.com.

THOMAS ALAN HOLMES grew up in a small north Alabama town and served on *The Black Warrior Review* masthead while a graduate student at the University of Alabama. His research and creative work have appeared in such journals as *Louisiana Review*, *Valparaiso Poetry Review*, *The Connecticut Review*, *Appalachian Heritage*, *Blue Mesa Review*, *Still: The Journal*, and *Appalachian Journal*. Alan and his family live in Johnson City, Tennessee, where he specializes in Appalachian and African American literature as a professor of English at East Tennessee State University. Iris Press released his *In the Backhoe's Shadow*, a poetry collection, in summer 2022.

JENNIFER HORNE served as the twelfth Poet Laureate of Alabama from 2017 to 2021. The author of three collections of poems, *Bottle Tree*, *Little Wanderer*, and *Borrowed Light*, she also has written a collection of short stories, *Tell the World You're a Wildflower*. She has edited or co-edited five volumes of poetry, essays, and stories. Her biography, *Odyssey of a Wandering Mind: The Strange Tale of Sara Mayfield, Author*, is forthcoming from the University of Alabama Press in early 2024. With Jay Lamar, she co-edited *Old Enough: Southern Women Artists and Writers on Creativity and Aging*.

RACHEL HOUGHTON graduated in 2022 from the University of Alabama Birmingham with a Masters in English. Her poetry has appeared in *Aura* and the *Vulcan Historical Review*, and her fiction can be found in *The Great Lakes Review*.

ANDREW HUDGINS was born in Killeen, Texas, in 1951 and educated at Huntingdon College and the University of Alabama. He earned his MFA from the University of Iowa in 1983. His volumes of poetry include *Ecstatic in the Poison* (Overlook Press, 2003); *Babylon in a Jar* (1998); *The Glass Hammer: A Southern Childhood* (1994); *The Never-Ending: New Poems* (1991), a finalist for the National Book Awards; *After the Lost War: A Narrative* (1988), which received the Poetry Prize; and *Saints and Strangers* (1985), which was a finalist for the Pulitzer Prize. He is also the author of a book of essays, *The Glass Anvil* (1997). Hudgins's awards and honors include the Witter Bynner Award for Poetry, the Hanes Poetry Prize, and fellowships from the Bread Loaf Writers' Conference, the Ingram Merrill Foundation, and the National Endowment for the Arts. Hudgins has taught at Baylor University, University of Cincinnati; and Ohio State University.

ELIZABETH HUGHEY is the author of *White Bull* (Sarabande Books), *Sunday Houses the Sunday House* (University of Iowa Press), and *Guest Host* (The National Poetry Review Press). She has received fellowships from the National Endowment for the Arts, the Sustainable Arts Foundation, and the Alabama Council on the Arts. Elizabeth is a co-founder and programming director of the Desert Island Supply Co., a literary arts center in Birmingham, Alabama, where she teaches poetry in Birmingham schools.

ASHLEY M. JONES is the Poet Laureate of the State of Alabama (2022-2026). She is the first person of color and the youngest person to hold this position in its 93 year existence. She holds an MFA in Poetry from Florida International University, and she is the author of *Magic City Gospel* (Hub City Press 2017), *dark // thing* (Pleiades Press 2019), and *REPARATIONS NOW!* (Hub City Press 2021). Her poetry has earned several awards, including the Rona Jaffe Foundation Writers Award, the Silver Medal in the Independent Publishers Book Awards, the Lena-Miles Wever Todd Prize for Poetry, a Literature Fellowship from the Alabama State Council on the Arts, the Lucille Clifton Poetry Prize, and the Lucille Clifton Legacy Award. She was a finalist for the Ruth Lily Dorothy Sargent Rosenberg Fellowship in 2020, and her collection, *REPARATIONS NOW!* was on the longlist for the 2022 PEN/Voelcker Award for Poetry. Jones has been featured on news outlets including *Good Morning America*, *ABC News*, and the BBC. Her poems and essays appear in or are forthcoming at *CNN*, *Poetry*, *The Oxford American*, *Origins Journal*, *The Quarry by Split This Rock*, *Obsidian*, and many others. She co-directs PEN Birmingham, and she is the founding director of the Magic City Poetry Festival. She is the Associate Director of the University Honors Program at UAB, and she is part of the Core Faculty of the Converse University Low Residency MFA Program. She recently served as a guest editor for *Poetry Magazine*. In 2022, she received a Poet Laureate Fellowship from the Academy of American Poets.

RODNEY JONES is the author of eleven books of poetry, including *Salvation Blues* (Houghton Mifflin, 2006), which was shortlisted for the Griffin International Poetry Prize, and *Elegy for the Southern Drawl* (Houghton Mifflin, 1999), which was a finalist for the Pulitzer Prize. He is the recipient of numerous honors, including the National Book Critics Circle Award, the Kenyon Review Award for Literary Achievement, and the Theodore Roethke Prize from Poetry Northwest, as well as fellowships from the National Endowment for the Arts and the John Simon Guggenheim Memorial Foundation. In 2016, he was inducted into the Alabama Writers Hall of Fame.

J. M. JORDAN recently began writing again after a twenty-year hiatus. He is a resident of the Old Dominion and a homicide detective by profession. His poems have appeared in *Arion, Carolina Quarterly, Image Journal, Louisiana Literature, Smartish Pace, The Potomac Review* and elsewhere.

AMELIE LANGLAND is a queer and trans poet who grew up in Alabama. As an MFA candidate in poetry at the University of Arkansas, she won the 2022 Carolyn F. Walton Cole Fellowship in translation. She currently serves as an associate editor at *Iron Horse Literary Review*. Her poetry has appeared, or is forthcoming, in *the minnesota review, Best New Poets 2018, RHINO, Susurrus, Measure Review, Waccamaw, Bayou Magazine, Beyond Queer Words*, and *Poetry South* among others. When she is not teaching or writing, she is most likely watching PBS.

Poet, librarian, raconteur; MATTHEW LAYNE has been poking hornet's nests and looking under rocks for lizards and snakes since he was knee-high to a peanut peg. A founding member of the 1990s improvisational poetry collective, The Kevorkian Skull poets, Layne believes in the radical transformative power found in the intersection of poetry and art, and he wants you to write your truth and share it out loud. A multiple Hackney Award winning writer, he has also been recognized by the National Society of Arts and Letters and been featured in *Peek Magazine, Birmingham Arts Journal, Steel Toe Review, B-Metro,* and elsewhere. His first collection of poetry, *Miracle Strip,* was published by Brick Road Poetry Press in 2023. Look for him at your local library.

QUINN LEWIS's poems appear in the *Southern Review, Cave Wall, Birmingham Poetry Review, Best New Poets,* and elsewhere. She's the recipient of a grant from the Elizabeth George Foundation, a Claudia Emerson Scholarship from the Sewanee Writers' Conference, and *RADAR Poetry's* 2019 Coniston Prize. She teaches in the English Department at SUNY Oneonta.

MCLEOD LOGUE is a poet from Birmingham, Alabama. She received her MFA in poetry from the University of North Carolina Wilmington, where she taught creative writing and read for *Ecotone*. Her work has appeared in *The Nashville Review, Gulf Stream Magazine, The Shore Poetry,* and elsewhere.

MAURICE MANNING has published five books of poetry, including *The Common Man,* which was one of three finalists for the 2011 Pulitzer Prize in Poetry. His first collection, *Lawrence Booth's Book of Visions,* was selected for the 2000 Yale Series of Younger Poets. He has had works in publications including *The New Yorker, Washington Square, The Southern Review, Poetry, Shenandoah,* and *The Virginia Quarterly Review.*

KWOYA FAGIN MAPLES holds an MFA in Creative Writing from the University of Alabama and is a graduate Cave Canem Fellow. Maples is a current Alabama State Council on the Arts Literary Fellow. She is the author of *Mend* (University Press of Kentucky, 2018) a finalist for the 2019 Hurston/Wright Legacy Award for Poetry and finalist for the 2019 Housatonic Poetry award. In addition to a chapbook publication by Finishing Line Press entitled *Something of Yours* (2010) her work is published in several journals and anthologies including *Blackbird Literary Journal, Obsidian, The Langston Hughes Review, Berkeley Poetry Review, The African-American Review, Pluck!, Tin House Review Online* and *Cave Canem Anthology XIII.* Maples is an Assistant Professor of Creative Writing in the MFA program for Creative Writing at the University of Alabama.

JASON MCCALL is the author of the essay collection *Razed by TV Sets* and the poetry collections *What Shot Did You Ever Take* (co-written with Brian Oliu); *A Man Ain't Nothin'; Two-Face God; Mother, Less Child* (co-winner of the 2013 Paper Nautilus Vella Chapbook Prize); *Dear Hero,* (winner of the 2012 Marsh Hawk Press Poetry Prize and co-winner of the 2013 Etchings Press Whirling Prize); *I Can Explain;* and *Silver.* He and P.J. Williams are the editors of *It Was Written: Poetry Inspired by Hip-Hop.* He holds an MFA from the University of Miami. He is a native of Montgomery, Alabama, and he currently teaches at the University of North Alabama.

ROSE MCLARNEY'S collections of poems are *Colorfast, Forage,* and *Its Day Being Gone,* from Penguin Poets, as well as *The Always Broken Plates of Mountains,* published by Four Way Books. She is co-editor of *A Literary Field Guide to Southern Appalachia,* from University of Georgia Press, and the journal *Southern Humanities Review.* Rose has been awarded fellowships by MacDowell and the Bread Loaf and Sewanee

Writers' Conferences; served as Dartmouth Poet in Residence at the Frost Place; and is winner of the National Poetry Series, the Chaffin Award for Achievement in Appalachian Writing, and other prizes. Her poetry and essays have appeared in publications including *American Poetry Review*, *The Kenyon Review*, *The Southern Review*, *New England Review*, *Prairie Schooner*, *Orion*, and *The Oxford American*. Rose is a professor of creative writing at Auburn University.

JAMES MERSMANN taught American literature and poetry writing at the University of Alabama at Birmingham where he won multiple awards for excellence in classroom teaching. Besides articles and poems in various journals, his publications include a literary biography of *Allen Ginsberg* for the Scribner's American Writers series; a study of poets and poetry against the war, *Out of the Vietnam Vortex*; and two books of poems, *The Isis Poems* and *Straying Toward Home*.

DANIEL EDWARD MOORE lives in Washington on Whidbey Island, but is from Selma, Alabama. His poems are forthcoming in *Notre Dame Review*, *The Meadow*, *Southern Humanities Review*, *New Plains Review*, *Temenos Literary Journal*, *Psaltery & Lyre*, *Radar Poetry Journal Plainsongs*, *Flint Hills Review* and *West Trade Review*. His book, *Waxing the Dents*, is from Brick Road Poetry Press. His recent book, *Psalmania* was a finalist for the Four Way Books Levis Prize in Poetry.

JIM MURPHY is the author of four books of poetry: *The Uniform House* (Negative Capability, 2014), *Heaven Overland* (Kennesaw State UP, 2009), *The Memphis Sun* (Kent State UP, 2000), and *Versions of May* (Negative Capability, 2023). His poems have appeared in journals including *Brooklyn Review*, *Cimarron Review*, *Gulf Coast*, *Painted Bride Quarterly*, *Mississippi Review*, *Puerto del Sol*, *Southern Poetry Review*, *The Southern Review*, and *TriQuarterly*. His critical articles have appeared in venues including *Modern Fiction Studies*, *MELUS*, and *Mississippi Quarterly*. He has also translated a chapbook of poems from Spanish, *Amazonia*, by Colombian American poet Juan Carlos Galeano, a portion of which appeared in *Mid-American Review*.

BRIAN OLIU shouts "Roll Tide" at random folks in his current city of Saint Paul, Minnesota. His newest book, *Body Drop: Notes on Fandom and Pain in Professional Wrestling* was released in September 2021 by The University of North Carolina Press. A chapbook with the poet Jason McCall, *What Shot Did You Ever Take*, was released by The Hunger Press in June 2021.

EM PALUGHI was born and raised in coastal Alabama and her poetry is often inspired by the Southern Alabama queer community. She now lives in Nashville, completing her MFA in poetry at Vanderbilt University. She is an editor of poetry and visual art at *Nashville Review* and her poems have appeared or are forthcoming in *Oakland Arts Review*, *The Loch Raven Review*, and *Black Warrior Review*.

CHARLOTTE PENCE's new book of poems, *Code*, received the 2020 Book of the Year award from Alabama Poetry Society and was a finalist for Foreword Reviews Indie Poetry Book of 2020. *Code* details not only the life cycle of birth and death, but also the means of this cycle: DNA itself. Her first book of poems, *Many Small Fires* (Black Lawrence Press, 2015), won Foreword Reviews' silver medal award in poetry. Both poetry books weave together personal experience and scientific exploration. She is also the author of two award-winning poetry chapbooks and the editor of *The Poetics of American Song Lyrics*. A graduate of Emerson College (MFA) and the University of Tennessee (PhD), she is now the director of the Stokes Center for Creative Writing at University of South Alabama.

RUSTY RUSHTON has recently retired from the position he held for the last twenty-five years at UAB as Associate Director of its University Honors Program, which he helped administer and where he lectured on and taught seminars in literature. He lives in Birmingham with his wife, their two cats, and the felt absence of their two children who are no longer children. Every now and again he writes a poem.

JOHN SAAD grew up on Alabama's Gulf Coast, but now lives in Homewood, Alabama. His poetry has appeared in *The Appalachian Review*, *Terrain.org*, *Raleigh Review*, *Hiram Poetry Review*, *The Pinch*, *Poetry South*, and elsewhere. He has contributed book reviews to *Birmingham Poetry Review* and online essays to *AL.com* and *The Progressive*. His chapbook, *Longleaf*, was the winner of the Hopper Poetry Prize and was published in 2017 through Green Writers Press. Besides poetry, John also manages his family's tree farm in Alabama's Black Belt region.

Originally from Birmingham, Alabama, AUSTIN SEGREST teaches at Lawrence University in Appleton, Wisconsin. He's the author of the collection *Door to Remain* (UNT Press, 2022).

JORDAN SHOOP graduated with a Bachelor of Arts in English at Samford University and earned the Vivian Lankford Campbell Creative Writing Award upon graduation. His poem "Tire Swing" won third place in the Northeastern Region of ASFA's Aspiring Minds Poetry Contest, and another poem "The Chamber" was released in Live Poets Society of NJ's "Inside My World." His work can be found in journals such as *In Parentheses*, *Wide Angle*, and *The Elevation Review*. His most recent work has been published in *New Note Poetry*.

LAUREN SLAUGHTER is a NEA Fellow in Poetry, the recipient of a Rona Jaffe Foundation Writers' Award, and author of the poetry collections, *Spectacle* (Panhandler Books) and *a lesson in smallness* (National Poetry Review Press). Her poems, essays, and short stories appear in *Image*, *Harvard Review*, *Tupelo Quarterly*, *Pleiades*, *Kenyon Review Online*, and *32 Poems*, among many other places. She is an associate professor of English at The University of Alabama at Birmingham where she is also Editor-in-Chief of *NELLE*, a literary journal that publishes writing by women. She lives in Birmingham, Alabama with her husband and three children.

R. T. SMITH's collections of poetry include *From the High Dive* (1983), *The Cardinal Heart* (1991), *Hunter-Gatherer* (1996), *Trespasser: Poems* (1996), *Split the Lark: Selected Poems* (1999), *Messenger* (2001), *Brightwood* (2003), *The Hollow Log Lounge* (2003), *Outlaw Style: Poems* (2008), and *Summoning Shades* (2019). He has received grants from the National Endowment for the Arts and the Virginia Commission for the Arts and has won the Cohen Prize from Ploughshares and a Pushcart Prize. Smith has taught at Auburn University and was coeditor of the *Southern Humanities Review*. From 1995 to 2018 he served as editor of *Shenandoah*, the literary magazine from Washington and Lee University in Lexington, Virginia, where he was writer-in-residence in the Department of English.

ANASTASIA SOROCHINSKY is in her second year in the English Language and Literature PhD program at Washington University in St. Louis, where she studies Cold War literature, language politics, and multilingual American fiction. She was born and raised in Birmingham, Alabama. Her work has appeared in publications such as *The Harvard Advocate* and *Birmingham Poetry Review*.

KIMBERLY ANN SOUTHWICK is an Assistant Professor at Jacksonville State University. She holds her PhD from UL Lafayette in English and Creative Writing. She is the founder and editor in chief of the literary-arts journal *Gigantic Sequins*, which has been in print since 2009. Her debut full-length poetry collection, *Orchid Alpha*, was released April 2023 from Trembling Pillow Press. She lives in Saks, Alabama.

CHEYENNE TAYLOR is a poet raised and based in Birmingham, Alabama. She received her BA & MA in English from the University of Alabama at Birmingham and her MFA in poetry from the University of Florida. Her work has appeared in several publications, including *Birmingham Poetry Review*, *Cimarron Review*, *The Cincinnati Review*, *NELLE*, *Poet Lore*, *Raleigh Review*, and the *Times Literary Supplement*.

JEANIE THOMPSON is founding director of the Alabama Writers' Forum, a statewide literary arts service organization, and a poetry faculty member of the Naslund-Mann School of Writing at Spalding University. Jeanie received her M.F.A. in Creative Writing from the University of Alabama and was founding editor of *Black Warrior Review*. She has published five collections of poems and three chapbooks, and has edited a collection of memoirs by Alabama authors, *The Remember Gate*, with Jay Lamar. Her latest work, *The Myth of Water, Poems from the Life of Helen Keller* (UA Press), was a finalist for the 2016 Foreword Indie Poetry Book Awards. Her awards include literature fellowships from the Alabama State Council on the Arts and the Louisiana Arts Council. Her current project is a collection of essays about collaborating with visual artists in Alabama. Her essay, "The Generous Becoming," is forthcoming in *Old Enough: Essays by Southern Women Artists and Writers* from UGA Press in 2024.

Born in Auburn, Alabama, ALLEN TULLOS is co-founder and senior editor of the open access journal *Southern Spaces* and co-director of the Emory Center for Digital Scholarship. His poetry has appeared in numerous publications including the British eco-anthology *Entanglements*, *Common Ground Review*, *Southern Quarterly*, *Broad River Review*, *Scoundrel Time*, *Appalachian Journal*, the *2020 Fish Poetry Anthology*, and the *North Carolina Literary Review*. Professor of history at Emory University, Tullos is the author of two books of American Studies: *Habits of Industry* (winner of the Sydnor Award of the Southern Historical Association) and *Alabama Getaway: The Political Imaginary and the Heart of Dixie*.

ADAM VINES is a professor of English and Director of Creative Writing at University of Alabama at Birmingham, where he edits Birmingham Poetry Review. He is the author of five collections of poetry, the latest, *Lures* (LSU Press, 2022) He has published poems in *The Southern Review, Kenyon Review*, and *Poetry*, among other journals.

JASON GORDY WALKER (he/him) has published poems in *Broad River Review, Cellpoems, Confrontation, Measure, Poetry South, Town Creek Poetry*, and other journals. He holds an MA in English from The University of Alabama-Birmingham, and he is an MFA student in poetry at The University of Florida. A recipient of scholarships from The New York State Summer Writers Institute, Poetry by the Sea: A Global Conference, and The Westchester University Poetry Conference, Walker has placed reviews and interviews in *The Alabama Writers' Forum, Birmingham Poetry Review, Poetry Northwest, Subtropics*, and the blogs of *NewPages* and Dos Madres Press. Born in Brookhaven, Mississippi, Walker was raised in Thomasville, Alabama, and he lived in Birmingham, Alabama for a decade.

RICHARD WEAVER lives in Baltimore City where he volunteers, when possible, with the Maryland Book Bank, CityLit, LightCity, and the Baltimore Book Festival. Post-Covid, he has returned as writer-in-residence at the James Joyce Pub. He's the author of *The Stars Undone* (Duende Press), and provided the libretto for the symphony, *Of Sea and Stars*, performed 4 times to date, 3 times in Alabama, and once at The Julliard School of Music in NYC. He admits to being one of the founders of the *Black Warrior Review*, now 47 years in service, and serving as its PE. His Alabama bona fides: 3 degrees from the U of A. He has published widely: his 1st poem appeared in *Poetry* (April 1975) and most recent in *Granfalloon* (summer 2023). His 200th prose poem since 2016.

PATTI WHITE is the author of four collections of poems, *Tackle Box* (2002), *Yellow Jackets* (2007), *Chain Link Fence* (2013), and *Pink Motel* (2017), all from Anhinga Press. Recent chapbooks include *A is for Aphasia* (2013), *Kontakion* (2014), and *District Flood* (2014). Her poetry has appeared in journals including *Iowa Review, North American Review, River Styx, Nimrod, DIAGRAM, Forklift Ohio, Missouri Review, Parcel, McNeese Review, Slippery Elm, Vine Leaves, Waccamaw*, and *New Madrid*; her nonfiction in *Gulf Coast* and *Mulberry Fork Review*. Her experimental novella *Particularly Dangerous Situation* was published by Arc Pair Press in 2020. A poetry/photography collaboration with the late Gaylin English, *NY/NY*, was published in 2022. She lives in Tuscaloosa, Alabama.

JAKE ADAM YORK authored four books of poems: *Murder Ballads* (Elixir Press, 2005); *A Murmuration of Starlings* (Southern Illinois UP, 2008); *Persons Unknown* (Southern Illinois UP, 2010); and *Abide*, published posthumously by Southern Illinois University Press in 2014. Originally from Alabama, he was educated at Auburn and Cornell. He received fellowships to serve as a Poet in Residence at the University of Mississippi (2009), to serve as the Thomas Visiting Professor in Creative Writing at Kenyon College (2011), and from the Mellon Foundation to serve as a Visiting Faculty Fellow at the James Weldon Johnson Institute for Advanced Study at Emory University (2011-2012). He was also a recipient of a fellowship from the National Endowment of the Arts. At the time of his death in 2012, he was an associate professor of English at the University of Colorado Denver and edited the journal *Copper Nickel*.

ACKNOWLEGMENTS

The editors wish to thank Christina Ellison & Miranda Ramírez for their assistance with this volume.

For contributors who supplied publication information, details are listed below. All poem copyrights have reverted back to respective authors, listed or otherwise, and Texas Review Press has permission to reprint poems included herein.

LANA K. W. AUSTIN: "Blood Harmony" originally appeared in *Columbia Journal*; "Walking the Manassas Battlefield, September 14th, 2001"originally appeared in *Mid-American Review*. **CAROLINE PARKMAN BARR:** "Moorland Hawker Dragonfly" originally appeared in *NELLE*. "Our Communion" originally appeared in *Two Hawks Quarterly*. **GABRIELLE BATES:** All poems are included in the book *Judas Goat* (Tin House, 2023). "Strawberries" and "In the Dream in Which I am a Widow"originally appeared in *The New Yorker*; "Dear Birmingham"originally appeared in the Acadamy of American Poets *Poem-a-Day*; "Sabbath" originally appeared in *Image*; "Anniversary" originally appeared in *New England Review*. **JOHN BENSKO:** "Independent Miner" and "Brookside, Alabama" appeared in *The Iron City* (U of Illinois P, 2000). "Snow Day" appeared in *Visitations* (U of Tampa P, 2014). **RANDY BLYTHE:** "For Aunt Louise, Who Never Liked Me" originally appeared in *Rattle*. "For Aunt Louise, Who Never Liked Me" and "Fluke" appeared in *The Human Part* (FutureCycle, 2014). "Instinct" originally appeared in *Concho River Review*. "Those Many Years" originally appeared in *Meat for Tea*. "Sami Painting" originally appeared in *Pleiades*. "Instinct," "Those Many Years," and "Sami Painting" appeared in *The Wish Furnace* (FutureCycle, 2023). **EMMA BOLDEN:** "Shower Season" appears in *House Is an Enigma* (Southeast Missouri State UP, 2018), reprinted with permission of the publisher. "Shower Season" originally appeared in *Nice Cage* 4, 2017. "Beatitudes" originally appeared in *8 Poems Quarterly* 4.1, 2021. "Hum City" originally appeared in *A Poetry Congeries*, 2018. "Finishing School" originally appeared in *Black Warrior Review* Online, 2018. **TABITHA CARLSON BOZEMAN:** An excerpt of "Sanatoria" part II, as "The Still", was published in *The Cardinal Arts Journal: The SPRING Issue*, 2021. **TINA MOZELLE BRAZIEL:** "Dandelion" originally appeared in *POETRY*, June 2021. "To the Coosa River at Clear Springs Marina and Trailer Court" originally appeared in *Duende*, Fall 2018 and was reprinted in *Known by Salt* (Anhinga 2019). **JOEL BROUWER:** Joel Brouwer, "Lines Written in Memphis Tennesee" from *Off Message*. Originally published in *Slate*. Copyright © 2010, 2016 by Joel Brouwer. Reprinted with permission of The Permissions Company, LLC, on behalf of Four Way Books, fourwaybooks.com. All rights reserved. **TAYLOR BYAS:** "The Black Girl Comes To Dinner" originally appeared in *The Shore*; "A Grocery Store in Alabama"originally appeared in *storySouth*; "Geophagia" originally appeared in *Glass: A Journal of Poetry (Poets Resist)*; "I Don't Care if Mary Jane Gets Saved or Not" originally appeared in *The Chattahoochee Review*; "My Twitter Feed Becomes Too Much" originally appeared in *Frontier Poetry*. **SHELLY STEWART CATO:** "Sonic Madonna, After the Storm" originally appeared in *Poet Lore*, Summer/Fall, 2021. "Maybe, Everything, Rewind, Reverse" originally appeared in *Jabberwock Review* (Winner, 2021 Nancy D. Hargrove Editor's Prize). "Anti-Ode to a Marriage: 'Why Antimatter Matters'" originally appeared in *Washington Square Review*, Fall 2022. "Snapchat at the Magical Arctic Puffin Exhibit" originally appeared in *New Ohio Review*, 2022. "Mega-" originally appeared in *Rattle*, 2020. **ALYX CHANDLER:** "Curses" originally appeared in *The Shore*, Issue 14. **CARRIE CHAPPELL:** "Windows" and "Lifeboat" originally appeared in the book *Loving Tallulah Bankhead* (Paris Heretics, 2022). **H. M. COTTON:** "Asterism" originally appeared in *The Greensboro Review*, Fall 2018. "Play the Line" and "Library: the week after my father's death" originally appeared in *Poetry South*, Fall 2018. "Honeysuckle" was the 2nd place winner of the 2021 Hackney Literary Award national poetry contest. **CHELLA COURINGTON:** "Lynette's War" originally appeared in *Amaryllis* (August 1, 2016) and *The Journal of Radical Wonder* (May 20, 2022). **T. CRUNK:** "Visiting the Site of One of the First Churches My Grandfather Pastored" and "Redemption" appeared in *Living in the Resurrection* (Yale UP, 1995). "from Summons" and "Prayer" appeared in *New Covenant Bound* (UP of Kentucky, 2010). "Ars Poetica" appeared in *Biblia Paupernum* (Accents Publishing, 2013). **LAURA DAVENPORT:** Davenport, Laura. "Quitting,"

"Why We Don't Write about Kudzu," "Porpoises," "Reconsider the Western." *Dear Vulcan*, Louisiana State University Press, 2020 "Love Poem as a Snake" originally appeared in *Boulevard*, Spring 2021. **WILL JUSTICE DRAKE**: "Intercession" originally appeared in *Trinity House Review*, #01: Michaelmas, 2020. **ANSEL ELKINS**: "Native Memory" originally appeared in Poem-a-Day, Academy of American Poets, 2016. "Blood on Your Saddle" originally appeared in *The Feminist Wire*, 2011. "Tornado" appeared in *Blue Yodel* (Yale University Press, 2015). **KRISTIN ENTLER**: "Injection Training" originally appeared in *Armstrong Literary*, Summer 2022. "A Tickle in Her Throat" originally appeared in *Citron Review*. **WILLIAM FARGASON**: "When My Father Tells Me My Great-Grandfather was in the KKK," "My Father's College Roommate," and "Sugar" were published in *Love Song to the Demon-Possessed Pigs of Gadara* (University of Iowa Press, 2020). "Sugar" was published by the Academy of American Poets on their website *Poets.org* in 2015. "When the Cop Tells Us" originally appeared in *The Boiler*, September 2021. **KATE GASKIN**: "A Small Sample of Snakes I Have Known" originally appeared in *The Southern Review* (Summer 2019). "Postpartum" originally appeared in *War, Literature and the Arts* (June 2019) and in *Forever War* (2020). "Ghazal for Alabama" originally appeared in *Alaska Quarterly Review* (Spring 2018) and in *Forever War* (2020). "Bad Fruit" originally appeared in *Cimarron Review* (Summer 2016) and in *Forever War* (2020). "Landscape with Logging Trucks and Invasive Species" originally appeared in *MumberMag* (Winter 2020). **JULIANA GRAY**: "Honeymoon Palsy" appeared in *Honeymoon Palsy* (Measure Press, 2017). "In Andalusia" originally appeared in *NELLE*, Issue Two, 2019. "A Trick of the Light" originally appeared in *Waccamaw*, No. 18, 2017. "Nobody's Mother" originally appeared in *The Chattahoochee Review*, Vol. 34, Nos. 2 & 3, 2019/20. **THEODORE HADDIN**: "Thoughts on the Mona Lisa" originally appeared in *Valley Voices*. "Grandpa Wears Neckties" originally appeared in *Poetry South*. "Van Gogh's Poem" will appear in *The Pendulum Moves Off* (Madville Publishing, 2023). **KATHRYN HARGETT-HSU**: "Petition for Naturalization" originally appeared in *Arts & Letters*. "Internal Dissident" originally appeared in *Crazyhorse*, no. 102. "At the Center of the Laogai 余烬" originally appeared in *TaiwaneseAmerican.org*. "Dark Peak" originally appeared in *Poets.org*. **JOSEPH HARRISON**: "Air Larry" appeared in *Someone Else's Name* (Waywiser, 2003); reprinted in *180 More Extraordinary Poems for Every Day* (Random House); *Poetry: A Pocket Anthology* (Penguin); *Literature: A Pocket Anthology* (Penguin). "Shakespeare's Horse" originally appeared on *Poets.org* and in *Shakespeare's Horse* (Waywiser, 2015). "Dr. Johnson Rolls Down a Hill" originally appeared in *The New Criterion* and in *Shakespeare's Horse* (Waywiser, 2015). "Mark Strand" originally appeared in *The New York Review of Books* and in *Sometimes I Dream That I Am Not Walt Whitman* (Waywiser, 2020). "To My Friends" appeared in *Identity Theft* (Waywiser, 2008). **CAROLYN HEMBREE**: "Ghazal for the Nomad" originally appeared in *New American Writing*, Issue 39. "A Cutter's Sestina (Prom '95)" originally appeared in *Contrary*, Winter/Spring 2017. "La Dictée" and "Prayer" originally appeared in *Beloit Poetry Journal*, Volume 71, No. 1 (Spring 2021). "Nocturne" originally appeared in *Mississippi Review*, Issue 46, 1&2 (Summer 2018). **RAYE HENDRIX**: "Pinson" originally appeared in *Columbia Poetry Review*, Issue 33, Fall 2020. "At Toomer's Corner, the Morning After the Iron Bowl (2019)" originally appeared in *The McNeese Review*, Winter 2020. "Blood in the Milk" originally appeared in *Southern Indiana Review*, Spring 2018. **THOMAS ALAN HOLMES**: "Belvedere" originally appeared in *Town Creek Poetry* 5.2 Fall 2011. "On Homer's Fox Hunt" originally appeared in *Appalachian Places*, November 2022. **JENNIFER HORNE**: "Morning Gift" originally appeared in *Borrowed Light* (Mule on a Ferris Wheel Press, 2019). **RACHEL HOUGHTON**: "Wading in Little Cahaba River" originally appeared in *Vulcan Historical Review*, Vol. 25, 2021. **ANDREW HUDGINS**: "The Unpromised Land," "New Headstones at the Shelby Springs Confederate Cemetery," and "Transistor Radio" appeared in *American Rendering: New and Selected Poems*, (Houghton Mifflin Harcourt, 2010). "Crucifixion" appeared in *Ecstatic in the Poison: New Poems* (The Overlook Press, 2003). "The God of Frenzies" appeared in *The Never-Ending: New Poems* (Houghton Mifflin, 1991). **ASHLEY M. JONES**: "greens&bread" and "candiedyams" originally appeared in *Oxford American*. "hoppinjohn: a blues" originally appeared in *Oxford American* and was anthologized in *New South Sonnets* (Belle Point Press). "WHAT IT REALLY IS" originally appeared in *SIERRA Club Magazine*. "On My Way to the Edmund Pettus Bridge, I Think of My Father" originally appeared in *Forum* (Pi Kappa Phi). **RODNEY JONES**: "The Peasant Poem" originally appeared in *Birmingham Poetry Review*, Spring 2023. **J. M. JORDAN**: "The Old Logging Road" originally appeared in *Modern Age*, Fall 2019. **MATTHEW LAYNE**: All works appear in Layne, Matthew. *Miracle Strip*. 1st ed., Brick Road Poetry Press, 2023. **QUINN LEWIS**: "Quarantine" and "Meanwhile, Flies" originally appeared in *The Southern Review*, Issue 55 Vol. 1, Winter 2019. "Meanwhile Flies" was reprinted on *Poetry Daily*, March 22, 2019. "Calypso Contemplates a Cowbird Mating Pair" originally appeared in *The Cincinnati Review*, Vol. 18, Issue 1, Spring 2021. "The River Ex" originally appeared in *32 Poems*, Issue 18.2, Fall/Winter 2020. "The Carnival Queen's First Understudy," originally appeared in *Birmingham Poetry Review*, Issue 47, Spring 2020. **MCLEOD LOGUE:** "Oh Honey, Bless Your Heart" originally appeared in *The Sonora Review*, Issue 80. **MAURICE MANNING:** All poems will appear in *Snakedoctor* (Copper Canyon Press, 2023). **KWOYA FAGIN MAPLES:** Maples, Kwoya Fagin. *Mend: Poems*, pp. 46-57. © The University Press of Kentucky. Used by permission. **ROSE MCLARNEY:** "Motionless," "American Persimmon," "Seasonal," and "On the Move" from *FORAGE* by Rose Mclarney, copyright© 2019 by Rose Mclarney. Used by permission of Penguin Books, an imprint of Penguin Publishing Group, a division of Penguin Random House LLC. All rights reserved. **JAMES MERSMANN:** "Watching My Mother's Breath" originally appeared in *Beloit Poetry Jornal*. "Mel Kneels Down in the Confessional Beside Bill and Carl" and "Breaking New Ground" originally appeared in *Straying Toward Home* (New South Books, 2007). "'For Counting Your Blessings,' She Said" and "Morning, Easter" originally appeared in *Birmingham Poetry Review* 42, 2015. **DANIEL EDWARD MOORE:** "God of Repeat" originally appeared in *Passengers Journal*. "Dear Body" originally appeared in *Manhattanville Review*. **JIM MURPHY:** "Junk Travel Through West Memphis" appeared in *The Memphis Sun* (Kent State UP, 2000). "River Minstrels, No Date Given" appeared in *Heaven Overland* (Kent State UP, 2009). **BRIAN OLIU:** "Alabama Basketball Fans Drown Their Sorrows In Arby's If They Lose, But Minnesota Timberwolves Fans Get a Free Arby's French Dip Sandwich if They Hit 12 Three-Pointers" originally appeared in *Words and Sports*, 1.4. **CHARLOTTE PENCE:** "Stingray Valentine" originally appeared in *The Southern Review*. **RUSTY RUSHTON:** "Humor Tends to Cowboy" originally appeared in *Cimarron Review*, #141, 2002. "Midnight Ride" and "The Bard's Glare" originally appeared in *Birmingham Poetry Review*, #27, 2006. "To a Waitress at Dreamland Barbecue" originally appeared in *The Cape Rock*, 34.1, 2001. "The Enunciation" originally appeared in *Licking River Review*, #32, 2001-02. "Athena, My Daughter" originally appeared in *Berkeley Poetry Review*, #30, 1995-7. **JOHN SAAD:** "Longleaf" - Saad, John. *Longleaf: Poems*. Brattleboro, VT: Green Writers Press, 2017. "100 Miles Out" - *The Pinch*, The University of Memphis, Vol. 41.1, Spring 2021. "Microburst on the Madison River" - *Terrain.org*, Terrain Publishing, March 25, 2020. **AUSTIN SEGREST:** "Yellowhammer" originally appeared in *Blackbird*. "Barrel Roll" originally appeared in *The Yale Review*. "Across the Street" originally appeared in *Poetry*. "Door to Remain" originally appeared in *Southern Humanities Review*. "Across the Street," "Door to Remain," and "The End of Analysis" appeared in *Door to Remain* (UNT Press, 2022). **LAUREN SLAUGHTER:** "The Neutral Ones" originally appeared in *On the Seawall*. "Alice the Corpse Flower Blooms at the Chicago Botanic Garden" originally appeared in *Rhino*. "Sometimes You Just Have to Grow Up" originally appeared in *Construction*. **CHEYENNE TAYLOR:** "Harvard researcher says dreams indicative of virus fears" originally appeared in the *Times Literary Supplement*, July 9, 2021, issue no. 6171. "Walker County Rites" originally appeared in another form at *New Ohio Review*, 2020 Summer Online Exclusive. **ALLEN TULLOS:** An earlier version of "Between Rivers, Years Between" originally appeared in *Southern Quarterly*, 52.2, Winter 2015. **ADAM VINES:** All poems appeared in *Lures* (LSU Press, 2022). **JASON GORDY WALKER:** "Elegy for a Friend" and "For the Woman Whose Name I Forget" originally appeared in *Town Creek Poetry*, Spring 2016, Volume X: Issue 1. "Villanelle in Blue" originally appeared in *Poetry South*, 2018, Issue 10. "Ode to a Dog Park" originally appeared in *Broad River Review*, 2019, Volume 51. **PATTI WHITE:** "Corn Maze" originally appeared in *Pink Motel* (Anhinga, 2017). "Thicketty, SC" originally appeared in *Yellow Jackets* (Anhinga, 2007). **JAKE ADAM YORK:** All poems appeared in *Murder Ballads* (Elixir Press, 2005). Reprinted with permission from the publisher.

Printed in the USA
CPSIA information can be obtained
at www.ICGtesting.com
CBHW011524021223
2204CB00002B/2

9 781680 033267